CRIMES OF PASSION

THE THIN LINE BETWEEN LOVE AND HATE

THIS IS A SEVENOAKS BOOK

Design copyright © Carlton Publishing Group 2006
Text copyright © Colin Wilson, Damon Wilson 2006

This edition published in Great Britain in 2007 by
Sevenoaks
An imprint of the Carlton Publishing Group
20 Mortimer Street
London W1T 3JW

A CIP catalogue for this book is available from the British Library

ISBN 978-1-86200-499-3

Printed and bound in Dubai

CRIMES OF PASSION

THE THIN LINE BETWEEN LOVE AND HATE

COLIN WILSON
DAMON WILSON

SEVENOAKS

Contents

	Introduction	06
1902	The Peasenhall Mystery	14
1906	The Murder of Stanford White	18
1906	The Chester Gillette Case	20
1907	The Camden Town Murder	22
1910	The Crippen Case	26
1910	Marie Tarnovska	30
1914	Madame Henriette Caillaux	34
1922	The Hall-Mills Murders	38
1922	The Lover in the Attic	42
1922	Bywaters and Thompson	46
1923	The Madame Fahmy Case	50
1924	The Vaquier Case	52
1924	Norman Thorne	54
1927	Ruth Snyder and Judd Gray	56
1927	Dr Dreher and Mrs Le Boeuf	60
1929	The Snook Case	62
1934	The Brighton Trunk Murder	66
1934	The Pyjama Girl	71
1935	Rattenbury and Stoner	73
1936	The Ruxton Case	76
1938	The Killing of Percy Casserley	80
1941	The Death of Lord Erroll	88
1941	The Corpse in the Chapel	90
1942	Murder in the Woods	94
1943	Who was the Woman in Sackcloth?	98
1946	Ley and Smith	102
1947	The Actress and the Steward	106
1949	The Guay Case	108
1949	The Shooting of the Baseball Star	112
1951	The Resistance Hero and his Wife	116
1951	Pauline Dubuisson	118
1953	The Emmett-Dunne Case	120
1954	Denise Labbé and Jacques Algarron	122

1954	Pauline Parker and Juliet Hulme	124
1954	The Bored Housewife	126
1955	The Ruth Ellis Case	127
1958	The Lana Turner Scandal	132
1962	Elizabeth Duncan	138
1964	Sharon Kinne	140
1967	The Death of Joe Orton	144
1968	The Max Garvie Case	146
1974	The Cape Town Scissor Killing	150
1976	The Lady in the Lake	151
1977	Joyce McKinney and the Manacled Mormon	153
1978	Sid and Nancy	160
1979	James and Freda Wilson	163
1980	Jean Harris	166
1980	Death of a Playboy Centrefold	170
1981	Susan Barber's Poisoned Pie	174
1982	Colin Thatcher	175
1983	The Professor and the Prostitute	178
1989	The Fatal Attraction of Carolyn Warmus	180
1991	The Pam Smart Case	184
1992	Amy Fisher, The Long Island Lolita	188
1993	John and Lorena Bobbitt	192
1994	The Trials of OJ Simpson	194
1994	Susan Smith	202
1999	Curry Wars and Red Herrings	206
2000	Jane Andrews, Dresser to the Duchess	210
2003	The Peterson Case	212
2004	The Side Effect	216
2005	Murder at Trewinnick Cottage	218

INTRODUCTION

The French call it crime passionel, and when these words are pronounced in court they imply that passion has overruled reason to the extent of making the culprit incapable of self-control. The British are inclined to take a sceptical view of this attitude, for they do not believe that self-control can be so totally undermined by emotion that a person becomes incapable of judgement. This is why a British jury sentenced Ruth Ellis to death for shooting her lover David Blakely, and why all attempts to reprieve her were unsuccessful. But, as this collection shows, many a Frenchman – and woman – has walked free because French juries accept the plea as a matter of self-evident truth.

It is worth noting at this point that not all crimes of passion involve jealousy. In fact, some of the most interesting have quite different motives. When Lorraine Clark's husband came home unexpectedly and found her in bed with a lover, she killed him, not *vice versa*, because he made it clear he expected her to give up wife-swapping parties. She obviously felt that adultery was an experience that brought colour and interest into her dull life, and shot him rather than comply.

So the general principle we have observed in this book is that if a couple have been involved in a love affair (or marriage), and its dissolution comes about because one kills the other, this counts as a crime of passion whether or not jealousy is involved.

This has allowed the authors to include, for example, the strange case of Professor James Snook and his one-time student mistress Theora Hix. Most readers may feel that the fact that she sank her teeth into a vulnerable part of his anatomy was sufficient reason to explain why he killed her. But the truth was almost certainly that this basically

moral man was deeply ashamed of his enslavement to a girl who seemed to embody the sexual freedom of the roaring 20s, so that when he snapped, it was with the force of a steel cable stretched beyond its limit.

This enables us to pinpoint another important recognition. In most love affairs the dominant role is assumed by the female – even, for example, in the case of Countess Marie Tarnovska, who got rid of unwanted lovers by persuading their successors to kill them. In the Snook case, Theora Hix remained the dominant one until Snook was goaded into shooting her, beating her and cutting her throat.

Dominance, one of the most important factors in animal behaviour, plays a central role in sexual relations. In 1936, a young psychologist named Abraham Maslow recognized just how central when he began a study of dominance in women. (He chose women because they were more honest than men.) His findings were significant – that they fell into three distinct categories: high-dominance, medium-dominance and low-dominance.

High-dominance women simply liked sex, and the kind of vigorous male who could satisfy them. Medium-dominance women attached great importance to tenderness and liked to be wooed by the kind of man who would take them to restaurants with candlelight and soft music. Low-dominance women tended to be scared of sex and preferred the kind of male who would admire them from a distance for a long period before daring to speak.

All three types of women, he found, preferred a male who was slightly more dominant than themselves, but not too much so. He even worked out tests that would enable a couple contemplating marriage to work out if the "dominance gap" was too great, too small, or of exactly the right size.

In the Snook case, the dominance gap was the wrong way round (Hix dominated Snook), so the outcome was almost foredoomed to be unsatisfying or tragic. The same applied to the Countess Tarnovska; Marie's manipulations ended by turning both her lovers against her and in jail for all three.

We can also see the central role played by dominance in some of the most important crimes of passion of the Victorian era. And since this book begins in the early twentieth century with the fascinating Peasenhall mystery, we will speak briefly of three cases in which dominance – or we should say, the lack of it – played a central role.

Madeleine Smith

In Glasgow in 1855, an attractive but bored 19-year-old named Madeleine Smith, daughter of a well-to-do architect, was introduced in the street to Pierre L'Angelier, a young Frenchman from Jersey, who had gone to considerable trouble to engineer the introduction. Soon afterwards, Madeleine received a letter from L'Angelier declaring his love; she replied encouragingly, using the maid as a go-between.

When her parents found out, they ordered her never to communicate with him again. But the lovers continued to snatch brief and frustrating meetings, during which they exchanged hasty kisses and

H.R.MILLAR

Madeleine Smith, the beautiful Scots girl who was accused of poisoning her lover, Pierre Emile L'Angelier, with arsenic, to prevent him carrying out his threat to reveal their liaison to her parents.

replied that their engagement was over: "My love for you has ceased."

L'Angelier's response was to threaten to write to her father revealing all. Madeleine hastily agreed to meet him again; again her letters address him as "dearest pet" and "sweet love"; but no longer as "my darling husband". For the truth was that she had come to loathe the ungentlemanly blackmailer. They had two more meetings, each in the basement of Madeleine's house, and on each occasion he drank a cup of cocoa prepared by Madeleine. After the first meeting, L'Angelier was ill; after the second, in March 1857, he returned home in agony, bent over and clutching his stomach; by 11 o'clock the next morning he was dead. His doctor insisted on a post-mortem, and 87 grains of arsenic were found in his stomach - the lethal dose being three grains.

Madeleine's letters were found; she immediately became the chief suspect, and was arrested on March 31, 1857. The notion of a young girl becoming the mistress of a Frenchman horrified Scottish public opinion. Her guilt seemed obvious. Yet although it was proved that she had purchased three lots of arsenic, as rat poison, they had been mixed with soot or indigo. And no signs of soot or indigo were found in the dead man's stomach - though one medical witness commented that the grains of indigo could easily be washed

caresses. By December she was addressing him as "My own darling husband". But no real intimacy was possible between them until the following summer, when the Smiths went to their country house at Row; here Madeleine had a chance to take unchaperoned country walks. A letter to L'Angelier in June 1856 begins:"If we did wrong

last night, it was in the excitement of our love", and goes on to note prosaically: "I did not bleed in the least but I had a good deal of pain during the night."

But later that summer, disillusionment - or perhaps merely satiety - began to set in. Madeleine was a practical and dominant girl, and L'Angelier was a romantic

and rather weak young man. Possibly she was also influenced by the attentions of a wealthy bachelor named William Minnoch, a close friend of her father's, who eventually proposed. She accepted. L'Angelier then played into her hands with a fit of petulance and self-pity that led him to return one of her letters; she promptly

introduction

from the arsenic with cold water. Madeleine insisted that her lover was in the habit of taking small quantities of arsenic for health reasons (arsenic is a stimulant and improves the complexion), but the defence offered no proof of this assertion. The jury eventually brought in a verdict of "not proven" – peculiar to Scotland – which implied that they regarded her as guilty, but found the proof insufficient. The crowd in court cheered, evidently feeling that L'Angelier deserved what he got.

Adelaide Bartlett

In the following case, the precipitating factor seems to have been a certain lack of dominance in a typical Victorian husband.

One day in the early 1870s, at the house of his brother, a grocer named Edwin Bartlett met a dazzlingly attractive 18-year-old girl named Adelaide Blanche de la Tremoile. She had dark curly hair, large appealing eyes and a French accent, and was staying with his brother's 16-year-old daughter. Edwin found her fascinating. Although 29, he had never thought of marriage because he had been working too hard building up a chain of grocery shops in south London, but the sight of Adelaide made him dream of romance.

In fact, she was "above" him socially, but when he learned that she had been born out of wedlock he decided he decided to pursue her with single-minded determination. Edwin called on her when she returned to the house of her guardian in Richmond, and persuaded

Adelaide Bartlett, the attractive French girl who was accused — and acquitted — of poisoning her husband with chloroform because there was no plausible way she could have introduced it into his stomach.

him that a virtuous and successful grocer would make a desirable husband.

To Adelaide he explained that his intentions were more than pure – there was no carnal desire in his feeling for her and, when they were married, their relationship would be wholly platonic. And by way of proving his good faith, Edwin Bartlett packed off his newly wedded bride to a ladies' finishing school in Stoke Newington, then to a convent school in Brussels. She came to stay with her husband during the school holidays but, according to Adelaide, their relationship was like that of father and daughter.

Things were not to remain that way. Four years later, in 1881, Adelaide had a stillborn baby. This was Edwin's fault; the nurse had begged him to call in a doctor. But the Victorian Edwin was rather shocked at the idea of another man "interfering with" his wife and, by the time a doctor was finally called in, the baby was dead.

Early in 1885 - the Bartletts had now been married 10 years - the couple decided to try another place of worship, and went to the Wesleyan chapel in Merton. The preacher that day was a young man named George Dyson. He had a black moustache, a receding hairline, and was of slight build. Dyson made a pastoral call soon after that. When he told Edwin Bartlett that he was about to go to Trinity College, Dublin, to take his degree, Bartlett was deeply impressed. He had an almost pathetic admiration for anyone with education - he himself was an avid, but disorganized, reader. He pressed the young man to come and visit them again as soon as he returned. Slightly overwhelmed - for he was modest and not very clever - Dyson agreed. And a warm, if rather peculiar, friendship began between these three rather lonely people.

Soon, Edwin proposed that Dyson should continue Adelaide's education, teaching her geography, history, Latin and mathematics. Dyson, who was making a mere hundred pounds a year, agreed. He would arrive in the morning while Edwin was out at business, and often stay all day. During most of this time, he was alone with Adelaide. Whether she became his mistress is not known, but

she often sat at his feet, with her head on his knee, and he often kissed her, alone and in her husband's presence. And, oddly enough, Edwin seemed delighted with the whole arrangement. He seemed to be trying to throw them into one another's arms.

He probably succeeded; their landlady noticed one day, after Dyson had left, that the window curtains were not merely drawn, but pinned together. It is hard to imagine why they should do this unless, at the very least, they had been engaging in some heavy petting.

And now, suddenly, Edwin became ill. One day he felt so exhausted at work that he hurried home. Adelaide went out to fetch a doctor named Leach, who diagnosed that Edwin was suffering from sickness, diarrhoea and bleeding of the bowels; he also had rotten teeth, due to an incompetent dentist. When the doctor looked into his mouth, he observed a blue line round the gums, a symptom of mercury poisoning. Leach's theory was that Edwin had, at some time, got a dose of mercury into his system, and that the sulphides produced by his rotting teeth had combined with it to form mercuric sulphide, hence the blue line.

Throughout December the patient remained in bed. On Christmas Day, 1885, he received an unpleasant shock when he went to the lavatory and passed a round worm. He was naturally something of a hypochondriac, and this gave him "the horrors". He swore that he could feel worms wriggling in his throat, and became deeply depressed.

On the last day of December, and the last day of Edwin's

life, he went to the dentist for yet another tooth extraction. When he returned home, his appetite had improved and he ate a large meal. He told the landlady that he would have a haddock for his breakfast. Obviously, he was at last on the road to recovery.

Just before 4 a.m. on New Year's Day, Adelaide knocked on the landlady's bedroom door. "Go and fetch Dr Leach. I think Mr Bartlett is dead." She explained that she had fallen asleep, holding Edwin's foot, which apparently soothed him, as she sat beside his bed. She had awakened and felt that he was cold. She had tried to revive him with brandy, but without success. Dr Leach observed a glass of brandy on the shelf, with a smell of chloroform.

A post-mortem revealed a baffling and astonishing fact: that Edwin Bartlett had died of chloroform poisoning. It was astonishing because chloroform is an unpleasant-tasting substance that would be almost impossible to swallow; moreover, it causes vomiting. If chloroform was poured down someone's throat when he was unconscious - for example, from the fumes of chloroform - it would get into the lungs. And there was no chloroform in Edwin Bartlett's lungs. Which seemed to point to the completely mystifying conclusion that he had drunk the chloroform voluntarily. Yet his cheerfulness before he went to sleep, and the fact that he had even ordered his breakfast, made it unlikely that he intended suicide.

The chloroform, it seemed, had been purchased by Dyson, who had bought it at Adelaide's request. He had even gone to three separate

chemists to get a fairly large quantity, claiming that he wanted to use it as cleaning fluid. Adelaide had told him she wanted it to make her husband sleep. And now, when he heard that chloroform had been found in Edwin's stomach, Dyson was panic-stricken. He saw it as the end of his career. He rushed along to see Adelaide, and she asked him to say nothing about the chloroform. Dyson refused, and said he was going to make a clean breast of it.

And so he did, the result being that Adelaide Bartlett found herself on trial for murder. When, in the spring of 1886, it became known that she was to be tried for poisoning her husband, and that the Reverend George Dyson would probably stand in the dock beside her, public excitement was intense, since the Victorians loved nothing so much as a good scandal.

In the event, Adelaide finally stood alone in the dock, because Dyson had managed to clear his own name by shamelessly doing his best to hand her over to the hangman. Her defence counsel, Edward Clarke, had an apparently impossible task: to convince a Victorian jury that this pretty Frenchwoman, quite probably an adulteress, was innocent of her husband's murder. He had only one thing on his side: the total mystery of how even the most cunning murderess could have got the chloroform into Edwin Bartlett's stomach.

And that is what finally cleared Adelaide. There was simply no logical way of explaining how the chloroform had got inside Edwin. To that question the prosecution had no answer. So there could be only one verdict. "Although we think there is the gravest suspicion attaching to the prisoner, we do not think there is sufficient evidence to show how or by whom the chloroform was administered." So the verdict was not guilty. The judge had to reprove the court sternly as it burst into cheers.

Sir James Paget, a well-known doctor, made the famous remark: "Now the case is over, she should tell us in the interests of science how she did it."

The answer surely is obvious. She persuaded Edwin that a dose of chloroform in brandy, gulped down, would destroy the worms once and for all. Which it did.

Dr Cross and the Catalyst Effect

In the Victorian age, women who were accused of murder tended to fare better than men, especially if they were pretty.

In the 1880s, a 63-year-old retired army surgeon, Dr Philip Cross, lived comfortably with his wife Laura and six children at Shandy Hall, near Dripsey, County Cork. His wife was 22 years his junior; they had been married 18 years, and it had been, on the whole, a happy marriage.

In October 1886, Mrs Cross engaged a new governess for the children, a 22-year-old girl named Effie Skinner. As soon as he saw her, the military, rather forbidding Dr Cross felt like a hawk eyeing a sparrow. For the first time, he realized that his marriage had been merely satisfactory, never ecstatic. It had never provided him with any real outlet for his male dominance.

Which is why one day, as Effie stood talking to him about the children, he bent and kissed her.

He was afraid she would tell his wife or leave immediately. But instead she stayed, and his desire to possess her only increased. His wife couldn't fail to noticed it, and she took what seemed to her the sensible course: she sacked Effie. The girl was shattered. She found another job and went to Dublin, and when Dr Cross visited her there, she finally gave herself to him. Possession did not cool his desire; he wanted to be married to her, living in comfort in Shandy Hall.

Early in May, 1887, Mrs Cross began to suffer attacks of vomiting. Her husband told her she had a weak heart. She died on June 1, and was buried three days later. Less than two weeks after this, Cross married Effie Skinner in London. At first, he decided that they had better keep the marriage a secret and live separately but, when he got back to Dripsey, he discovered that Effie's mother had told one of his neighbours. And since there seemed no point keeping Effie in London, he moved her to Shandy Hall.

Inevitably, there was gossip, and the police finally decided to act. Laura Cross was exhumed, and the coroner found 3.2 grains of arsenic in her body, as well as strychnine. There was no trace of heart disease.

The police were also able to trace the supplier from whom Dr Cross had bought arsenic "for sheep dipping". Tried at the Munster Assizes in Cork, he was found guilty on December 18, 1887, and hanged the following January.

Effie was so shocked by the realization that she had been the cause of the murder that she refused to see him in the condemned cell. It is said that Cross's hair actually turned white overnight.

Once more we are made aware of that all-important factor of dominance, which – as we shall see in the course of this book – plays a very central role in crimes of passion. Cross was apparently a happily married man who was fond of his family – although his rather abrupt manner may have concealed this – but the moment he saw Effie, some kind of chemical reaction took place. She was not a pretty girl, but there must have been some quality of innocence and vulnerability about her that brought out the dominant and protective male in him in ways that his wife never had.

This quality might, we suggest, be called "the catalyst effect" for, like a chemical catalyst, it has that ability to bring about a basic transformation in a person. In the case of Dr Cross, it changed a respectable Victorian gentleman into a man who was capable of killing his wife of 18 years.

Readers of the Crippen case will note that Ethel Le Neve also had that same catalyst quality, which may explain how a mild and rather quiet little man was able to poison his wife and then hack her to pieces and remove the bones before burying her in the cellar.

Truly, as Sherlock Holmes might have put it, the complexity of human passions makes the combinatorial analyses of inorganic chemistry seem obvious and crude.

The Praslin Case

Finally, a remarkable French case of the early 19th century, which happens to be one of the first to be solved by medical detection.

Charles-Louis Theobald, the Duc de Choiseul-Praslin, married his wife Fanny – a daughter of one of Napoleon's generals – in 1824, when she was 16 and he 19. She was a woman of fiery temperament, with lesbian inclinations. By the time she was 34, and had borne nine children, she was corpulent and wrinkled. The duke, an introverted, withdrawn man, found her dominant ways intolerable, and ceased to frequent her bed. Yet there can be no doubt that the duchess continued to love her husband. Matters became increasingly strained when an attractive girl named Henriette Deluzy was engaged as the children's governess, and it soon became clear that the duke was strongly attracted to her. Whether she became his mistress is not known, but it seems certain that the duchess thought the worst. She told her husband to dismiss the girl; he replied that if Henriette left, he would go too. The duchess wrote him a number of pathetic letters, which make it clear that this was not the first time the duke had shown interest in other women, but in spite of this she still loved him.

Finally, the duchess got her way; Henriette Deluzy was dismissed – without even a reference. The duke continued to call on her, and the affair became the talk of Paris society. In June 1847, the duchess announced that she intended to seek a divorce, on the grounds of her husband's

introduction

adultery with the governess. The duke was mad with fury; he would lose his children and his position at one blow.

On the evening of August 17, he went to see Henriette Deluzy, returning home in the early hours of the morning. As dawn was breaking, the servants were electrified by a piercing scream. Then the bell connected to the duchess's bedroom began to ring. There was another scream. It looked as if burglars had broken in. The duke's valet and the duchess's maid crept to her door, and heard the crash of something falling over. They knocked and called, but there was no reply. They tried another door, but it had been wedged. A number of servants rushed to the garden, and looked up at the bedroom window; as they did so, the shutter opened, and several of them saw a man they recognized as the duke. It seemed that he had also heard the burglars and had entered his wife's bedroom. The servants rushed back indoors to help him fight the intruders.

To their surprise, the bedroom door was now open. The room was in chaos and there were splashes of blood on the walls. The duchess was sitting on the floor, half-propped against her bed; she was obviously dead. Her throat had been slashed, and her face battered.

As they were examining her, the duke walked into the room, and screamed as he saw his dead wife. "Some monster has murdered my beloved Fanny! Fetch a doctor." He claimed that he had only just been awakened by the noise.

Two passing gendarmes noticed the front door was open, and came in. Soon the house in the Rue Faubourg-St-Honoré was full of policemen, including M. Allard, Vidocq's successor as head of the Sûreté. It took him little time to dismiss the theory about burglars - to begin with, the duchess's jewels were untouched. Under the sofa, he found a Corsican pistol, covered with blood.

"Does anyone know whom this belongs to?", asked Allard. To his surprise, the duke answered: "Yes, to me." So Allard asked: "But how did it get here?"

The duke's story was that he had heard cries for help, and rushed into his wife's bedroom, brandishing his pistol. Seeing she was covered in blood, he had dropped the pistol to raise her up. Consequently, he had become covered in blood. Seeing that his wife was dead, he went back to his bedroom to wash off the blood...

It was just plausible - except, of course, that he had told the servants that he had only just awakened. Allard went to the duke's bedroom, and pointed out that bloodstains led to his door. The duke replied that he had been dripping with his wife's blood as he had returned.

But the state of the duke's bedroom left little doubt of his guilt; there was a bloodstained handkerchief, the blood-stained hilt of a dagger, and a piece of bloodstained cord. When the severed end of the bell-pull from the Rue duchess's bedroom was found under his shirt, Allard told the duke he was under arrest.

But suppose his story were true? Or suppose, at any rate, that he continued to insist that it was true? Was there any point at which his account could be positively disproved? He could claim that the servants had mis-understood him when they thought he said he had only just been awakened by the noise. He could claim that the shock of discovering his wife's dead body had led him to act in a strange and confused manner, carrying off the blood-stained cord and the bell-pull. A court might disbelieve him, yet still have difficulty proving that he murdered his wife.

The bloodstained pistol was turned over to the eminent pathologist Ambroise Tardieu, who had written the first treatise on hanging. What the police wanted to know was whether the pistol had been dropped in the duchess's blood, or used as a weapon to batter her to death. With characteristic thorough-ness, Tardieu studied the pis-tol, first under a magnifying glass, then a microscope. The first thing he discovered was a chestnut hair close to the butt. Near the trigger guard, he found fragments of skin tissue. Further micro-scopic examination revealed a bulb, or root, of human hair, and more fragments of flesh. One of the fragments melted when heated, and formed a grease spot on a piece of paper. Moreover, some of the contused wounds on the dead woman's forehead had been made with a blunt instrument like the butt of the pistol. In short, there could be no possible doubt. The micro-scope revealed that the duchess had been battered to death with the pistol.

Tardieu's medical investiga-tions revealed exactly what had happened that night. The Duc de Praslin had slipped into his wife's bedroom, probably through the bath-room, intending to kill her with one sweep of a sharp knife. But his nerve failed him, or perhaps she woke up as he bent over her. The blade made a deep cut in her throat, but failed to sever the windpipe; she screamed, and began to fight. He stabbed her again and again with a dagger, then began to beat her with the butt of the pistol; as she writhed on the floor, she bit his leg (a medical examination revealed her teeth marks). By this time the whole house was aroused; the servants were knocking on the door. His original plan - of killing her, then opening the front door and making it look like a burglary - had to be abandoned; instead, he decided to leave an open window. But as he threw back the shutters, he saw the servants in the garden. At least this allowed him to escape back to his own bed-room. And now he made yet another mistake. He rushed into his wife's room, pretending that the noise had awakened him, and screamed at the sight of his wife's body. And when the police arrived, and he was forced to change his story, he knew that his last chance of getting away with murder had vanished...

Before being taken to the Luxembourg prison, the duke swallowed a dose of arsenic. He died three days later, still refusing to admit to the murder. But Tardieu's microscope had made such a confession superfluous.

Truly, as Sherlock Holmes might have said, the complex-ities of our human passions make the combinatorial anal-yses of inorganic chemistry seem obvious and crude.

Colin Wilson
Damon Wilson
January 2006

1900s

THE PEASENHALL MYSTERY

In 1902, Queen Victoria had been dead for a year, but Victorian morality was as dominant as ever. So crimes in which there was even a hint of sex aroused prurient interest. Which explains why a murder that took place in the otherwise unmemorable Suffolk village of Peasenhall, near Saxmundham, received such widespread coverage in the British press.

Around 8 o'clock on the morning of June 1, 1902, a carter named William Harsent walked to Providence House, the home of a retired couple, William and Georgiana Crisp, carrying a parcel of newly ironed linen for his 23-year-old daughter Rose, who was a live-in maidservant. It was a bright, sunny day after a night of storm, and Harsent found the back door open. What he saw inside made him drop the linen. Rose lay at the foot of the stairs, half-naked. Her throat had been cut from ear to ear, and deep gashes covered her bare shoulders. She had been wearing a nightdress, but this had been partly torn from her, and partly burnt away. A broken medicine bottle lay on the floor beside the body, as well as a broken paraffin lamp. The bottle had contained paraffin, which had burnt the nightdress. Its label showed that it had originally contained medicine for the children of a local man, William Gardiner.

Constable Eli Nunn arrived at 8.40, and made notes about the crime scene. Although

the nightdress was around her knees, Rose was wearing stockings, and only the

> **THE FIRE, INTENDED TO GUT THE ROOM AND DESTROY EVIDENCE, WENT OUT AFTER THE INTRUDER HAD LEFT**

upper part of the nightdress was burnt; it seemed the fire,, intended to gut the room and destroy evidence, went out after the intruder had left.

The girl's bed had not been slept in, but there were three letters in the room, one of which – unsigned – made an appointment to come and see her at midnight.

Police also found some obscene poems from a 19-year-old youth, Fred Davis, who lived next door; it seemed that Rose had asked him to write them out for her. She was clearly not the prudish type. Fred later admitted he was hoping to seduce Rose, but claimed he had not succeeded. However, that may have been because he did not want to be suspected

of being the father of her unborn child – for the medical examination, which revealed that Rose Harsent had been dead at least four hours, also showed that she was six months pregnant. She had been stabbed in the throat as well as slashed about the shoulders, the implication being that she wrestled in the dark with her attacker, and the assailant could not see what he was doing.

No one had any doubt that the father of the unborn child was the 45-year-old Sunday school teacher, William Gardiner. He had been the choir-master, and Rose had been a member of the choir. It was true that the popular Rose had many admirers in the past, but, at the time, her name was linked only with that of Gardiner, a married man with seven children.

This came about because in the previous year, he and Rose had been the subject of scandal. Two youths, George Wright and Alphonse Skinner, had seen them walking towards the building known as the "Doctor's Chapel", which stood alone in

a field. The youths had hidden behind a hedge until the couple went inside, then crept closer. They were unable to see what was happening, but the sounds made it clear. There was a rustling of clothes, then the girl gasped "Oh, oh."

The silence that followed suggested a state of mutual satisfaction. Gardiner was heard to ask her what she was thinking about. She answered: "What you were reading last Sunday." He asked her what he had been reading, and she replied: "About what we are doing now." She then went on to quote the verses from Genesis, chapter 38, about how Onan "spilled his seed on the ground". Although the "sin of Onan" has now become a synonym for masturbation, the Bible makes it clear that it was actually an act of *coitus interruptus*.

The scandal was so great that an inquiry had been

The murder of Rose Harsent was widely reported in the British press. This artist's impression of Rose's father discovering his daughter's body. on the front cover of the *Police News* dated 14 June, 1902, added furher drama to the case.

THE ILLUSTRATED POLICE NEWS.—JUNE 14, 1902.

DESPERATE MURDER BY LONDON "HOOLIGANS."

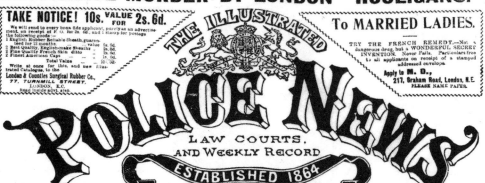

THE ILLUSTRATED
POLICE NEWS
LAW COURTS.
AND WEEKLY RECORD
ESTABLISHED 1864

No. 2000. [REGISTERED AT THE G.P.O. AS A NEWSPAPER.] **SATURDAY, JUNE 14, 1902.** **Price One Penny.**

THE HOUSE IN WHICH THE BODY WAS FOUND.

ROSE HARSANT.

SENSATIONAL CRIME IN SUFFOLK.

conducted by the Reverend John Grey; Gardiner had denied the story, saying that he had been in the "Doctor's Chapel" with the girl only to help her move a stiff door. He was so furious with the two youths that he publicly called them liars, and paid for a lawyer to write them a letter demanding an apology. The young men ignored it. The inquiry ended with Gardiner being told, "Let this be a warning to you for life", and he had appeared to be suitably chastened.

Yet although he appeared to have nothing further to do with the girl, it was plain to people who observed them closely (as villagers are inclined to) that they were still on intimate terms. They were observed walking together in the dusk, and Gardiner was even seen with his feet in Rose's lap in chapel. The chapel elder who rebuked him for this was told that it would not happen again.

The day after Rose Harsent's body was found, Superintendent George Staunton called on Gardiner, and asked him if the handwriting on one of the letters

The victim Rose Harsent – a somewhat idealized newspaper impression.

ROSE HARSANT.

was his; Gardiner denied it. The policeman asked if the envelope in which another letter was contained was not identical with those used by Gardiner's firm; again he denied it. But the next day, he was arrested and charged with Rose's murder, then taken to Ipswich Prison.

Certainly, the case against him looked black. His clasp knife was found to be stained with blood, and the inside scraped out (which he denied doing). He claimed he had been cutting up rabbits;

in 1902, there was no way of testing whether a bloodstain was from a human being or an animal.

Gardiner's defence was an alibi, supported by his wife; he said he had been at home all evening. At 11.30 his wife had gone in to see their next-door neighbour, an old lady who was frightened of thunder, and Gardiner had joined her later. They both stayed until 1.30 a.m., then went to bed.

There was another piece of evidence that pointed to his guilt. Early that Sunday morning, after the storm had passed, the unpaved village street was a sheet of mud. A gamekeeper named James Morris, walking down the street soon after dawn, noticed footprints that ran 200 yards from Gardiner's cottage to Providence House, then back again. As a gamekeeper he was trained to notice such things. He even noticed that the footprints were of rubber soles with a bar across.

An artist's impression of Rose's father, William Harsent, discovering his daughter's body.

Gardiner proved to possess such a pair of shoes.

In the two trials that followed, Gardiner was lucky. In those days the jury's verdict in a murder trial had to be unanimous, and one member of the jury stubbornly refused to be convinced of his guilt. The judge had to order a retrial, and once again the jury failed to agree.

Gardiner should have been tried a third time; but the authorities decided he had been through enough, and entered a *nolle prosequi*, which meant no further prosecution would take place. It was equivalent to the Scottish verdict of "not proven". Gardiner and his wife moved to a London suburb, where they opened a shop. Whether they prospered or not has never been recorded, but Mrs Gardiner's hair had turned white from her ordeal. Gardiner died in 1941.

Who killed Rose? The puzzle surely responds to simple logic. Whoever came to her room that night was hoping for a pleasant half hour in her bed. Instead she told him she was pregnant and asked him what he intended to do about it. But he must have known – as we now know – that she was not some innocent maid who had shyly surrendered her virginity, but a woman who thoroughly enjoyed sex and had had several lovers. Why should he be expected to take the responsibility, or find the money to send her away for an abortion? There were angry words hissed in the darkness of the kitchen, where she had been waiting for him; he flew into a fury and hit her – the Crisps heard a scream around midnight, but failed to investigate – then, to stifle her cries, cut her throat. Hours later he went back with the paraffin bottle and tried to burn the evidence, then fled.

A simple country lad, like the youth next door, would probably have agreed to marry her. Whoever killed her could not do that, probably because he was already married, and her threats filled him with rage. So he knelt on her, pulled out his rabbiting knife, and silenced her.

This version of events fits William Gardiner perfectly.

Fingerprint evidence could probably have determined his guilt, but in 1902 it was not used outside London. So, when one juryman refused to accept his guilt, the likeliest suspect in Rose Harsent's murder walked free.

Appointment for murder?

Was Gardiner guilty? Certainly, he was not the only man who might have made Rose pregnant. To begin with, there was Fred Davis, who wrote out the highly indecent verses found in her room. She was no blushing wallflower, but a forthright country girl who, as the indecent verses showed, took sex for granted and enjoyed reading and thinking about it. One writer on the case has compared her to Dylan Thomas's promiscuous Polly Garter in *Under Milk Wood*. She had almost certainly had other lovers besides Gardiner.

Nevertheless, the evidence against Gardiner is strong. The sheer fury with which he reacted to the story of the two youths reveals a man of quick temper, and whoever killed Rose did so in a fury. The evidence shows that this good-looking man with a black Edwardian beard became the lover of Rose Harsent, and could have been the father of her unborn child and the writer of the letter making the appointment with her at midnight.

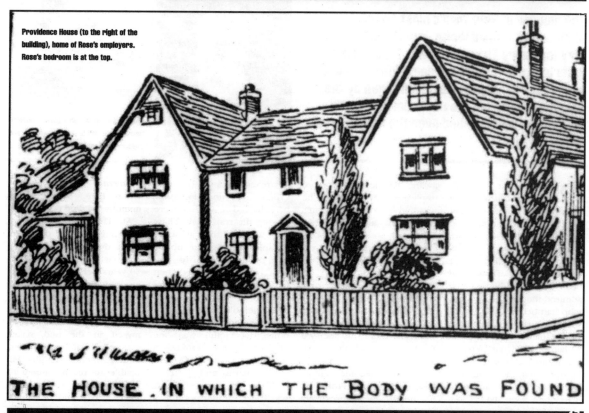

Providence House (to the right of the building), home of Rose's employers. Rose's bedroom is at the top.

THE HOUSE IN WHICH THE BODY WAS FOUND

THE MURDER OF STANFORD WHITE

Evelyn Thaw, née Nesbit – the ex-showgirl whose "rape" led to murder, and (left) her seducer Stanford White.

The murder of New York's most famous architect, Stanford White, by the wealthy playboy Harry Thaw, was one of the greatest American scandals of the early 20th century. This sense of scandal was heightened by the salacious details of the seduction of Thaw's wife that were splashed over the front pages of the tabloids.

On the night of June 25, 1906, a wealthy young rake named Harry Thaw sat beside his beautiful wife on the roof of Madison Square Garden, New York, watching a new revue. Before her marriage, Mrs Thaw had been Evelyn Nesbit, a much admired model and showgirl, who had been only 16 when she met Thaw. After she had almost died of appendicitis, he had succeeded in persuading her to accompany him to Europe – with her mother as chaperone – and finally to marry him. Soon she became aware of one of his more unpleasant peculiarities: he was addicted to flogging. Having no alternative, she submitted, and on one occasion was whipped so severely that she was confined to bed for two weeks.

The flogging episode may have been connected to her admission that she had been seduced seven years earlier, when she was 15, by Stanford White, the architect of Madison Square Garden. Thaw had become almost insane with jealousy. From then on, he dreamed obsessively of revenge. And on that evening of June 25, 1906, he achieved it. As they were leaving the roof show, Thaw saw White sitting alone at a table. He walked up to him, pulled out a pistol, and shot him three times. Then he calmly walked away and allowed himself to be escorted to the police station.

The scandal was tremendous. His victim was one of New York's best-known socialites, a man of enormous charm and generosity. Thaw, on the other hand, was looked down upon as a *nouveau riche* playboy whose father had made his millions building railways.

At Thaw's murder trial, Evelyn gave lurid details of her seduction by the architect (who was more than 30 years her senior), describing how he had taken her virginity after getting her drunk on champagne. ("When I came to I found myself in the bed, naked except for an abbreviated pink undergarment.") The jury was unable to reach agreement. At the second trial, in 1908, Thaw was found not guilty

Sanity on trial

Determined to prove his sanity – a difficult matter since he was undoubtedly weak in the head – Thaw paid a battery of lawyers to institute an appeal. This was turned down in 1909, but he kept on trying. Evelyn testified at several hearings, and it became clear that she had perjured herself at the original trial. She had claimed to be the victim of a brutal seducer, when in fact she had been in love with Stanford White, who had treated her as much as a daughter as a mistress, even sending her to finishing school. Large bribes from her mother-in-law, however, guaranteed that she never told the truth in court.

A brothel madame also testified that Thaw paid her well for prostitutes who were willing to endure sadistic beatings, and that she had received $40,000 to keep quiet during his first trial.

Harry Thaw (centre) in the Supreme Court, when Justice Hendricks granted him a new trial by jury to determine his degree of mental responsibility for the murder of Stanford White.

by reason of insanity and sent to an asylum in Matteawan, in upper New York state, where his wealth allowed him to live very comfortably.

In 1913 it was Thaw's money that facilitated his escape from the asylum, and he fled over the border to Canada. He was soon arrested, and waved at the large crowd that had gathered to see the famous fugitive. The justice minister himself ordered Thaw's deportation back over the border.

Followed by reporters to Concord, Massachusetts, he fought off extradition to New York until, in 1914, his lawyers succeeded in obtaining another trial – in which, no doubt due to plentiful bribes – he was found not guilty and released.

Even then he could not stay out of trouble. In 1915 he met a youth named Fred Gump in an ice cream parlour and obviously found him attractive. On Christmas Eve 1916, he lured Gump to a New York hotel with a job offer, then burst into his room in the middle of the night and flogged him with a whip until he was almost unconscious. The following day Gump escaped, and Thaw was

arrested in Philadelphia after attempting suicide by slashing his wrists and throat with a razor. Once again his mother paid vast bribes and the proceedings were dropped.

Evelyn, by now divorced (and briefly remarried), tried unsuccessfully to get her hands on more of the Thaw fortune, then became a night club entertainer, and in 1926 attempted suicide by drinking Lysol. This led Thaw to renew their acquaintance, and there was even some talk of their reconciliation. This never happened. Evelyn raised the money to open a café in New York, where Thaw brought a party of showgirls, and when he saw the size of the bill,

overturned a table of bottles.

During the remainder of his life – he died of a heart attack in 1947 – he was sued many times, usually for violence when drunk. In 1934, Evelyn wrote a book in which she admitted to many more affairs than the one with Stanford White. She also admitted that she originally encouraged Thaw in an attempt to make White jealous.

Gerald Langford's book *The Murder of Stanford White* (1962) states that "At last report, Evelyn, in her late 70s, was living in modest circumstances in California." In fact, she lived on until 1967, when she died in a nursing home in Santa Monica, aged 82.

1906

THE CHESTER GILLETTE CASE

Theodore Dreiser's novel *An American Tragedy* is about a young man who is executed for the accidental death of his mistress in a boating accident. But in the real case on which the book was based, there can be no doubt that the crime was deliberate and premeditated murder, so the killer could marry another woman.

As a boy, Chester Gillette had helped his parents preach for the Salvation Army; he and his siblings went on soul-saving missions in Washington, Oregon, Wyoming, California and Hawaii. In 1901, when he was 18, his uncle Noah, who owned a skirt factory, sent him to Oberlin College, where he spent two years. After that he tried a number of jobs, including railroad brakeman, but when his uncle visited him in 1905 in Chicago, Chester was glad to accept an offer to go and work in the skirt factory in Cortland, NY – although his uncle warned him that he had to start at the bottom. But he proved bright, intelligent and hard-working, and had soon established a secure position.

Also working in the factory as a clothing inspector was a pretty farm girl named Grace Brown, known as Billie, who was three years his junior.

There was a strong mutual attraction, and soon Chester and Billie were seeing one another regularly, and he was visiting her in her lodgings. Then the inevitable happened, and they became lovers. She had put up some resistance, telling him in a later letter: "I said no many times."

He probably began to regret this fairly soon, for his position as the nephew of a factory owner gave him an entrée into Cortland society and, since he was good-looking and well-dressed, he was popular with mothers of marriageable daughters. He was also dating other girls from the factory. And a girl named Harriet Benedict, whose family were well-to-do, was more than interested in Chester Gillette. Life was suddenly opening up.

The good-looking Chester Gillette, who killed his pregnant girlfriend and tried to make it look like accidental drowning.

But in the following spring, his world collapsed when Billie told him she was pregnant. For a while she returned to her parents' farm, but kept her condition a secret. And their letters reveal a sudden deterioration of their relationship, with Billie accusing him of wanting to be rid of her. Undoubtedly, he felt trapped. Their strained relations were noted by others in the factory, and Billie was seen in tears.

Chester, though, soothed her by talking about some future trip they would take together, and she hoped that what he had in mind was a secret wedding.

Back at her parents' home Billie once more turned up the pressure, announcing that she wanted to die. "Please come and take me away…" And she added a veiled threat: "I will come straight back to Cortland if you don't come before [Saturday]."

On Sunday July 8, Chester arrived in the small town of DeRuyter, and registered at a hotel as Charles George. Billie joined him there the next day, and they took a train to Utica, NY, where Chester registered at a hotel as "Charles Brown and Wife". He left without paying the bill.

By this point, Billie had realized that there would be no immediate wedding. At the next hotel – the Glenmore in Tupper Lake Village – she had hysterics at breakfast and had to be helped from the room by a waitress.

Their next stop was intended to be the town of Old Forge. But they decided to rent a rowboat and take a trip out on Moose Lake, a popular tourist attraction. The boat owner, Robert Morrison, was curious why the young man should climb into the boat with two suitcases and a tennis racket.

That afternoon the couple were seen going ashore for a picnic, but they failed to return. The next morning, Morrison embarked on a search by steamboat, and eventually came upon the overturned boat. A young boy spotted a body lying on the bottom of the lake, and it was dragged up on a spiked pole. Billie Brown proved to have lacerations on her face and forehead that were clearly the result of blows.

In the Glenmore Hotel, the visitors' book named the couple as Grace Brown of South Otselic and Carl Grahm of Albany. Grace was soon identified as an employee of the Gillette Skirt Factory in Cortland. Her companion was assumed to be the young man with whom she was "keeping company", Chester Gillette.

A fellow employee, Bert Gross, read the newspaper account of the tragedy and decided to join the search, now two days old. He and a team that included the District Attorney George W. Ward tracked Gillette to the Arrowhead Hotel in Inlet, and he seemed shocked at the news of Grace's death. Then he declared that it had been the result of an accident.

Quite clearly, it was an open-and-shut case against him. If Billie had simply fallen in the water, why had he fled instead of reporting it?

His trial began on November 12, 1906, in the Herkimer Courthouse, and George Ward pointed out that the evidence of the aliases in hotel registers was damning. The defence – that Grace had committed suicide – convinced no one. It took the jury only six hours to find Gillette guilty.

Spoilt for choice

When Dreiser decided to write *An American Tragedy* in 1921, he had not made up his mind on which of three cases to base it. He was fascinated by the American phenomenon of murderers whose motive was to "rise in the world", and all three cases fitted this description.

In New York in 1890, a young medical student named Carlyle Harris, determined to become a wealthy society doctor, became involved with 18-year-old student Helen Potts and secretly married her when she became pregnant. The baby was stillborn. In January 1891, after an evening reading aloud with the school principal, Helen complained of numbness. A doctor who examined her noticed that her pupils were dilated, and saw by her bed a book with Carlyle Harris's initials. Harris admitted to giving her morphine capsules "for a headache". As the girl was dying, Harris performed a tracheotomy, but it only hastened her death.

Despite the vigorous advocacy of his mother, a temperance orator, Harris was found guilty and electrocuted in 1893.

In 1911, the Rev. Clarence Richeson, the handsome pastor of the Baptist church in Hyannis, Massachusetts, seduced a young choir singer named Avis Linnell, and got her pregnant. Then he was offered a church in fashionable Cambridge, and became involved with Violet Edmands, a girl of a higher social status. He went to the local YWCA, where Avis had moved, and offered her pills to abort her baby – they contained cyanide and she died. When it was learned that Richeson had purchased cyanide he was arrested. In custody he tried to emasculate himself with a jagged tin lid but failed; he was electrocuted in 1912.

An appeal heard in February 1908 was rejected, in spite of the efforts of Gillette's mother Louise to persuade the governor of New York to intervene personally. Gillette was electrocuted at Auburn on March 30, 1908.

1907

THE CAMDEN TOWN MURDER

For reasons we now find hard to understand, the Camden Town Murder caused the same morbid excitement in 1907 as Jack the Ripper's crimes 19 years earlier.

On the morning of September 12, 1907, 23-year-old Phyllis Dimmock, a prostitute of 29 St Paul's Road, Camden Town, was found by Bert Shaw, the man who was living with her, lying with her throat cut. Shaw worked nights as a railway cook, and believed that his "wife" had abandoned her old trade. This was wishful thinking.

The naked body lay on the bed and the room had been ransacked. An album of postcards lay on the floor.

For the past three nights, the police learned, she had slept with a sailor named Roberts, but he had a sound alibi. He told the police that Phyllis had shown him a postcard signed "Alice" which asked her to meet someone in her favourite pub, the Rising Sun.

When Bert Shaw found the postcard, it was printed in the *News of the World*, with a caption: "Can you recognize this writing?" An artist's model named Ruby Young, who lived in Earls Court Road, recognized the handwriting as that of her lover, an artist named Robert Wood. Wood called on her before she could post

a letter to the *News of the World*, and told her how he came to know the murdered girl. He had met her casually, he claimed, in a Camden Town pub, and had bought her a drink. When Phyllis told him she liked postcards, he offered to let her select one from a batch he happened to have in his pocket. She asked him to write "something nice on it", and he scrawled the appointment at the Rising Sun for Monday. She asked him to sign it "Alice", and he had gone off with the card, promising to post it to her, which he did the next day.

Wood must have been a good talker, because Ruby Young believed his unlikely story, and agreed not to claim the £100 reward. But she could not resist telling a friend "in absolute confidence". The friend repeated it to a journalist who terrified Ruby into admitting it, then went to the police. Wood was arrested as he left the offices of the London Sand Blast Glass Works in Grays Inn Road, where he worked, on October 4, 1907.

He was identified by several women as a friend

of Phyllis Dimmock, and a car-man, named MacCowan, said he had seen Wood leaving 29 St Paul's Road at 4.45 on the morning of the murder. Wood tried out a fake alibi, which he had previously arranged with

Ruby Young, but by this time she had already told the police the truth.

The case for the prosecution depended on circumstantial evidence. This consisted mainly of the postcard, and of a burnt fragment of a letter, which Phyllis Dimmock had also shown to Roberts, making an appointment at the Eagle on Wednesday, the evening of the murder, and signed "Bert". The handwriting, the prosecution claimed, was identical on both.

The trial took place at the Old Bailey on December I2, 1907, with the famous Marshall Hall defending. There was much evidence against Wood, all pointing to premeditation. He had a peculiar walk, with jerking shoulders, and MacCowan had recognized this. Phyllis Dimmock had kept her hair in curlers on the evening of the murder, which showed she was not expecting any clients. Many people had seen Wood with her in the Eagle pub, opposite Camden Town station.

Marshall Hall succeeded in throwing doubt on MacCowan's evidence, and declared that the character of many of the Crown witnesses – brothel-keepers, gin-sodden sluts, etc. – indicated the weakness of the Crown's case. He argued that there was no credible motive for Wood committing the crime, and that none of the stolen articles was ever traced to Wood. The weapon was never found, and Wood had no blood on his clothes.

The final witness for the defence was Wood himself, a handsome and quiet-spoken young man, who made an excellent impression in contrast to most of the Crown witnesses. It was obvious that public opinion was strongly on his side. (Wood's father and brother had already testified that he returned home at 11.30 on the evening of the murder.) The jury returned after 17 minutes to declare the prisoner not guilty. There were cheers and demonstrations.

The unfortunate Ruby Young was extremely unpopular and had to be smuggled away from the Old Bailey in a charlady's uniform.

Robert Wood, the young commercial artist, whose good looks undoubtedly played a role in his acquittal of the murder of Phyllis Dimmock.

29 St Paul's Road, Camden Town, where Phyllis Dimmock's common-law husband found her body.

Was this a crime of passion?

If Wood was the murderer – and it seems highly likely – then there is no other solution. The jury rightly dismissed robbery as the motive. So the murder must have been unplanned, the result of a quarrel. What would they have been quarrelling about except the fact that Phyllis was now "married", and Wood passionately objected to having his nose pushed out? He later changed his name and faded into obscurity.

1910s

THE CRIPPEN CASE

Harvey Hawley Crippen, known as "Peter", was an American doctor of homoeopathy who was 30 when, in 1892, he met a 19-year-old Polish girl named Cora Turner, and was galvanized into marrying her when she told him that a stove manufacturer – her present lover – wanted her to run away with him. They were badly suited; Crippen was the kind of person who wanted a quiet life, while Cora was a born party-goer. She was also convinced that she could be a great singer.

In the American Depression of 1893 they were forced to live with her parents, and she told him firmly to forget his Hippocratic oath and become a quack. Accordingly he took a job with a patent medicine company and was soon promoted to manager of their London branch. When they moved to London in 1897 he was on the huge salary of $10,000 a year.

However, a handbill advertising Mrs Crippen under her stage name Belle Elmore, and naming her husband as her manager, came to the attention of Crippen's employer in America, who felt that the manager of a comedienne was little better than a pimp, and fired him.

For many months Crippen floundered. He reached a new low when he learned that Belle had taken a lover. Finally, he found another – but worse paid – job with a firm of quacks, and moved into an office in Oxford Street. His new employer would soon go bankrupt, but not before Crippen had met a pretty 18-year-old named Ethel Le Neve, who was his secretary.

"Peter" Crippen, the little quack doctor, whose affair with his secretary led him to plan the murder of his wife, and eventually to the gallows.

Belle Elmore, the plump comedienne whose cheerful nature endeared her to her friends, but whose talents failed to impress London music-hall audiences.

Although Ethel (whose real name was Neave) was a moaning hypochondriac whose endless complaints of headache and catarrh had earned her the nickname "Not very well thank you", she was certainly better suited to Crippen than Belle. Although he was 13 years her senior, they were strongly attracted to one another. This is presumably why he did not divorce Cora when he found she had taken an ex-prize-fighter as a lover, and why he put up with a series of lodgers who shared his wife's bed. With bankrupt stock purchased from his ex-employer, he set up his own business, with Ethel as his bookkeeper.

Ethel was soon in love with her employer, and

Ethel Neave ("Le Neve"), Crippen's mistress, disguised herself as a boy in her bid to escape with her lover to a new life in Canada.

A friend of Marie Lloyd

Failing to become an opera singer, Cora lowered her sights to the music hall. But although her fellow artistes loved her effervescent personality, audiences found this short, plump diva unappealing. As Belle Elmore, Mrs Crippen eventually became a moderate success in the London music halls. The British liked the American act, and Belle seems to have been the sort of person that everyone liked anyway — immensely vital, good-natured, embarrassingly frank. She earned the enduring friendship of Marie Lloyd and many other music-hall artists. But at home, she became inclined to bouts of screaming temper. And most of her friends detested her husband, regarding him as a weakling.

The coal cellar in which Cora Crippen's dismembered body was uncovered.

Crippen then became a dentist, and Ethel his assistant. At one point, Ethel became pregnant; she was determined to have the baby, and for a while it looked as if it might transform their lives, and bring about the inevitable break with Belle. Then she had a miscarriage. And to make things worse, Belle went around telling the Music Hall Ladies' Guild members that no one was sure which of Ethel's many lovers was responsible. This may well have been the last straw. Instead of leaving her, which would obviously have been the sensible course, Crippen decided to murder her. (Another reason was Ethel's determination to achieve the respectability of marriage.) On January 17, 1910, he bought no fewer than 17 grains of hyoscine, a vegetable poison that he had seen administered to calm the violently insane at London's Royal Bethlehem Hospital. There is a strong probability that Ethel knew her lover inten-ded to kill his wife – she may even have helped plan it.

On the evening of January 31, 1910, two of Belle's music-hall friends came to dinner at the Crippens' house at 39 Hilldrop Crescent, Camden Town. They said goodbye to Belle at 1.30 the next morning; it was the last time she was seen alive. The following day, Crippen pawned Belle's diamond ring and earrings, and Ethel slept at Hilldrop Crescent. The next day, letters were received by the Secretary of the Music Hall Guild, signed Belle Elmore and resigning her membership; they explained she was

leaving for America to nurse a sick relative. Just before Easter, in the third week of March, Crippen told his friends that Belle was very ill in Los Angeles; soon after, he announced her death.

Belle's friends were suspicious. One checked with the shipping lines and discovered that no one of that name had sailed for America in February. A music-hall performer called Lil Hawthorne paid a visit to New York with her husband, John Nash, and they also made enquiries, which achieved no positive result. Back in London, they talked to Crippen, who sobbed convincingly, but told contradictory stories about where Belle had died. The Nashes decided to go to Scotland Yard. There they spoke to Chief Inspector Walter Dew of the CID, who agreed to go and talk to Crippen. The doctor smoothly admitted that his wife was still alive. She had simply walked out on him and gone to join her former prize-fighter lover in Chicago. Dew was completely taken in. A thorough search of the house convinced him that there were no suspicious circumstances. When Dew left the house, he was more than half convinced that Belle was alive.

Then Crippen made his greatest mistake; he decided to flee. He and Ethel left for Antwerp, and there took a ship for Canada. Ethel was dressed as a boy. When Dew returned two days later, and found the house deserted, he called in his team of diggers. Beneath the coal cellar floor, buried in quicklime, he found the remains of Mrs Crippen.

On board the SS *Montrose*, Crippen's secret had already been discovered by Captain

in some ways they were well suited. Crippen was a con-man, although as a result of weakness rather than moral delinquency, and Ethel was a pathological liar, whose biographer, Tom Cullen, writes that she "lied from sheer perversity – in fact she seemed incapable of telling the truth". But she was also determined not to yield her virginity until they were legally married. It was not

until Crippen discovered his wife in bed with a German lodger – and Ethel, presumably, had reason to feel that his marriage was at an end – that she consented to become his mistress. The date was December 6, 1906, seven years after their first meeting. It seems to have happened in a hired hotel room during the day, as did their subsequent intimacies, and Crippen continued to return home at night.

Henry Kendal, who quickly realized that "Mr Robinson's" son was a woman in disguise. In a copy of the *Daily Mail*, the captain found a picture of the wanted "cellar murderer". He handed his radio operator a message that began: "Have strong suspicion that Crippen London cellar murderer and accomplice are among saloon passengers." So it came about that Crippen was the first murderer to be caught by means of wireless telegraphy, for which Marconi had received the Nobel prize in the previous year. On the morning of July 31, 1910, as the ship lay off the mouth of the St Lawrence river, Crippen went on deck and was greeted by Dew, who approached him

with the words "Good morning, Dr Crippen."

The trial opened on October 18, 1910, at the Old Bailey. As an accused wife-killer, Crippen was his own worst enemy. His only chance of escaping the rope was to admit everything except intent to kill. But if Crippen pleaded guilty, the whole sordid story about Belle and Ethel would emerge. Crippen chose to protect Ethel and enter a plea of innocence. His defence was that Belle had left him, just as he said, so the body in the cellar must be that of some other woman, buried by some previous tenant, or hidden there during his tenancy. It was obviously an absurd story, and it amounted to suicide. And, of course, it left to the prosecution the fairly light task of proving that the corpse was that of Cora Crippen. This depended largely upon whether a certain piece of skin, which appeared to contain an operation scar, was from the stomach. If so, it was almost certainly Cora Crippen. Dr Turnbull, for the defence, said it was from the thigh, and that the scar was actually a fold.

The brilliant young pathologist Bernard Spilsbury, an expert on scar tissues, had no doubt whatsoever that the fragment of skin was from a stomach, not a thigh. And when they found part of a rectus muscle of the abdominal wall attached to the skin, the identification was proved beyond doubt. In court, Turnbull identified the skin as coming from the thigh, and the scar as a fold. Spilsbury, with the calm, grave manner that later led juries to think

him infallible, pointed out the older man's errors with a pair of forceps, and the harassed Turnbull left the box with an embarrassed flush. His colleague Dr Wall then admitted that he had changed his mind about the piece of skin, and that it came from the abdomen.

The poison hyoscine had been found in the remains, and Crippen was proved to have bought 17 grains of the drug not long before his wife's disappearance.

Crippen's downfall was not entirely due to medical evidence. Part of the body had been wrapped in a piece of pyjama jacket, and it had the maker's name on it. One pair of Crippen's pyjamas had a missing jacket, but Crippen insisted that these had been purchased years before, in 1905 or 1906 – the intervening years explaining why the jacket was now missing. But the prosecution was able to establish that the pyjamas to which the jacket belonged had been purchased in 1909, because the design was not made earlier. Crippen was caught out in a direct lie, and this convinced the jury of his guilt.

It took the jury only 27 minutes to reach their verdict. Crippen was hanged on November 23, 1910. Ethel was tried separately, but acquitted of the charges.

Ethel Le Neve emigrated to Canada, but she returned to England in 1916, took a job in a furniture store in Trafalgar Square, and married an accountant there. Her husband is said to have borne a strong resemblance to Crippen. She died in 1967 at the age of 84, telling her friend, the novelist Ursula Bloom, that she still loved Crippen.

Inspector Walter Dew escorts Crippen off the SS *Montrose*.

MARIE TARNOVSKA

Countess Marie Tarnovska, sometimes called the Siren of the Adriatic, was charged in Venice in March 1910 with conspiring to murder an unwanted lover. She appeared in court together with her maid Perrier, and two of her lovers – Donat Prilukov, a lawyer, and Dr Nicolas Naumov. They were charged with conspiring to murder a third lover, Count Paul Kamarovsky, who was actually shot by Naumov.

At 13 Marie was sent to a school for noblemen's daughters at Kiev. By the time she was 15, adolescent gawkiness had turned into remarkable beauty, and she was much admired by the young men at the local cavalry school. Among these was Count Vassili Tarnovsky, a man-about-town known for his conquests. So was a Russian prince, whose estate was heavily encumbered, and a baron who was even less well-off.

A nymphomaniac looking for love

Marie Tarnovska's life involved many emotional tangles. She was a beautiful but highly dominant woman, with more than a touch of sadism in her make-up, who found most men weaker than she was, and spent her life searching without success for the great love that would satisfy her.

The daughter of Count O'Rourk, she was the descendant of an Irish soldier of fortune who had emigrated to Russia when Peter the Great was looking for capable officers. From this ancestor she inherited a fiery romantic nature – a polite way of saying she was a nymphomaniac. Her mother was a beautiful Russian woman of unexcitable temperament.

All three approached Count O'Rourk to ask for his daughter's hand. When he told his daughter, he commented that the prince or the baron would make a tolerable match, but not Tarnovsky. Naturally, he was the one Marie preferred. And since her father was so set against him, she eloped and married him. She was then 16.

For a while they were happy, and were received in Kiev society. Tarnovsky fathered two children. But Marie's father was right. Tarnovsky loved women too much to be faithful to one. When he took mistresses, Marie was too

In real life, Marie Tarnovska was far less dowdy-looking.

sensible to upbraid him; she simply took lovers. But she took care to prevent her husband finding out for, like many obsessive seducers, he was pathologically jealous.

One day Pietro, the younger brother of the count, came to stay with them. He was only a boy when his brother married Marie; now he was a young man, tall, studious and with a romantic reverence for women. He saw Marie as an angel, and worshipped her. But he could not fail to observe how his brother neglected her. For Marie, he provided a chance for revenge. There was a certain sweet pleasure in seducing this shy and inexperienced

The victim, Count Paul Kamarovsky.

young man, and even more in the thought that she was cuckolding her husband with his own brother.

However, she was revealing a certain lack of foresight. Seducing Pietro was easy enough. But what did she want to do with this solemn and idealistic young man once he was her slave? A brief affair would have been perfect, but an adoring lover was too much of a responsibility.

Things became more complicated when he announced his intention of telling his brother the truth, and asking him to release Marie so he could marry her.

Her natural guile provided the answer. She told Pietro that she wanted him to be sure this was not a brief infatuation, and to prove it by going away for six months; then, if he still felt the same, she would come to him. Sorrowfully, he agreed and left.

Six weeks later she wrote to him to say that she could not bring herself to leave her children, and that they must renounce one another. In the best tradition of nineteenth-century Russian lovers, Pietro hanged himself. "Foolish boy!" said Marie, but she went to the funeral with her husband.

Her next lover was a wealthy financier who showered her with jewels and begged her to go with him to his estate in the Urals. But Marie had

no intention of condemning herself to a dreary life in the countryside. Besides, she had already found a lover she preferred - an officer of the Russian Imperial Guard named Alexis Bosevsky. So she ordered the financier to go back home and forget all about her. Grief-stricken, he returned to his estate and shot himself.

Soon she was bored with her guards officer, who was proving to be as demanding as a husband. His ardour convinced her that he would never leave her of his own accord. Then the solution occurred to her – that her husband would certainly kill him if he suspected that they were lovers.

She told Bosevsky that her husband was going away, and they could finally spend a night in one another's arms. When he entered her bedroom he found her waiting in a transparent negligée. She surrendered to his caresses until she heard the sounds of her husband coming, then she screamed. The count did what any Russian husband would do - drew his pistol and shot the would-be rapist.

Bosevsky did not die at once, however. At his deathbed, Marie had to pretend that she had screamed to save her honour, and that she was still in fact in love with him. At least poor Bosevsky died without realizing what a dupe he'd been.

During his final hours Bosevsky was attended by a doctor named Dmitri Stahl, who was also a drug addict. Watching Marie embracing her dying lover suggested to him the idea of supplanting Bosevsky. He introduced her to cocaine, and Marie soon became his mistress. The affair left her an addict.

Meanwhile, her husband had been arrested and charged with Bosevsky's killing. Marie approached an old acquaintance, a wealthy and influential lawyer named Donat Prilukov, and asked him to pull strings to get her husband exiled to Siberia. Prilukov was a married man with three children, but the hint of a night of love with Marie was enough to make him agree.

However, in Tsarist Russia, a husband who shoots a man who is trying to rape his wife is virtually untouchable. All Prilukov's efforts came to nothing. Worse still, the investigation revealed that

The room (marked with an "X") in which Count Kamarovsky was murdered.

Bosevsky had been Marie's lover for some time. The outraged count thereupon told Marie that their marriage was over, and drove her from his house with a horsewhip.

But she still had the faithful Prilukov, and had no difficulty inducing him to desert his family and take her on a tour of Europe. They went to Vienna, Paris, Algeria and Marseilles. Unlike her former lovers, Prilukov was not a willing victim; the thought of his wife and children tormented him. In Marseilles he left her and took a train to return to his wife. But, as he later testified at the trial, he was unable to go through with it and, a few stations later, got off the train and returned to Marie.

Back in Russia, she met and enslaved a colonel, Count Paul Kamarovsky, who had just returned from the Russo-Japanese war. Prilukov knew all about the new lover, but was so in love that he gave her 100,000 francs that he had embezzled to run away with. She used them to accompany Kamarovsky to Warsaw.

There she sighted another potential victim, Kamarovsky's friend Dr Nicolas Naumov. Kamarovsky made the mistake of telling Marie that Naumov was a woman-hater. Such a challenge was irresistible, and soon Naumov was so violently and romantically in love with her that he fired a bullet through his hand to prove it, and allowed her to engrave her initials on

his arm with a dagger. (She admitted that the sight of his blood thrilled her, evidence of her peculiar pathology.)

Tiring of Kamarovsky, she brooded on the simplest way of getting rid of him. Since Naumov was the romantic rather than the homicidal type, she sent for Prilukov, who hastened to her side. Then it struck her that perhaps Naumov, after all, might do her bidding if she made him jealous enough. She made sure that Naumov heard that Kamarovsky had been seen leaving her bedroom in his nightshirt. He wrote in despair a letter that would later be read in court:

"I was and am and would have liked always to be thy slave. Thou hast deceived me. All is now finished and thou hast opened an abyss before me. My life is now impossible…"

Marie lost no time in assuring him of her love, then went on to show him a fake telegram from Kamarovsky (who was in Venice), declaring that Naumov was a worthless blackguard and she was little better. That, and Marie's renewed surrender, was all that was necessary to make him swear that Kamarovsky would die.

She, Prilukov and Naumov went to Venice, discussing various schemes for killing Kamarovsky, including chloroform and a dagger. Meanwhile, Marie persuaded Kamarovsky to insure his life for £20,000 in her favour.

The murder took place on September 3, 1907. Naumov went to the villa that Kamarovsky had rented on the Campo Santa Maria, strode past the maid, rushed upstairs, and burst into Kamarovsky's bedroom with a cry of "Paul, you

scum!"Then there were shots. Moments later, Naumov rushed down the stairs holding the smoking revolver, and vanished through the front door.

Outside, the police, tipped off by Prilukov, were waiting, and placed him under arrest. And Naumov, aware of the deception, lost no time in confessing, and implicating Marie and Prilukov. Already in

Marie Tarnovska arrives at court in 1910.

Vienna, they were extradited.

Prilukov's legal skills delayed the trial until March 1910. And Marie, who had hoped to get rid of two lovers at a stroke and end up £20,000 the richer, stood in the dock to hear her love life exposed and described in explicit detail by the well-prepared prosecution, while press men scribbled it all down for the fascination of readers all over the world.

All three defendants did

> **I was and am and would have liked always to be thy slave. Thou hast deceived me. All is now finished and thou hast opened an abyss before me. My life is now impossible.**
>
> Dr Nicolas Naumov

their best to blame the other, but none of them stood a chance. Marie was sentenced

to eight years in prison, Prilukov to 10, and Naumov – in spite of the fact that he had fired the shots – to only three, on the grounds that he was clearly not entirely sane.

Marie Tarnovska was sent to Trano prison, but served only two years of her sentence – she was released due to ill health in August 1912. She finally died in Paris, still a cocaine addict, in 1923 at the age of 45.

1914

MADAME HENRIETTE CAILLAUX

Madame Caillaux's shooting of a newspaper editor, because he had libelled her husband, could actually be said to have been one of the contributory causes of the First World War.

Gaston Calmette, editor of *Le Figaro*, who was shot by Mme Caillaux.

Joseph Caillaux was a Leftist who outraged his opponents with his suggestion that Frenchmen ought to pay income tax. Nowadays, that suggestion does not raise an eyebrow, but in the early twentieth century, only the British and the Germans paid tax, and the very idea enraged the French middle classes. That was one of the reasons Caillaux got sacked from his premiership in 1912. But he was back in 1914, this time as finance minister.

The conservative press hated him. And since a public figure could not sue for libel, they could invent any smears they liked. The chief offender in this respect was *Le Figaro*, and its editor Gaston Calmette. He called Caillaux just about everything except a rapist and child molester.

He had another reason for hating Caillaux. Because Germany had a strong socialist party, Caillaux was inclined to regard them with sympathy. The rest of France had detested them since the Franco-Prussian war of 1870, which had ended with total French defeat.

Certainly, the German Kaiser Wilhelm was about as irritating a figure as it is possible to imagine – stupid, conceited and belligerent – and his attempts to humiliate the French by interfering in Morocco, which they regarded as their own backyard, caused national indignation. Most Frenchmen believed – rightly – that he wanted to provoke a war. In fact, Caillaux believed so too, but he also wanted to prevent this from happening. And the French right regarded him as a weak-kneed appeaser.

In two months, *Le Figaro* devoted 138 sneering articles and cartoons to Caillaux. He

Mme Henriette Caillaux, who was willing to face life imprisonment to avenge slurs on her husband's honour.

had divorced his former wife to marry his much younger mistress Henriette, and his ex-wife had retaliated by passing on to the press various indiscreet personal letters, both to her and to Henriette. As she saw her husband sinking into despair, Henriette decided to do something about it. Calmette had attacked her too, so she felt she had the right to be angry.

On March 16, 1914, she bought a Browning revolver, and tried it out in the shooting gallery in the shop's basement. She went home and changed into an expensive gown, – then wrote her husband a note. Since the law would not give them justice, she said, she would go and obtain it herself. Then she ordered her chauffeur to take her to the offices of *Le Figaro*

in Rue Druot. She asked to see the editor, and was told to take a seat outside his office. While there, she heard an employee chortling about another story on her husband that would be published the following day. Then Calmette's voice was heard asking her to be shown in.

Scandal in court

Henriette's husband, of course, had to resign, and did so the evening his wife killed Calmette. But the scandal had damaged his reputation; his sexual habits, such as kissing Henriette "all over", had been detailed in court, to the delight of the French public. Above all, one of France's most effective advocates for peace was removed from influence, a result that would have delighted Calmette.

Caillaux, now re-elected, failed to express regret for the death of the editor: "If Calmette had walked up to her to disarm her, as any man of courage would have done, instead of running away, or even if he had not crouched down, he would only have been wounded in the legs."

He was a model of Gallic politeness. When she said, "No doubt you are surprised to see me?" he replied, "Not at all. Please be seated."

She wasted no time. As Calmette walked back to his desk, she pulled the revolver out of her handbag and pulled the trigger. The editor's assistants dived to the floor, and Calmette tried to hide behind his desk. She stood over him and fired four more shots. The office boy tackled her and wrenched the gun away.

As excited employees rushed into the office and helped Calmette into his chair, he gasped out to them: "Forgive me for causing you so much trouble, my friends."

Mme Caillaux watched the commotion. And when there was silence, she told the reporters: "It was the only way to end it all. There was no justice, so I administered it."

As a reporter tried to grab her, Henriette explained with

Mme Caillaux in the dock.

dignity: "My car is waiting below to drive me to the police station."

Calmette died a few hours later in hospital from a bullet that had entered his stomach. By the time he was dead, Henriette was already in jail.

Three months later, on July 20, Mme Caillaux's trial opened in Paris amid unprecedented publicity. Her defence was that the killing was not premeditated, and that the gun had gone off accidentally ... five times. It was obviously preposterous, but the jury was as charmed by this pretty, slightly plump lady as her husband had been. The jurors were unanimous in proclaiming her innocent – obviously, for in France, anything less would have been regarded as ungallant behaviour. And Henriette was allowed to leave the court and return home.

1920s

1922

THE HALL-MILLS MURDERS

On the morning of Saturday, September 16, 1922, a 15-year-old girl named Pearl Bahmer was taking a stroll in the New Jersey countryside with a youth called Raymond Schneider when she saw two bodies lying on the grass near a crabapple tree. They raced to the nearest house and told the owner, who rang the police.

Eleanor Mills, choir singer and mistress of the Reverend Edward Hall.

What they had found were the corpses of the local minister, Edward Wheeler Hall, who was 41, and of one of his choir singers, Mrs Eleanor Mills, 34. He had been shot once in the head, she three times. Her throat had also been slashed from ear to ear and maggots infested the cut – it later emerged that the killer had cut out her tongue and vocal cords. Scattered around the bodies were torn, pencilled letters. The minister's calling card had been propped against one of his feet and his panama covered his face.

The letters proved to be love letters from Mrs Mills to the Reverend Hall, and revealed conclusively that she had been his mistress for some time. In fact, their affair was widely known, and a few people were even aware that they planned to elope.

Clearly, this was a *crime passionel*, which suggested that the person responsible was either the Reverend Hall's wife, or Mrs Mills's husband. The wife was Frances Hall, seven years her husband's senior and from a wealthy and aristocratic background. But then, she was a woman known to have a kindly disposition, hardly the type to mutilate her husband's mistress. As to Mrs Mills' husband, Jim, he was generally reckoned to be feeble and inadequate, and completely under his wife's thumb. Not only did he know about the love affair, and had made no objection, but his wife had warned him that one day she would leave him for the minister. Neither seemed a likely killer.

The investigation that followed was something of a farce. Two lots of country police squabbled about their jurisdiction and seemed to have no idea of where to start – they even arrested the couple who found the bodies, whereupon Pearl Bahmer provoked scandal by accusing her father of incest. This had nothing to do with the case, but did lead to the revelation that he had been carrying a revolver on the night of the murders. A vast crowd of eager reporters – more than 90 – added to the wild confusion at police HQ.

Two more logical suspects were Mrs Hall's brothers Willie and Henry – the latter an expert shot. But concrete evidence was lacking, and finally police incompetence and sheer muddle led a Grand Jury to decide that there was insufficient evidence to charge anyone with murder.

So the case marked time for four more years. Then, on the evening of July 17, 1926, police surrounded Mrs Hall's

The wronged wife, Frances Hall, wealthy, aristocratic, and known to have treated the victim with kindness.

house and arrested her. It seemed that the husband of a parlourmaid in her house had tried to get his marriage annulled, and made some amazing accusations. Arthur Riehl stated that the parlourmaid, Louise Geist, had learned that the minister and his mistress had planned to elope, and had passed on this information to Mrs Hall. On the night of the murder, Mrs Hall, her brother Willie Stevens and Louise Geist drove out to the lovers' lane where the couple planned to meet, and killed the two of them. Louise received $5,000 for her part in the crime and for her silence. The newspapers made the accusation into front-page headlines after Mrs Hall and her brothers were arrested.

Some of the most telling evidence against them came from a bizarre lady who became known to the press as the "Pig Woman"; she was Mrs Jane Gibson, who ran a pig farm near De Russey's Lane, the scene of the murder, and who claimed that at 10.30 on the night of September 14, 1922, she had passed close to the crabapple tree under which the bodies were later found, and heard a quarrel, followed by shots. But the Pig Woman's mother faced her in the courtroom corridor and declared that her daughter was a pathological liar, administering such a tongue-lashing that the hefty Pig Woman collapsed – she later proved to be suffering from cancer – and had to give her evidence from a hospital bed in the courtroom. From this, she croaked out a story

of how she had been chasing a prowler when she saw a Dodge sedan – the Halls had such a car – and a middle-aged woman and a man. The woman shouted angrily: "Explain these letters!" Then there were screams and shots.

But perhaps the most impressive evidence concerned the visiting card propped by the dead man's foot. It had been in a safe in the State

Prosecutor's office since the day after the murder. And when examined in the Middlesex County fingerprint laboratory, it had been found to contain a print.

Lieutenant Fred Drewen mounted the stand and testified that he had taken the fingerprints of Willie Stevens, and that the print on the visiting card was that of Stevens's left index finger. Next, the head of

the Bureau of Records of the Newark Police Department, Edward H. Schwartz, testified that he had examined the card and found that the print was that of Willie Stevens. Finally, Joseph Faurot, who had been New York's Deputy Police Commissioner, mounted the stand. He not only testified that the fingerprint was that of Willie Stevens, but produced transparencies

of the accused man's fingerprints, which he projected on to a screen, explaining to the jury his reasons for having no doubt.

In an English or French court of law, that would have settled the case; unless Willie Stevens could explain how his fingerprints came to be on the minister's calling card, the jury would have concluded that it was he who had placed the card against the dead man's foot.

Fortunately for the defendants, there was a dramatic interruption. Alexander Simp-

Choir singer Eleanor Mills (left), poses with Mrs Frances Hall, wife of the pastor of their New Brunswick church.

The "Pig Woman", Jane Gibson, was carried into court in bed, to give her sensational evidence.

son, the peppery little prosecutor, announced that the Pig Woman was at death's door, and about to sink into a coma. So Faurot stood down to make room for the Pig Woman's doctor, and the judge announced that the trial would be adjourned for the time being.

Back on the stand, a few days later, Schwartz and Faurot again insisted that the fingerprint on the card was that of Willie Stevens, although they agreed that being exposed to the weather for 36 hours might have impaired the print.

When the maid, Louise Geist, appeared on the stand, she testified that, on the morning after the murder, Willie had told her that "something terrible happened last night". And another witness, Marie

Demarest, told how a private detective hired by Mrs Hall had tried to bribe her to suppress part of her testimony.

Things looked black for the defendants. Yet, incredibly, the defence made no real attempt

> ## " I CHARGE WITH ALL THE SOLEMNITY THAT IS INVOLVED IN IT THAT THE CARD IS A FRAUD. "
> Robert J. McCarter

to discredit the most serious piece of evidence: the calling card. Robert J. McCarter told the jury: "I charge with all the solemnity that is involved in it that the card is a fraud." But he failed to explain how a fraudulent fingerprint could be fabricated, or how, if the card itself was a fraud, Willie

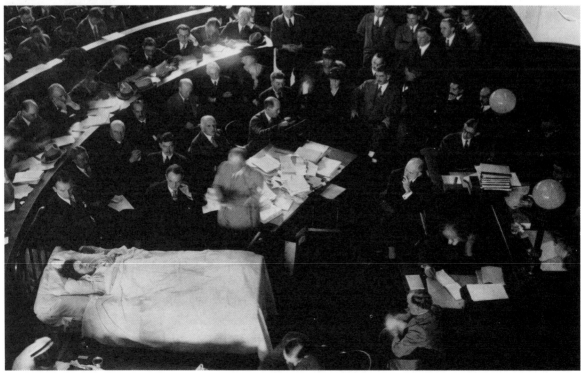

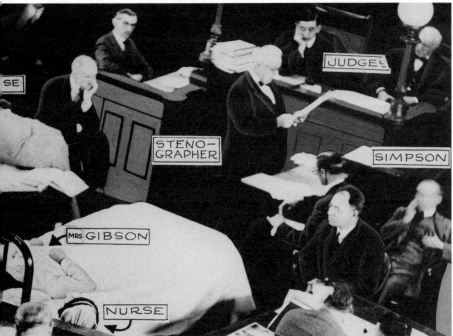

SE

JUDGE

STENO-GRAPHER

SIMPSON

MRS GIBSON

NURSE

In this general view of the courtroom, the participants are labeled.

wife slit her throat and removed the vocal cords that had been responsible for the sweet voice that had seduced her husband.

So why was she acquitted, when all the evidence pointed to her guilt? It may be that the upper-class status of the three defendants made the jury feel they were unlikely killers. Another is certainly the irritatingly flamboyant manner of the prosecutor, a native of Jersey City, who had referred to the residents of Somerset County, where the trial took place, as country bumpkins. During the trial, his extrovert city manners grated on the jury. It seems probable that the verdict was a gesture of defiance and contempt towards State Senator Alexander Simpson rather than an affirmation of belief in the innocence of Mrs Hall and her brothers.

Stevens had been induced to put his fingerprint on it. The jury was apparently incurious about this vital point. On December 3, 1926, after deliberating for five hours, they returned a verdict of not guilty. James Mills, sexton and husband of the murdered woman, remarked that he was not surprised, as money could buy anything.

At this distance in time, the solution to this "unsolved" murder case seems obvious. The defence was correct about one thing: Frances Hall had no idea that Eleanor Mills was her husband's mistress. When she found out - probably from overhearing a telephone conversation about an elopement - she summoned her brothers, and they hurried off to administer summary justice. Mrs Hall may have been doubly enraged because she genuinely liked Eleanor Mills and had always

treated her with kindness. If the Pig Woman's testimony is correct, Hall was shot first, above the ear, while Eleanor

ran away; they found her with the aid of a torch, dragged her back and shot her beside her lover. Then the infuriated

The Klan did it ... possibly

In the best book on the case, *The Minister and the Choir Singer* (1964), William H. Kunstler has another interesting suggestion. Flatly dismissing the notion that Mrs Hall and her brothers were guilty, he goes on to suggest that the culprits were the Ku Klux Klan. And he disarms scepticism by going on to talk about the Klan and its activities, and pointing out that the modern Klan had spread swiftly since its formation in Georgia in 1915 – where it was a white supremacist organization – to the northern states, where American Puritanism was showing disgust at post-war immorality and the onset of the roaring 20s. By now Klan membership had expanded to over a million. Many "loose" women were stripped, then tarred and feathered, and notorious seducers kidnapped and flogged. The open adultery of the Reverend Hall and his mistress was just the kind of abomination that outraged Klansmen.

But there is one major objection to this scenario – that when the Klan administered "justice", it usually left a calling card – sometimes even branding the offender with KKK. Which seems to dispose of an otherwise promising solution.

THE LOVER IN THE ATTIC

In 1930 the case of Walburga Osterreich made America roar with laughter. Perhaps that was why the Los Angeles district attorney did not have the heart to pursue the prosecution, and let her go.

In spite of her name, Walburga, known as Vally, was not in the least like a typical German *hausfrau*. In 1903 she looked much younger than her 36 years, and had a superb figure and a smile that made men forget that her face was plain.

No one in Milwaukee's German community could understand why Vally had married her husband Fred, who looked like what he was – an unromantic, overweight businessman who drank heavily, but not heavily enough to prevent him from becoming rich (a millionaire by to-day's standards) by giving unremitting attention to the manufacture of aprons.

Walburga had the misfortune to lose her only son Raymond

when he was a teenager. She was fond of one of Raymond's friends, a skinny, pale orphan named Otto Sanhuber, who worked as a sewing machine repairman, and who occasionally went to service machines in Fred's factory.

Otto had developed a crush on his friend's kindly mother, so after Raymond's death he continued to call on her, and daydreamed of resting in her arms. As to Vally, she had Spanish blood, and when she observed his Oedipal fixation, probably decided that it was not such a bad idea.

One day Walburga asked Fred to send someone to look at her sewing machine. As she had hoped, it was Otto. She was wearing a thin silk dressing gown, silk stockings, and a fetching perfume as she led him to her bedroom where the machine was located. It is likely that it was Vally who took the lead in the seduction, since Otto was inexperienced, shy and unaccustomed to attracting female attention. All we know is that by the time he left, he had ceased to be a virgin, and Vally now knew how much she enjoyed adultery.

Thereafter the machine, like Vally, required frequent servicing. But not often enough for Vally, who even risked visiting Otto in his uncomfortable lodging, where the bed was far less soft than her own. They found an excuse to take a holiday together in St Louis, but spent most of the nine days in bed.

Finally, Fred began to suspect that his wife had a lover. However, when he confronted her, the scornful

nobility of her denials convinced him that he was mistaken. But the prospect of having to break off with her lover or risk being found out made her determined not to lose him. One day Fred came home to find her gone.

A private detective reported that Vally and Otto had taken a train to Chicago. Attempts to track them down failed, but Vally soon returned of her own accord; she admitted her infidelity and asked for a divorce. Her husband refused, on the grounds that his alimony would benefit "that shrimp".

Three years later, in 1911, Fred Osterreich decided that his rival had left town, and dismissed the private detective. In fact, Otto Sanhuber was by then spending most of his nights in the bed of their deceased son Raymond, and his days in the bed of Vally Osterreich. Eventually, he moved into the attic room in the Osterreichs' house, rendered confident by the knowledge that Fred was too corpulent to climb the ladder and through the trapdoor.

During the First World War, Otto announced that he was going to fight for his country; Vally's tears and pleas dissuaded him - temporarily. Finally, patriotism triumphed, and he went and enlisted. The sergeant's jibes about his size sent him scurrying back to his attic within hours. Now he was a deserter, he made doubly sure that no one suspected his presence.

Soon after that, Fred decided to retire, and the Osterreichs moved out to Los Angeles. Otto went on ahead, and hung around until they arrived. He was trailing them as they went house-hunting in Los Angeles. Vally rejected several houses

because they had no attic. Finally, they found a suitable place, and Otto moved into his eighth attic in 14 years.

The end came some months later, on August 29, 1922. Neighbours heard shots, and a woman screaming. They rang the police, who had to break into the house through the bolted front door. Fred Osterreich was lying dead on the floor, shot through the head with a .25, a lady-size gun. Vally was found locked in the closet in her locked bedroom. She told how she was getting undressed in the clothes closet when she heard shots; then the closet door was locked behind her. That was all she could tell them...

At first, nothing seemed to be missing. Then Vally recalled her husband's diamond-studded watch, and the large bankroll he habitually carried around. This must obviously have been the burglar's objective. The investigation soon went cold.

A year later, the diamond-studded watch turned up - in the waistcoat pocket of an estate attorney named Herman Shapiro. He happened to bump into Chief Inspector Herman Cline, who had handled the Osterreich mystery and recognized the watch Shapiro pulled out to consult from its description. Shapiro said Mrs Osterreich had found it, not bothered to tell the police - who seemed to have lost interest - and had given it to him. Vally confirmed this - she said she had found the watch under a mat.

An actor named Bellows now came forward to offer evidence that seemed to incriminate Mrs Osterreich. He told how, soon after the murder, she had asked him to destroy a small revolver

by filing it into pieces. He had dumped these into the famous tar trap of La Brea on Wilshire Boulevard. An enterprising newspaper succeeded in recovering the rusting pieces. Then another neighbour of the Osterreichs described how Vally had asked him to dispose of yet another revolver soon after the murder. This was also located. It began to look as if Vally Osterreich could have killed her husband, then, with a certain amount of ingenuity, locked herself in the closet.

Vally was questioned for days. But eventually, the police had to release her. However, before they did this she asked to see her estate attorney Herman Shapiro...

Eight years later, in 1930, Mr Shapiro went to the police and told them that his conscience was troubling him. When he had spoken to Mrs Osterreich, she had told him that her dissolute younger brother was living in the attic of her home. Would he please go there, scratch on the wall, and take him food and water? Shapiro did as she asked, and was confronted by a small man with a receding chin, who admitted that he had been living in various attics for years. But he complained that he was tired of his situation, and was anxious to leave. Besides, if the police found him now, it would incriminate Mrs Osterreich. So Shapiro drove Otto Sanhuber to San Francisco. And Herman Shapiro became Vally's new lover. It was after they had quarrelled and broken up that he went to the police.

They searched Vally's former home - she had moved by now to a smaller residence - and found that the attic

The lover, Otto Sanhuber, is embraced by his wife after his acquittal.

showed signs of long-time habitation. Soon after that, Otto Sanhuber was arrested. He was now married, and was working as the caretaker of an apartment building.

Back at the police station, he admitted shooting Fred Osterreich. But, he said, it had been an accident. Ever since the Osterreich home had been burgled, he had kept a revolver close to hand. That night in August, he had heard the couple returning from an evening out, then quarrelling. Fred had slapped his wife so hard she fell down. So he, Otto, had hastened downstairs, to find Fred standing over his prostrate wife. When Fred saw his rival, he exploded: "You little rat! What are you doing here?" There was a scuffle, and the gun had gone off. When the struggle was over, Fred Osterreich lay dead, and Vally was wailing: "Gee this is terrible!" Otto saw the answer: lock Vally in her closet, then lock the bedroom door and retreat to his attic...

The five-week trial of Otto Sanhuber caused a sensation – the story of the "phantom lover in the attic" gripped the imagination of America. But a moving speech from his attorney, the famous Jerry Giesler, ensured the sympathy of the jury for the poor orphan. They decided that he was not guilty of murder, only of manslaughter, and Otto received a sentence of three years. The truth was, nobody had the heart to see him executed. And since the death of Fred

Osterreich had taken place eight years earlier, a statute of limitations meant that he was free. He went back to his wife and their apartment building.

Walburga Osterreich was tried separately on a charge of conspiracy. But when the jury failed to reach agreement, the district attorney decided he couldn't face it all over again, and begged to be excused. So she also walked free. She had lost most of her money in the stock market crash of 1929, but with what remained she opened the first Beverly Hills supermarket on Wilshire Boulevard, and made her home in a kind of attic above it. She lived there peacefully until her death.

Walburga Osterreich being arraigned in court in 1915, with Detective Cline on the left.

Lover by day, writer by night

One day, Fred looked up from the garden, and saw a face looking down at him. He went and tried to open the attic trapdoor, but it was locked from above. Vally told him he was imagining things, and he reluctantly decided he must be suffering from overwork or alcoholic delusions. During the day, Otto would make love to Vally and help her with the housework, a combination of pet, houseboy and stallion. Meanwhile, Fred's business had become so prosperous that he now employed 1,500 people.

In his attic, Otto spent his days reading magazines and library books, and even scribbling adventure stories, which began to sell. Fred's increasing prosperity led them to change house a number of times; whenever that happened, Vally had to smuggle Otto into the new attic.

BYWATERS AND THOMPSON

The most widely publicized British *crime passionel* of the period between the two world wars is the case of Bywaters and Thompson.

Frederick Bywaters, Edith Thompson's young lover.

Around midnight on October 4, 1922, having enjoyed an evening at the theatre, Edith and Percy Thompson were returning to their home in Ilford, Essex, when a man jumped out from the shadows. Brandishing a knife, he drove it several times into Percy Thompson's chest. Thompson collapsed to the pavement. His wife screamed and cried for help. But it was too late. By the time help arrived the assailant had fled and Thompson was dying. Escorted home by the police his wife seemed to be in shock, and told them she had no idea what had happened.

The next morning, Edith was told that her husband had died of his wounds. She continued to maintain that she had no clear memory of what had happened.

But by now, a neighbour had given the police a name that interested them: Frederick Bywaters, a young man who had once lodged with the Thompsons, but had left after a quarrel with the husband. Percy Thompson's brother Richard believed that Bywaters – a laundry steward on a P&O liner – was at present

away at sea. But Superintendent Frederick Wensley soon learned this was not true. In fact, Bywaters, a young man of 20, was soon traced to the home of Edith's parents. Brought in for questioning, he seemed arrogant and irritable; in spite of his youth, he was obviously a highly dominant character. But when marks on the sleeve of his jacket were identified as blood, Wensley informed him that he was going to be detained.

By this time, the police had obtained a search warrant; and what they found in Edith Thompson's home would eventually condemn her to death: a series of letters written by Edith to Bywaters, that made it clear that these two were lovers.

It was Edith who broke first. While crossing the yard at the Ilford police station, she caught a glimpse of Bywaters through the library window. She suddenly cried: "Oh God, what can I do? Why did he do it? I didn't want him to do it. I must tell the truth." Minutes later she had admitted that the man who stabbed her husband was Frederick Bywaters.

Soon afterwards, Bywaters also confessed. He admitted lying in wait for the couple at the end of the road, then grabbing Thompson as he walked past and asking him to divorce his wife. They grappled, he said, and he pulled out a knife. "He got the worst of it." Mrs Thompson, he insisted, knew nothing about the murder as she had been standing at some distance and had been "spellbound, at the time..."

If that had been all, Frederick Bywaters would have hanged alone. But the letters shed a more sinister light on the affair. For, if they were to be believed, Edith had been trying to get rid of her husband by poisoning him with ground glass – a light bulb pounded into pieces – "big pieces too" – but he had found one of them in his porridge.

The dead man was exhumed, and his stomach examined – by Dr Bernard Spilsbury – for signs of poisoning with powdered glass. Spilsbury concluded that Edith's acc-ount was pure imagination.

Nevertheless, when the trial opened on December 6, 1922, Edith Thompson stood beside her lover in the dock. The jury heard how, in the summer of 1921, the love affair had started on holiday on the Isle of Wight. The Thompsons had gone there with Edith's younger sister, Avis Graydon, and her boyfriend, Frederick Bywaters, who was a friend of her brother. Edith had known him since he was a schoolboy (even now he was only 18).

Two months later – in August – Percy Thompson realized that he had made a mistake in inviting Bywaters to live with them. The young man was unmistakably sweet on Edith, and she encouraged

The street corner where Percy Thompson was stabbed to death.

and told her lover that she had given way and "surrendered to him unconditionally" – a phrase that sounds as if it was intended to arouse jealousy. Now the letters begin to contain daydreams of getting rid of her husband. How about poisoned chocolates? Or hyoscine, the drug Crippen had used? She might poison him with gas if they had gas in the house... But perhaps a ground electric light bulb would serve just as well? Or an overdose of opium? It was soon after this that she told her lover that she had tried powdered glass three times, but that she had decided to give up these attempts at murder after her husband found a large piece of glass in his porridge; further attempts could wait until Bywaters returned. She reassured Bywaters that if Percy died, there would be no suspicion because of his bad heart.

The ship was away on a long voyage – to Australia – so Edith had plenty of time to daydream. But finally – on September 23, 1922 – the long wait was over. They met at a restaurant opposite her office in Aldersgate Street. On

him by allowing him to fetch and carry for her. In fact, this was what led to the quarrel that caused Bywaters to leave. One warm afternoon, as they sat in the garden waiting for the arrival of Avis Graydon, Edith, who was sewing, asked for a pin. Bywaters rushed in to get one. Percy Thompson was in a bad mood, and made some sarcastic remark about her desire to have people at her beck and call. The two began to bicker. Later, at tea (Avis was late), Thompson continued to be grumpy, and made some critical remarks about Edith's family. In the garden, Bywaters heard a crash as a chair overturned, and a gasp of pain from Edith as she was thrown across the room. Bywaters made the mistake of intervening, and was told to pack his bags and go.

How the love affair continued is not clear – except that the lovers now had to meet secretly. Neither is it known when she cast aside her inhibitions and became his mistress. But from September 9, 1921, Bywaters was away at sea, and Edith wrote to him at every opportunity ("Darling, your old pal is getting quite a sport. On Saturday I was first in the egg and spoon race and first in the 100-yard flat race and third in the 50-yards last race...").

When he returned, they began to meet secretly again. Percy Thompson, now thoroughly suspicious, waited at the station one day, and saw Edith get off the train with Bywaters. He waited until later, at home, to upbraid her, sneering that Bywaters had seen him at the station and "run away". When Edith reported this to her lover, he lost no time in calling at the house and insisting that he had not run away – he had simply not seen Thompson. When Bywaters told Percy Thompson that he was making Edith's life hell, the husband replied: "I've got her and I'll keep her."

In November Bywaters went back to sea, and there were more letters. Thompson wanted his wife to have a baby; she refused angrily. Then she suddenly decided she preferred domestic peace,

Mr dull-but-reliable

Edith had married Percy Thompson when she was 22, in 1915; he was a shipping clerk and was two years her senior. Percy had joined the London Scottish Regiment, and his wife, who was a romantic young woman, inclined to hysteria, had taken to her bed. However, Thompson proved to have heart trouble, and was soon invalided out. Thompson seems to have been dull but reliable, and his pay was poor; in fact, Edith contributed more to the family budget with her pay as the manageress of a millinery firm in the City, for which she received the generous (for the time) salary of £6 a week.

It seems that the lovers were first attracted to one another on holiday in the Isle of Wight, and when Bywaters kissed Edith, she made no protest. But Thompson noticed nothing of the flirtation – he probably regarded Bywaters as little more than a child – and liked the young man enough to suggest that he come and lodge with them. Freddy accepted the suggestion, and a week later told Edith he was in love with her. They sealed their love with a kiss – but, at this stage, it went no further.

Saturday morning she got time off from work and they spent the morning in the park. They even seem to have found an opportunity to make love, for she writes tenderly about "what happened last night".

She was remorseful about going to the theatre with her husband, and advised her lover to "do something to make you forget" – perhaps take Avis out. "I'll be hurt, I know, but I want you to hurt me – I do really..."

In fact, Bywaters spent the evening with her parents in Upper Norwood. Then, with a sheath knife in his pocket, he had made his way to Ilford to meet them on their return from the theatre...

This, then, was the evidence presented before Mr Justice Shearman, who was clearly horrified by the letters and all they implied. "Right-minded persons will be filled with disgust," he told the jury. The Solicitor-General, Sir Thomas Inskip, who presented the case for the prosecution, found it an easy task to convince the jury that Edith Thompson was a wicked and abandoned woman who had planned the murder of her husband. The letters – presented by the prosecution in telling but misleading extracts – left no doubt of it. Edith spoke in her own defence, alleging that she was deliberately misleading her lover into thinking she wanted to kill her husband when her real motive was to keep his love. (She might have been more honest if she had said "keep him interested".)

After a hostile summing-up from the judge, the jury took only two hours to find both defendants guilty. When Mr Justice Shearman read aloud the death sentence, Edith cried: "I am not guilty. Oh God, I am not guilty."

The execution was set for January 6, 1923. Three days before this, Bywaters told his mother that, although he was guilty and deserved to hang, Edith had no idea he intended to attack her husband that night. But a last-minute appeal to the Home Secretary, based on this "confession", was rejected only hours before the execution. Both were hanged at precisely 9 a.m., she in Holloway women's prison, he in Pentonville. By the time of the execution Edith Thompson was in such a state of collapse that she had to be carried to the scaffold.

Frederick Bywaters arrives at the Old Bailey in December 1922, where he would be sentenced to death.

1923

THE MADAME FAHMY CASE

The night of July 9, 1923, was stiflingly hot, and ended in a violent thunderstorm. It was during this storm that a beautiful Frenchwoman, Madame Marguerite Fahmy, killed her Egyptian playboy husband, Prince Ali Fahmy, in their luxury suite in London's Savoy Hotel, by shooting him in the head three times. The subsequent trial, with its tale of stormy passion and sexual perversion, kept the British public breathless with morbid fascination.

The couple had met the previous year. Ali was 21 and, on the death of his father, a wealthy industrialist, had become a multi-millionaire. She was 32, and the daughter of a cab driver named Albert and a charlady; after a convent education, she had given birth to an illegitimate child at 16 (it was placed in an orphanage) and become a prostitute, then a hostess at the Folies-Bergères, and found herself a rich lover. She went on to marry another wealthy lover when she was 29, but the marriage soon collapsed. And it was while she was waiting for her divorce that she met the wealthy young prince in Egypt. He pursued her passionately, spent a fortune on her, and persuaded her to marry him early in 1923.

It was a mistake. He was a spoilt child; she was a woman of the world with an imperious temper. Soon they were quarrelling all the time as she showed her irritation at his immaturity, under the eyes

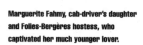

Marguerite Fahmy, cab-driver's daughter and Folies-Bergères hostess, who captivated her much younger lover.

Wealthy playboy Prince Ali Kamel Fahmy, whose passion for the French ex-prostitute proved to be his undoing.

of his male private secretary Said Enani, who was probably also the prince's lover.

On the evening of the killing, they had quarrelled at dinner; she wanted to go to Paris for a minor operation, and he wanted her to have it in London. She was heard to say (in French – she spoke no English): "You shut up or I'll smash this bottle over your head." When the bandleader asked her if there was any tune she would like to hear, she replied: "I don't want any music – my husband threatened to kill me tonight." Later, her husband asked her to dance but she refused.

At about 1.30 the following morning, a porter was passing their suite when the prince came out in his pyjamas. "Look what she has done," he said, indicating a red scratch on his cheek. Madame Fahmy, still in evening dress, came out of the room, and said something the porter did not understand. He warned them

The Savoy Hotel, scene of the shooting on a hot July night.

that they might wake the other guests, and they went back into the room. As the porter turned away, a little dog ran out, and the prince bent down and whistled for

it, snapping his fingers. A few moments later, three shots rang out. The porter ran back to the open door and saw Madame Fahmy throwing down a pistol, and her husband lying on the floor and bleeding from the head. A few hours later the prince died in hospital, and Madame Fahmy was arrested. Her trial opened less than two weeks later, on July 23, 1923.

Her advocate, the famous Edward Marshall Hall, based his defence on the argument that she was a poor, oppressed woman who had made the mistake of marrying a despotic oriental of perverted sexual tastes, who often beat and kicked her. The secretary denied that his master had ever kicked her, but he conceded that the prince had once hit her so violently that he had dislocated her jaw.

The manager of the Savoy, giving evidence, described how Madame Fahmy had said to him, in French: "I lost my

head." Marshall Hall suggested that a better translation of "J'ai perdu la tête" would be: "I was frightened out of my wits." The manager agreed.

The firearms expert, Robert Churchill, testified that although the pistol with which Fahmy was shot was an automatic the trigger had to be pulled for each shot.

In a dramatic final speech, Marshall Hall described Madame Fahmy, crouching like a terrified animal, with the gun in her hand, and then the weapon exploding – to her horror and consternation.

He enacted the scene, pointing the gun at the jury, then dropping it dramatically. "Members of the jury, I want you to open the doors so this Western woman can go out..." he declaimed, in a flagrant appeal to racial prejudice. They were convinced, and took a little over an hour to acquit her.

It was no accident

Marshall Hall's version was pure fiction. A few moments before his death. Prince Fahmy was whistling for a little dog; the porter had only walked a few yards when the shots rang out – three of them. The firing of the gun was obviously no accident – she pressed the trigger three times. But a sentimental British jury preferred to believe that a pretty Frenchwoman killed her violent, Egyptian husband when in a state of terror. (Marshall Hall made doubly sure of an acquittal by hinting that the quarrel was really about the prince's desire for anal sex, which his wife had refused.) So Madame Fahmy walked free, and went on to become a film star, playing the part of an Egyptian wife.

THE VAQUIER CASE

In January 1924, Mrs Mabel Theresa Jones went to Biarritz to recover from strain due to financial problems. She was the wife of the landlord of the Blue Anchor Hotel, at Byfleet, in Surrey.

The lover, accomplished con-man Jean-Pierre Vaquier, followed his mistress back to England.

At that time of year her hotel – the Victoria – was half-empty. There, Mabel Jones met a Frenchman named Jean-Pierre Vaquier, a 45-year-old inventor, who was employed to service the radio in the lounge, which he himself had constructed. He spoke no English and she spoke no French, but she purchased a dictionary and they succeeded in communicating, and became friendly.

They managed to tell one another about their backgrounds. She said she was married with two children; he said he was divorced, and that his wife and children were dead. (This later proved to be untrue.) When she went off on a tour of the Pyrenees, she sent him postcards beginning "Dear Friend". Against her better judgement, Mabel found herself thinking about the attentive Frenchman.

Back in Biarritz, Vaquier told her he loved her, and persuaded her to move with him to another hotel, where they became lovers. He was undoubtedly in love with her, and she probably found the holiday affair an exciting way of passing the time.

When her husband wrote saying he needed her at home, Vaquier begged her not to go. When she told him she had to, he said that he would go too. He had invented a sausage machine, and the patent rights would make him rich. To establish these

False name in the poisons book

Alfred Jones still had congestion of the lungs when he returned. He made no objection to the dapper foreigner, obviously having no doubts about his wife's fidelity. He did not even seem to mind when Vaquier made trips to London, accompanied by Mabel Jones. On one of those trips, Vaquier went to a chemist close to the Russell Hotel and bought some strychnine, with the strange excuse that it was for his experiments with radio. He signed the poisons book with a false name: "Wanker".

Throughout March Vaquier lived at the Blue Anchor, borrowing money from Mrs Jones and assuring Alfred Jones that his bill would be settled promptly when his money arrived from America.

rights he had to go to London. Mabel recommended him to try the Russell Hotel.

When Mabel Jones went to London to visit the Bankruptcy

> ## " You assassinated my husband! "
> **Mabel Jones accused her lover**

> ## " Yes, Mabs, for you! "

Receivers' Office, she met Vaquier at the Russell, and spent the night with him.

She arrived back at the Blue Anchor, but her husband Alfred was not there, having gone to Margate and been laid low by a severe cold. That evening, Vaquier arrived at the Blue Anchor. He explained that he would have no money until he received £500 from America for his patent, and asked if he could meanwhile live on credit. She sent a telegram to ask her husband, and he agreed. Mabel Jones also lent Vaquier the money to pay his account at the Russell, so he could get his luggage back.

On March 28 there was a party at the Blue Anchor, and the landlord, as usual, drank heavily. Vaquier was not there – the regulars found him irritating, and looked askance at his assiduous attentions to the landlord's wife. The next morning Alfred Jones needed a bromo seltzer, which he kept in the bar. As he drank it down he gasped: "My God, they're bitter". Not long after, Jones became ill. By the time a doctor arrived around

midday, he had been carried up to his room. There he lapsed into convulsions, and gasped for air. In half an hour he was dead.

When the doctor was told about the bitter bromo, he asked to see the bottle. But it seemed Vaquier had already asked for it. It was now empty, and had been washed out. When it was submitted to a Home Office pathologist, however, it was still found to contain traces of strychnine.

A post-mortem revealed that Alfred Jones had died of a huge dose of strychnine.

Mabel Jones accused her lover: "You assassinated my husband!" He replied: "Yes, Mabs, for you."

Questioned by the police, Vaquier soon became chief suspect. He tried to throw suspicion on the barman, but every customer knew the true state of affairs.

Curiously, he also seemed to enjoy the limelight, and allowed the press to take photographs of him. This was a mistake. One of them was seen by the chemist from whom he had purchased the strychnine.

Vaquier went on trial at Guildford Assizes on July 2,

1924. He revealed himself as histrionic, vain and almost comically untruthful. Marshall Hall appeared for the prosecution, but his formidable persuasive powers were unnecessary. It was clear that Vaquier had decided to murder his mistress's husband while in London, which is why he had bought poison under a false name.

No one was surprised when, after two hours, the jury returned a verdict of guilty. Vaquier's last words as he stood on the scaffold at Wandsworth on August 12, 1925, were "Vive la France!"

Mrs Mabel Jones, whose husband was the landlord of the Blue Anchor in Byfleet, made the mistake of taking a French lover while on holiday in Biarritz.

NORMAN THORNE

Norman Thorne made the supreme mistake of dismembeing his victim – always a sure method of alienating a British judge and jury. Yet, despite his actions, he seems to have been a man of decent character, so that, in retrospect, it is almost possible to feel some pity that the law demanded the supreme penalty for his crime.

Norman Thorne was a 24-year-old poultry farmer, whose activities also included Band of Hope speaker, Sunday school teacher and boys' club enthusiast. In December 1924, he was tiring of an affair with a Kensal Green, London, typist, Elsie Cameron.

Thorne had been in the navy in the last year of the First World War, but had since been a victim of the post-war slump, losing his engineering job through redundancy. After living at home with his parents he bought the chicken farm in 1922, but by 1924 was still scarcely able to make ends meet.

On December 4, Elsie set out for Crowborough, Sussex, to visit Thorne at his smallholding, meaning to ask him what he intended to do about her pregnancy (which she had invented for the purpose of putting pressure on him).

On December 10 her father wired Thorne asking for news of his daughter, and heard by return: "Not here ... can't understand." Two farmworkers said they had seen Elsie Cameron, attaché case in hand, walking towards Thorne's farm on the evening she vanished, but Thorne insisted they were mistaken. He appeared to welcome police inquiries – "I want to help all I can" – and eagerly showed

them around his poultry farm and the broken-down shack where he lived. He posed for press photographers feeding the birds in their wire-enclosed pen.

A female neighbour, who unaccountably had been unaware of the publicity, finally came forward a month after Elsie Cameron's disappearance to say she had seen the missing girl walking through the gate of Thorne's farm on December 5; as a result, Crowborough police asked for help from Scotland Yard. Digging up the poultry farm began in earnest, and on January 15 Elsie's corpse, with head and legs severed, was found.

Thorne now admitted that Elsie Cameron had indeed arrived at his farm. But there

had been a quarrel about another woman, and he had stormed out of the hut; on his return, at 11.30 p.m. he found

Elsie Cameron, the neurotic London typist who claimed to be pregnant.

Norman Thorne, the 24-year-old poultry farmer from Crowborough in Sussex.

her dangling from a beam. He panicked. "I got my hacksaw ... sawed off her legs and head by the glow of the fire..." In the morning he buried the remains in one of his chicken runs. It was the spot where he had posed for his photograph.

At his trial for murder at Lewes (before Mr Justice

Finlay, prosecution led by Sir Henry Curtis-Bennett, KG; Thorne defended by Mr J. D. Cassels, KG) there was controversy between the pathologist Sir Bernard Spilsbury, who had examined the remains on January 17, and Dr Robert Bronte, the pathologist called by the defence, who inspected them a month after Spilsbury's post-mortem. Spilsbury had found signs of injuries to "the head, face, elbow, legs, and

Norman Thorne and Elsie Cameron pose for a formal photograph. In fact, he was already tiring of her.

feet, which together were amply sufficient to account for death from shock…", but no evidence of hanging. (Nor had the police found any trace of rope-markings on the wooden beam.) His opinion was that the bruising – on the back of the head and on both temples, and the leg – indicated that Elsie

Why claim suicide?

It was certainly Thorne's stubbornness in insisting on the suicide defence that hanged him. He might well have pleaded manslaughter, of quarrelling with Elsie Cameron and killing her in a fit of temper (which is very probably what happened). Elsie Cameron was known as neurotic and unstable, and had been unemployed for six or seven months preceding her death because of her "nervous condition". Before that she had been under medical supervision for neurasthenia and loss of energy. On a visit to Thorne's parents, she had been hysterical and "difficult". (She arrived at the chicken farm without even a change of underwear, but with a baby dress.)

The bruises on her legs support the view that her death was unpremeditated; a man who intends to murder an unwanted mistress does not cover her in bruises; he strikes a single blow.

Spilsbury's disproving of the suicide defence should have made it obvious to the jury that Thorne had killed her during a quarrel, and allowed him a certain benefit of the doubt. Unfortunately, Spilsbury's quietly confident manner of giving evidence tended to leave the jury feeling slightly cowed. So in a sense, Thorne was not hanged by the medical evidence, but by Spilsbury's reputation. It was for this reason, rather than professional jealousy, that a certain resistance to Spilsbury began to build up during his later years.

Cameron had been attacked with considerable violence, probably with a heavy instrument with a smooth surface. (Thorne possessed a pair of Indian clubs.) Spilsbury contradicted Bronte's suggestion that the "creases" or "grooves" found on the victim's neck were due to hanging, saying

Norman Thorne poses for reporters on the precise spot where he had buried Elsie Cameron's body

they were natural marks to be found on most female necks.

Spilsbury prevailed, and Thorne was found guilty and sentenced to death. When the case was taken to the Court of Criminal Appeal, application was made for the medical evidence to be reviewed by a commissioner appointed by the court, but it was rejected, as was the appeal, and Thorne was ultimately hanged in April, 1925.

RUTH SNYDER AND JUDD GRAY

It is sad that an affair that began so romantically should have ended so tragically, in three deaths.

Ruth Brown was a 19-year-old telephonist, of Swedish origins when she mis-routed a call from art editor Albert Schneider, who upbraided her irritably. She apologized so charmingly that he rang her back to apologize, too, and ended by offering her a job on the Hearst magazine *Motor Boating*. She proved pretty and pert, and they were soon dating.

The truth is, their personalities were bound to clash. He was of German origin, efficient, dominant and inclined to be impatient. What he needed was an undominant mate who would adore him. Instead, he chose a romantic dreamer who fanta-sized about faraway places and passionate lovers. Schneider was hoping Ruth would become his mistress, but she held out for marriage. So in July 1915 he gave in, and married her 10 months after their first meeting. She was 13 years his junior.

Predictably, they were not soulmates. The excitement-starved Ruth found this efficient German tedious and dictatorial, and was soon dreaming of lovers. She found life as a housewife in Queens,

Long Island, a bore, and she enlivened it with bridge and luncheon parties. In 1918 she gave birth to a daughter, Lorraine, but it failed to improve her marriage; even Albert – who had changed his name from Schneider to Snyder because of wartime anti-German feeling – made it clear that he found fatherhood tiresome.

For seven years she kept herself amused with bridge parties and sunbathing, and conceivably with love affairs – at least, a notebook found in her home contained the names of 28 men. These included that of Henry Judd Gray, a rather quiet little corset salesman who wore thick tortoise-shell spectacles. Ruth had been introduced to him in a cheap Swedish diner in New York in June 1925. A few weeks later, after a quarrel with her husband, she went to dine with him.

After the meal, they called in at Gray's office, where Ruth complained of sunburned shoulders. Gray produced a remedy called camphor ice, which he rubbed on her bare skin. Ruth burst into tears, explaining that she was unaccustomed to such

gallant behaviour. Judd kissed her. Then he offered her a corselet as a gift and, with an audacity probably due to drink, offered to fit it there and then. She agreed, and became his mistress, probably on the office floor. Soon she began spending nights with him in hotels, her husband accepting her explanation that she was staying with a friend. He even made no objection when she invented a friend in Albany and went off there for several days.

The lovers made an odd pair. Gray was of English puritan stock, and was puritanical by nature. He seemed to enjoy being dominated – he liked to embrace her ankles, and called her "Momsie". The more they made love, the more he wanted her. In fact, he already had a spouse who would have suited Albert Snyder down to the ground, a "home girl" whose major virtue was that she was "a careful and exceptionally exact housekeeper".

Gray's salary was considerably smaller than Snyder's, and his new role as a lover demanded more money than he earned. Ruth seems to have lent – or given – him a

number of sums, including a cheque for $200.

In the following months, Albert Snyder narrowly escaped death on a number of occasions. One evening, when he was tinkering underneath the car, the jack slipped and he was almost crushed to death. Possibly this was an ac-

room was full of coal gas. Ruth explained that she must have accidentally stepped on the tube connecting the gas cock to the fire, and pulled it off. In the following January she gave Albert a medicine to cure hiccups; it was not Alka-Seltzer but bichloride of mercury, and it made him seriously ill.

When Ruth first raised the subject of killing her husband, Gray was deeply shocked. But when she announced, in September 1926, that she had definitely decided to kill Albert, he asked how she intended to do it, and listened with fascination to her plan to knock her husband unconscious with a sleeping powder, then turn on the gas. In the following month, when she asked for his help, he blanched and told her she was foolish to entertain such ideas. But when she emphasized how much she hated having sex with her husband, and how often he demanded his marital rights, Gray began to waver.

After so much planning, the murder itself was almost criminally incompetent. Gray, who had been drinking heavily to give himself courage, entered the house late on the evening of March 20, 1927, and hid himself to await their return from a party. He concealed himself in her bedroom and drank more whiskey.

At 2 a.m. the Snyders returned, with eight-year-old Lorraine. Ruth was sober, but she had made sure that her husband had drunk more than enough. By 2.30 a.m., Snyder was asleep, and Ruth

cident – it made Ruth realize how convenient it would have been if Albert had in fact been crushed. Not long after this, Snyder was running the car engine in the garage when Ruth brought him a glass of whiskey. It made him oddly dizzy, so that he hardly noticed when the garage door closed.

He was almost unconscious from carbon monoxide fumes when he staggered outside.

Yet, although Snyder told his brother that he thought his wife had tried to kill him, he nevertheless accepted her suggestion that he should insure his life. Perhaps he thought that no harm would

come to him for the sake of a mere $1,000. In fact, the policy which he signed in triplicate was actually three policies, which would pay out more than $100,000. It was Ruth who paid the premiums.

A few months later, Snyder awoke from a doze on the settee gasping for air; the

had sneaked out of her twin bed to summon her lover. Judd entered their bedroom with a sash weight, and took an almighty swing at the head of the sleeping man. In his excitement, however, he missed his target, grazing Snyder's skull, and the intended victim was shocked awake. Gray hit him again, then staggered as Snyder punched him – Snyder, the fit and healthy boating fanatic, was far bigger than Gray. They struggled and, as Gray tried to free his necktie from Snyder's powerful grip, he dropped the sash weight. "Momsie, help me!" he gasped, Ruth found the sash weight and hit her husband on the back of the head. Snyder now finally went limp.

The lovers now stuffed chloroform-soaked rags into Snyder's mouth and nostrils, then wound picture-wire around his throat. They disarranged the furniture to lend weight to their burglar story, and pulled open the drawers.

Gray changed into one of his victim's shirts – his own was bloodstained – and finally left, after tying Ruth's hands and ankles and binding a gag around her mouth. He declined her request to knock her unconscious, which proved to be another major mistake.

Lorraine Snyder was woken by a tapping on her bedroom door, and opened it to find her mother lying on the floor, her wrists and ankles still bound. Ruth told her to summon the neighbours, and the child ran across the street to awaken Mr and Mrs Mulhauser. The latter found that Ruth had untied her hands, but not her ankles.

Among the police who were summoned was Detective Arthur Carey, who soon smelt a rat. Ruth claimed that she had been attacked by a big man with a moustache, but failed to explain how she saw him in the dark. Carey decided that no professional burglar would have knocked Snyder unconscious, then strangled him with picture wire; this

was obviously the work of someone who wished him dead. And surely Ruth would have untied her own ankles after she had freed her hands, not waited for the Mulhausers to arrive? A gun left on the bed also aroused Carey's suspicions – surely no burglar would have left it behind? Finally, the bloodstained sash weight was found in the tool chest; why should a burglar go to the trouble of concealing it when he could simply drop it on the floor?

As the interrogation continued, Ruth was left in no doubt that the police knew she was lying. She stubbornly denied this, and also denied – what was equally obvious – that she must have had an accomplice. With typical incompetence, Gray had left behind a tie pin with his initials. When they found the notebook containing the name Judd Gray, they lost no time jumping to the correct conclusion.

In the police station, she was told that Judd Gray

had confessed. It was untrue – he had not even been found – but it convinced her. Believing herself betrayed, she felt outraged. So when Police Commissioner McLaughlin stated: "Gray helped to kill your husband, didn't he?", she answered defiantly: "Yes."

Gray was arrested at half past the following midnight in a Syracuse hotel. He told the police that he had not been in the Snyders' house that night, but they found the train ticket that proved he had travelled from Syracuse to Long Island. By now, Ruth's confession was in all the headlines. Gray went on to tell the whole story.

The trial lasted from April 18, 1927, to May 9. Ruth's defence blamed Gray; Gray's defence blamed Ruth. The jury reached a unanimous verdict of guilty.

Courtroom scene showing Ruth Snyder (B) sitting beside her co-accused, Judd Gray (A). Ruth, sitting with her back to the camera, is wearing the fur coat she wore throughout the trial.

Ruth makes the front page

Gray went to his death calmly and philosophically on January 12, 1928. Ruth died hard; a few days before her execution she began to scream for hours every night. A reporter on the *New York Daily News* had a camera strapped to his ankle, with a shutter release in his pocket. As all eyes were fixed on the straining body, hurled against the straps by the thousand-volt current, he stepped into the aisle and raised his trouser leg. The picture was published the following morning over the whole front page of the *Daily News*; it was subsequently syndicated all over the world.

The most famous death photograph ever taken, by photographer Thomas Howard, of the *New York Daily News*, which catches the moment Ruth Snyder is thrown forward against the straps by the 2,000-volt current.

DR DREHER AND MRS LE BOEUF

On July 6, 1927, boys hunting for frogs around the shallow Lake Palourde, in Louisiana, saw a body floating in the water. Police found that it was attached to two railway angle irons, one tied to the neck and one to the ankles. These had not been quite heavy enough to prevent the body floating to the surface. The stomach had been slashed open with a knife, obviously to release gases. However, the face was unidentifiable because the man had been shot in the head – twice – with a shotgun.

The corpse was buried without being identified. Then it struck someone that this might be Jim Le Boeuf, head of the local light and power company, and one of the leading citizens of nearby Mason City, who had not been seen for a week. When his wife Ada was asked to come to see if she could identify the body, she flatly refused, on the grounds that her husband was simply away on business. However, when pressed further, she showed embarrassment and explained that he had run away with a red-headed woman who lived in a hut on the bayou (river outlet), and with whom gossip declared that Jim Le Boeuf had been seen bathing naked.

The police went to the lady's hut, and found her still there, denying that there had been any intimacy between her and Jim Le Boeuf. Further investigation suggested that the gossip had been started by a man named James Beadle, who rented boats on the lake. He and Le Boeuf had been

well acquainted, since Le Boeuf was an enthusiastic sportsman, who often hired a boat to go fishing. Beadle admitted that he had not seen Le Boeuf bathing with the redhead; what he had actually seen was Ada Le Boeuf bathing naked with Jim's old and close friend Dr Tom Dreher. It seemed that Ada had paid Beadle to spread the rumour about Jim and the redhead.

It was beginning to look more and more as if Ada was the key to this mystery.

Her husband had, by this time, been identified through his dental chart. The police now probed among Jim Le Boeuf's neighbours, and learned that his wife's name had been coupled with that of Dr Dreher for some time.

Beadle confirmed this. In fact, he admitted that it was he who had brought the rumours to Jim Le Boeuf's attention. It seemed that Le Boeuf had come to hire a boat one day and, finding Beadle away, had borrowed one without permission, and then

returned it so late that there was an irritable exchange. "Just because you're careless with your property," said Beadle, "you can't be free with mine." Le Boeuf had asked him what he was talking about, whereupon Beadle told him about the rumours of an affair between Ada and Tom Dreher. Le Boeuf had dismissed the notion. His wife suffered from migraines,

he said, so Dreher was often at their house in attendance. But so what? Dreher was 52, not the age when a man starts seducing his friends' wives. In fact, they were all middle-aged…

Le Boeuf, it seemed, had then gone to his wife and asked her if there was anything between her and Dreher. She indignantly denied it. She needed Dreher, she said,

Ada's story

Questioned about the murder, Ada Le Boeuf told a strange story. She claimed that on the night of the murder, she and Jim had taken separate boats – as was their custom – to go across the lake for dinner with relatives. On their way back around midnight, another boat had approached with two men, one of whom had shot her husband. She had no idea of their identity because it was too dark to see. She had kept silent because she was afraid Tom Dreher would be accused of the murder.

because sedatives did not work, and he gave her injections that cured her. And ever since then, he had been available to call on her whenever she needed medication.

The police then called on Dreher, and he immediately admitted that he was behind the murder. Beadle, he said, had done the actual shooting. Ada had told Dreher that she and Jim were going to supper at their relatives. He and Beadle had waited for them and killed Le Boeuf. But when it came to sinking the body, they found that the three railway irons they had left nearby had been reduced to two – a passing youth, it emerged later, had tossed one into the lake. So they had been forced to make do with two.

At the trial, all three defendants tried to throw the blame on the others. But few observers were left with any doubt that it was the determined Ada who had been the moving force behind the murder plot.

Dreher and his mistress were sentenced to be hanged, Beadle to a long term in jail. Governor Huey Long rejected an appeal to commute Ada's sentence, and the two were hanged together on February 1, 1929.

The amiable Tom Dreher, regarded by many inhabitants of Mason City, Louisiana, as a victim of the predatory and strong-minded Ada Le Boeuf. Accused of the murder of his friend Jim Le Boeuf, Dreher confessed immediately, obviously relieved to be able to clear his conscience.

THE SNOOK CASE

The Snook murder case was one of the most celebrated scandals of the late 1920s, largely because an enterprising court stenographer took down the lurid and otherwise unprintable sexual details in shorthand, and published them in a booklet.

James Snook, executed for the murder of his student mistress Theora Hix, was an unlikely candidate for the electric chair, being a respectable professor of veterinary medicine in Columbus, Ohio. Born in 1880 on a farm, he was an expert shot, and participated – although without distinction – in the Olympics in 1920. A charming and good-looking man, he began to go through a mid-life crisis in his 40s, with the result that he was summoned before the dean to explain why he had given narcotics to a female student. He was let off with a caution.

In June 1926 he met a pretty medical student, Theora Hix, 23, in an office at the Ohio State University, where she was working as a stenographer, and accepted a lift from her. Within weeks they were lovers.

A year after their affair began, Snook took her to the rifle range and taught her to shoot; in due course he gave her a Derringer, which she kept in her handbag. And two

The gentle, mild-mannered Professor James Snook stood little chance when marked down by the man-eating, nymphomaniac student, Theora Hix. He is holding the Derringer gun he had given her.

Sex and drugs in the back seat

Professor Snook, although he had been married for only four years and had a daughter, was soon hopelessly addicted to Theora's body, and had abandoned his dignity to the extent of having sex and taking drugs in the back of his car. At Theora's own request he sterilized her.

Their love was not entirely free of ups and downs, for Theora was wilful, moody, and inclined to brutal frankness, telling Snook that she had another lover, Bill Miller, whose large penis gave her more pleasure than his. But the drugs they took — not only cocaine but also cannabis, which they consumed rather than smoked, and the aphrodisiac Spanish Fly — seemed to make up for it. Theora was well on her way to becoming a drug addict.

years further on, he hired a "love nest" (as the newspapers were to call it) in downtown Columbus, telling the landlady, Mrs Margaret Smalley, that he was a salt salesman, and that his wife would sometimes be with him.

Theora was the aggressive one. She liked to fellate him, and she liked him to hurt her. And this seems to be why, on June 29, 1929, she asked him to take her to some remote spot "so I can scream". She was also concerned in case their love-making was interrupted by a policeman. (She and a student named Marion Myers had been caught recently and fined $20 each.)

Both of them were fairly high, having taken both cannabis as well as Spanish Fly. So on the edge of the rifle range, they moved into the back seat of the car and began the preliminaries to sex. But Theora was in a foul mood, and complained that the car was too cramped. Argument soon turned to a quarrel, in which she returned to her old complaint about the size of his penis and the superiority of the organs of Bill Miller and Marion Myers. Then, when he said that he would not be around that weekend because he was taking his family to see his mother, she shouted: "Damn your mother and damn Mrs Snook. I'm going to kill her and get her out of the way." Then, obviously still sexually excited, she said: "You've got to help me", and took his erection into her mouth. But she was still angry and began to bite it and to squeeze his testicles. He struggled, howling with pain, and freed himself by twisting her arm back. This made her shout: "Damn you, I'm going to kill you too."

At this point she began to get out of the car, taking her handbag, and Snook experienced the sudden conviction that she was about to take out the Derringer and shoot him. He grabbed a hammer that he kept in the tool box, climbed out after her, and hit her on the head. Then, probably carried away by the pleasure of hitting the woman who tormented and bullied him, he went on to open a penknife and cut her throat. After sitting for a while on the running board of his car, he drove off.

When her body was found, Bill Miller was the first suspect; but he had an alibi. Someone, however, reported seeing Theora in a blue coupé, which led the police to the professor. His landlady saw his picture and identified him as the salt salesman. Forensic analysis revealed bloodstains on his suit, even though it had been dry cleaned.

At his trial, which began on July 24, 1929, the jury was

Snook looks less than happy as he sits in his cell. Note the bandaged hand, which he claims he hurt the day before the murder.

stunned by the depravity of their goings-on, which Snook recounted with a certain naïve frankness, feeling that the court would feel he was justified in killing such a vicious, sex-mad harpy, and pass a lighter sentence. It had the opposite effect, and on August 14 he was sentenced to die. He was electrocuted on February 28, 1930.

1930s

1934

THE BRIGHTON TRUNK MURDER

The Derby Day rush hour – June 6, 1934 – saw Brighton railway station crammed with people. So it was hardly surprising that when a large trunk was deposited in the left-luggage office, the attendants later failed to remember anything about the owner. Eleven days later, when a foul smell filtered out of the trunk, they decided to call in the police to break the locks. Inside, wrapped in brown paper, was the rotting, disarticulated torso of a woman. Her legs were found the next day in a suitcase in the left-luggage office at King's Cross station, but her arms and head remained missing. The autopsy showed that the victim had been five months pregnant.

It was decided to conduct a door-to-door investigation in the area surrounding the station – it was possible that the killer, or killers, might have been observed if they

Prostitute and ex-showgirl Violette Kaye, murdered by her pimp Tony Mancini.

had arrived on foot. Unfortunately, no one remembered seeing anything unusual that day. Nevertheless, the police did turn up a possible lead. A prostitute called Violette Kaye had disappeared early the previous month – long enough that she could have been the Brighton station victim.

Over 40 women had been reported missing from Brighton that summer, so it took the police until mid-July to get around to interviewing Violette's pimp, a small-time crook called Tony Mancini. In his statement, Mancini insisted that, as far as he knew, Violette was alive and working in France. They had quarrelled on May 10, and Violette had left for Paris. The last he had heard of her, he said, was a telegram sent to her sister-in-law saying: "GOOD JOB – SAIL SUNDAY – WILL WRITE – VK".

The police were not fully satisfied with this version of events and, on July 15, called at Mancini's lodgings at 52 Kemp Street for a second interview. The landlady told them that he was not at home, but invited them in to wait in his flat. As they entered the room the officers became aware of a foul smell. It seemed to be coming from a large trunk and, thinking grimly about the missing head and arms, the officers forced it open. Inside was Violette Kaye – over two months dead, but otherwise complete and unmutilated.

The following day a police patrol picked up Mancini as he hitchhiked along the Maidstone Road in Kent. Under interrogation, he admitted that he had concealed Violette's death, but he denied the charge of murder. He had come home from work on May 10 and found her lying dead. He had known his bad record would make him a prime suspect as the murderer, he said, so he had covered up her death.

The bedroom at 52 Kemp Street, where the decomposing body of Violette Kaye was found in the trunk shown left.

Mancini was 26 years old and spoke in a working-class London accent, but this was a front. His father was actually a Whitehall civil servant. Mancini's criminal career had started when he deserted from the RAF as a teenager. While hiding from the military police he had become mixed up in London's underworld, eventually working as a strong-arm man for the gangster "Harry Boy" Sabini.

He and Violette Kaye had met in 1932. Mancini was working as a "collection agent" in Sabini's protection racket. Violette, whose real surname was Saunders, was an attractive showgirl but for her, at 42, work was increasingly hard to find. She turned to prostitution to support her alcohol and morphine habits, and needed a pimp for protection. Mancini, although 16 years her junior, was glad to oblige and they decided to move to Brighton – "the place where it was all happening".

Violette was by no means a common prostitute though. Her good looks and show business connections earned her a well-to-do clientele. However, her trade brought other problems. Landlords soon guessed what the stream of male visitors meant and the couple had to move home regularly – as much as once a fortnight. Eventually, after living at 12 other addresses, she and Mancini moved into 44 Park Crescent, an unfurnished basement flat, down a narrow flight of steps.

Of course, when she was entertaining a client, Mancini had to make himself scarce, and it was probably boredom that prompted him to take a job as waiter and cook in the Skylark Café, under the promenade. Five days after he had started work, on Thursday, May 10, 1934, Violette arrived at the Skylark drunk. It was a slack period, so Mancini made her a meal and sat talking to her. After a while, he got up to make tea for the rest of the staff. As he handed a cup to a young waitress called Florence Attrell, he made the mistake of saying: "Here you are, mate."

Violette, overhearing the remark, shouted: "I won't have that! Don't call her mate!" A shocked silence fell over the café, Mancini told her to pull herself together. Violette burst into angry tears and stormed out. Mancini later claimed the incident cost him his job, but this did not stop him going to the café the next morning to tell everyone that Violette had left him and gone to Paris. It was at this time also that Violette's sister-in-law, planning to come down to visit the following Monday, received the telegram. In fact, Violette was already dead, her body wrapped in a blanket and propped in a cupboard at 44 Park Crescent.

Mancini seems to have kept his cool, even though he was obviously at a loss as to what to do with Violette's corpse. About a week later he told Mr Snuggs, his landlord, that since Vi had left him he couldn't afford to keep the flat on himself. As they talked, Snuggs noticed a large trunk in the middle of the room, waiting to be packed.

Mancini moved into 52 Kemp Street with Violette's body still in the trunk. He seems to have been unable to shake off the indecision about what to do next, and made no attempt to dispose of the body. It was a hot summer, and as the smell got worse a friend asked him if he was keeping rabbits in his room. The growing stench and the police enquiries were enough to make him eventually lose his nerve and go on the run.

Mancini's trial began on December 10, 1934. Prosecuting counsel J. D. Cassels delivered a seemingly unanswerable case. The telegram slip, on which the faked message sent to Violette's sister-in-law had originally been

Mancini's good fortune

Following Mancini's arrest, the newspapers were of one mind in portraying him as a vicious thug (and quite possibly a foreigner as well). The general opinion was that only a monster could have lived for two months, without apparent guilt, sleeping a few feet from the rotting body of his girlfriend. But Mancini had at least one piece of good fortune: he was to be defended by Norman Birkett, KC, one of the most brilliant advocates of his time.

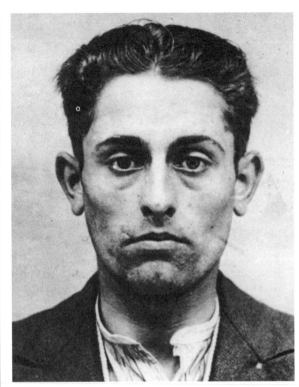

London gangster and pimp Tony Mancini, Violette Kaye's lover, a man capable of sudden violence.

written, was in the same handwriting as the menus Mancini had written out in the Skylark Café. Witnesses came forward to give evidence that Mancini and Violette often quarrelled. Several even claimed that they had heard him say: "What's the good of knocking a woman about with your fists? You should use a hammer, same as I did…" And, in fact, a partially burned hammer was one of the objects found at 44 Park Crescent.

When Henry Snuggs, the landlord of 44 Park Crescent, was called to identify the trunk he had seen in Mancini's room as the one that had

contained Violette's body, Birkett cross-examined him on quite different matters. He elicited the admission that the landlord had never seen or heard the couple quarrel – in fact, Snuggs admitted, they had seemed noticeably affectionate. He even told the court that he had always found Mancini a "perfect gentleman"; a far cry from the heartless gangster portrayed by the prosecution.

Birkett was particularly clever in demolishing the evidence of the three witnesses who claimed that Mancini had bragged about hitting a woman with a hammer. By simply leading them in the right direction, he let them contradict each other and blacken each other's characters. The first, a stall-keeper, admitted that he

had sacked his assistant, the second witness, for theft. The third witness then refused to admit that he had heard Mancini mention a hammer at all.

The prosecution called the

> **❝What's the good of knocking a woman about with your fists? You should use a hammer, same as I did… ❞**
> Tony Mancini

previous tenant (who claimed that he had left a hammer behind when he moved out) to identify the charred hammer that had been found in the fire-grate. The implication was that a hammer had been in the flat when Violette

had received her injuries, and afterwards had been burned. Birkett showed this to be pure supposition when he made the witness admit that he could not be sure if the charred hammer was the one he had left behind. The prosecution could no more prove that there had been a hammer in the flat at the time of Violette's death than Birkett could prove that there had not been.

When the prosecution called Dr Roche Lynch, the Home Office pathologist, to give evidence about the skull damage that had apparently killed Violette, Birkett again started his cross-examination on a tangent. He asked Dr Lynch if he had found morphine in the body. Lynch agreed that an amount "distinctly greater than a medicinal dose" was present in Violette's corpse. Birkett asked him if this might have been the actual cause of death, and Lynch acknowledged that he could not be sure. In admitting this he exposed a large hole in the prosecution's case; the corpse in the trunk had been so decomposed, it had proved impossible to ascertain the cause of death. It was only a supposition that she had been beaten to death.

On the first day of the trial, Birkett had cross-examined a police inspector who had given basic, technical evidence as to the lay-out of the basement flat at 44 Park Crescent. Birkett had asked him if the stairs down to the flat were narrow and worn, and the inspector replied that they were. He was then asked

Addicted to violence

On November 28, 1976, the *News of the World* had a scoop. Under the headline I'VE GOT AWAY WITH MURDER, Tony Mancini was interviewed by Alan Hart. Hart began: "A man acquitted of killing his mistress, after one of the most famous murder trials in British history, has now confessed to me that he was guilty. Ex-gangster Tony Mancini has lived 42 years with the secret that he was responsible for what became known as the Brighton Trunk Murder."

Tony Mancini, the article said, had actually been an extremely vicious criminal, but he had simply never been caught for his more serious crimes. While working for "Harry Boy" Sabini, he had been ordered to mark a man for life for informing to the police. Mancini had walked up to him as he leaned on the bar of his local pub and had lopped off his left hand with a hatchet, then walked casually out of the bar leaving the axe embedded in the counter. On another occasion he had gleefully turned the handle of a meat mincer as the hand of a fellow crook was forced into the grinders. He admitted that, for him, violence "was like a drug addiction".

About Violette's death, Mancini told Hart a very different story to the one he had given to the court in 1934. When he and Violette had argued in the Skylark Café, he said, he had been sacked on the spot. They had then taken a taxi back to 44 Park Crescent. During their on-going argument, Violette had complained of being cold. As Mancini knelt to make a fire she stepped up behind him and hit his head a glancing blow with a hammer. He

leapt up, took the hammer from her and started to walk away. She screamed, "Give me that hammer!" and he, in a fury, turned and threw it at her head. It knocked her to the ground and he grabbed her shoulders and started to bang her head down shouting, "You stupid bitch! Look what you made me do!" It was only when he saw blood trickling from her mouth that he realized that her head was hitting the brass fender, not the carpeted floor. "I honestly didn't mean to kill her," he said. "I had just lost control of myself in the heat of the moment."

About the trial he said: "When I gave evidence I had carefully rehearsed my lines like an actor. I had practised how I should hold my hands and when to let the tears run down my cheeks. It might sound cold and calculating now, but you have to remember that my life was at stake. I was charged with murder, and in those days the penalty was death."

This is the trunk in which the dismembered body of an unknown woman was found at Brighton station in June 1934.

what the floor at their foot was made from. The inspector replied it was made of stone.

The reason for this apparently pointless line of questioning became clear when Sir Bernard Spilsbury, a legend in the field of criminal pathology, took the stand. It was Spilsbury's opinion that Violette Saunders had been killed by repeated blows to her head from a blunt instrument – quite possibly a hammer. Prompted by Cassels, he demonstrated on a human skull just where, and with what effect, the blows were administered. He even presented a piece of Violette's skull into the evidence that, he said, proved his view of the case.

Not even bothering to ask what Spilsbury thought the fragment to prove, Birkett dem-anded why, if the autopsy had taken place five months earlier, had the bone fragment only just been brought to the attention of the defence? In a similar vein, why had there been no doctor for the defence at that autopsy?

Spilsbury could answer neither question satisfactorily. Birkett then returned to the question of the high dose of morphine found in the body. Spilsbury was forced to admit that he had no definite evidence that Violette had not been killed by the drug. Birkett then turned to another possible cause of death. Could Violette, in a drunken or possibly drugged state, have fallen down the narrow flight of stairs that had been described earlier in the trial, and sustained the possibly fatal head injuries on the stone floor beneath? Spilsbury had to agree that it was possible. Birkett had, in effect, neutralized the prosecution's star witness.

The defence still had one move to make before starting their own case. Cassels had called Chief Inspector Donaldson to answer some routine questions on police procedure. Birkett, who was cross-examining, asked him to tell the court of the defendant's previous criminal record – something defending counsels are usually keen to conceal. The chief inspector had to read the rather mild list of convictions: two for petty theft and one for loitering with intent. The prosecution's claim that Mancini was a brutal, professional criminal now seemed rather thin.

Beginning the defence case, Birkett called his chief witness: Tony Mancini himself. On the stand, he appeared chastened and unsure of himself – more a penitent than a monster. As he answered Birkett's gentle questioning he became increasingly emotional, and occasionally wept. This behaviour clearly made a strong impression on the jury.

He told the court that he and Violette had loved each other and never quarrelled. If there had been any stress in the relationship, he said, it was purely due to her profession. The constant moves from one flat to another and the fear of arrest had caused her to drink excessively and use morphine to help her sleep.

Mancini then went on to tell the court about the events of May 10. Violette had clearly been drunk when she arrived at the Skylark Café, so he was not surprised to find her lying on the bed when he eventually got home. It was only when he tried to wake her, and saw blood on the pillow, that he realized that she was dead.

Mancini explained that he had kept Violette's death secret because he knew that the police would be biased against him. After his initial hesitation, each day that passed increased the necessity of concealment as it also increased his chance of being hanged. And his fear that he would be misjudged

by the authorities seemed to have been fully borne out.

In his final summing-up, Birkett reminded the jury that it was their duty to release his client if there was so much as a shadow of a doubt as to his guilt. He ended on a ringing note: "People are not tried by newspapers, not tried by rumour, not tried by statements born of a love of notoriety, but tried by British juries, called to do justice and decide upon the evidence."

On December 14, after two-and-a-half hour's deliberation, the jury found Mancini not guilty and the judge ordered him freed. The Violette Saunders case has since gone down as one of the most brilliant defences in

The left-luggage department of Brighton station, where a body-in-a-trunk murder in the summer of 1934 led to the discovery of the body of Violette Kay in the cheap basement room where she had died.

legal history – but it is now known that the verdict was completely wrong.

As for the body that was found in a trunk in the left-luggage department of Brighton station – the corpse that had started the ultimately botched Violette Kaye case – it remains one of the most notorious unsolved crimes of the period. Despite a massive police investigation, which extended over four countries, the identities of the victim and her presumed murderer were never discovered.

THE PYJAMA GIRL

On the morning of September 1, 1934, a farmer called Tom Griffiths was leading a bull along the grass verge of the Howlong Road, near the town of Albury in New South Wales. As he stopped to light a cigarette he glanced towards a nearby storm culvert and spotted an odd bundle, lying half concealed in the pipe. Moving closer, he discovered that it was the corpse of a young woman dressed in yellow, Chinese-style silk pyjamas.

The police were called and inspected the body. She was lying face down and was partly naked – the pyjama trousers had been dragged down around her knees. Her head was wrapped in a blood-soaked towel over which a potato sack had been pulled to hold the wrapping in place. Whoever had dumped the body had also tried to burn it using kerosene or petrol, but the flames had done little damage to the body (since the human body is mainly made up of water, attempts to burn corpses with anything other than a furnace or a large bonfire generally end in failure; a forensic scientist once joked that setting fire to a corpse is like trying to set fire to a bucket of water).

At the morgue the head was unwrapped, and proved to be that of a woman in her late teens or early 20s. She had been on the short side – only five feet one inch tall – with a slim body and small breasts. Her face was oval-shaped and, even in death, was noticeably pretty. Her bobbed hair had been dyed blonde with per-oxide and her eyes were blue. There was a .25-calibre bullet wound beneath her right eye, but she had been killed by a brutal attack to the left side of her head – seven or eight blows with a blunt object had smashed in her skull. As the body showed no signs of decomposition, she had presumably been killed no more than a day or so before she was found.

The authorities were optimistic that they would soon identify the victim. Attractive young women tend to be noticed and remembered, even by passing strangers. Thanks to the minimal decomposition her finger-prints were in perfect condition, and were sent to be checked against police records. Additionally, her mouth had been undamaged by the attack that killed her, allowing an imprint of her teeth to be checked against dental records. The .25 bullet had been fired from a Webley Scott automatic pistol. Since gun ownership was tightly controlled in Australia, the number of licensed handguns in the country was relatively small and all such weapons could be checked to see if one matched the scoring on the bullet.

But a year later, despite nationwide interest in the case, the "Pyjama Girl" remained unidentified. Her fingerprints were not on file, so she probably didn't have an Australian police record.

The bullet did not match any licensed Webley Scott .25 automatic, so must have been fired from an illegal weapon. No dentists recognized the dental imprint circulated by investigators, but that was hardly surprising because she didn't have any fillings or evidence of other dental work. Even the fact that she had evidently been an eye-catching woman in life did not help. Her body was dis-played, preserved in a bath of formalin, at the University of Sydney. Thousands of residents of New South Wales – and thousands more who were merely morbid sightseers – shuffled past her body and tried to recognize her placid face (the gruesome damage to the side of her head was tastefully hidden by a bandage). In fact, the unknown woman became the chief tourist attraction in Sydney for some time. But every suggestion as to who she might be turned out to be a dead end.

For almost 10 years the mystery remained unsolved, and the unnamed woman floated in her bath of formalin – a spectacle now only for the odd tourist with an interest in gruesome mysteries. But the Pyjama Girl was not forgotten by the Australian public or media;

the investigators' failure to identify her or her murderer was brought up every time someone wanted to question the efficiency of the police.

Ironically, it was the very man who had taken the brunt of the press criticism over the years, Sydney Police Com-missioner Bill Mackay, who apparently cracked the case. The chronology of events is somewhat muddled, not least by Mackay himself. One version is that, in March 1944, Mackay was eating in Romanos, one of Sydney's more expensive Italian restau-rants, and noticed that one of the waiters, Antonio Agostini, seemed particularly gloomy. Mackay had been on nodding terms with Agostini some years before the war, when the Italian immigrant had run the restaurant's coat-check concession. Mackay asked him what the matter was and Agostini broke down and said that he had something to confess. Back at the station he admitted to killing his wife…

This version of events is perhaps a bit too pat for some commentators – making Mackay himself the officer who succeeded when so many others had failed. Another version of events has Mackay, sick of the continuing press criticism, assigning two new investigators to the Pyjama Girl case. These came across Agostini's name as someone who had been questioned over the disappearance of his wife at about the time the Pyjama Girl was found, but the lead had never been fully followed up. It was these officers who, some say, were responsible for locating Agostini and then convincing him to confess.

Tony Agostini claimed that the Pyjama Girl was his English-born wife Linda. Originally from Bromley in Kent, Linda Platt had run a sweet shop with her sister until an unhappy love affair had driven her to emigrate to the other side of the world. She had met Tony Agostini while he was also "just off the boat" from Europe and they had married in 1930.

The marriage had started as a happy and loving relationship, but, according to Tony, Linda had become increasingly alcoholic and, when drunk, was insanely suspicious that he was having affairs. One night after a particularly savage argument, Tony claimed that he had been wakened by something cold and hard pressed to his face. He opened his eyes to find Linda holding the barrel of a gun to his flesh. They had struggled. The gun went off. Linda fell dead.

Convinced that an Italian could get no justice at the hands of the Australian police, Tony said, he had driven the body out to the storm drain, dumped it and tried to burn it with petrol.

At his trial, though, evidence emerged that seriously undermined Agostini's version of events. The prosecuting counsel asked him: if, as he claimed, Linda had died of an accidental gunshot to the head, how had the left

> **For almost 10 years the mystery remained unsolved and the unnamed woman floated in her bath of formalin – a spectacle now only for the odd tourist...**

side of her skull come to be so badly battered? Evidently flustered, Agostini replied that he had been carrying her dead body downstairs when he had tripped and she had crashed, head-first, down the wooden steps, landing hard against a plant pot on the lower landing.

Even in the 1940s, forensic science was advanced enough to blow this ridiculous story out of the water. The Pyjama Girl had been killed by at least half-a-dozen blows to the head; a tumble down a single flight of stairs could not have done so much damage. Yet the police offered no specialist testimony to corroborate this fact, and the jury found Agostini guilty of manslaughter not murder. He served almost four years of a six-year sentence then, paroled, returned to Italy.

Was the Pyjama Girl really Linda Agostini? The answer is almost certainly no. Although there were many similarities between the description of Linda at the time of her disappearance and of the mystery victim, there were also some decisive differences. Linda had been a full-breasted woman of 29; the Pyjama Girl

had been almost flat-chested and appeared to have been in her late teens or early 20s. More importantly, Linda had brown eyes and was known to have several fillings in her molar teeth; the Pyjama Girl was blue-eyed and had no fillings. The police effectively covered up these points by failing to call as witnesses the two dentists who had examined the Pyjama Girl's teeth and reported no fillings, then arguing – against all known evidence – that brown eyes can turn blue after death.

So why did Tony Agostini risk execution by confessing to a crime he had not committed? The answer is probably that he was, in fact, a murderer, but not that of the Pyjama Girl. The story of his spontaneous confession to Police Commissioner Mackay might well be true, but Agostini may have added that he had successfully disposed of his wife's body. Faced, on the one hand, with a murder case that he could not convict on – the only evidence against Agostini was his own confession, which he could withdraw at any time – and, on the other, the ongoing embarrassment of the Pyjama Girl mystery, it seems likely that Mackay decided to kill two birds with one stone. If Agostini could be persuaded to insist that the Pyjama Girl was Linda, then Mackay would see to it that the prosecution case would be slanted to bring a conviction for manslaughter rather than murder. Agostini – unaware that with the police having no evidence and no witnesses, he was already safe from a murder conviction – agreed.

So the question remains – who was the Pyjama Girl? We will probably never know.

Death of a good-time girl

Socially, Australia was still a very staid limb of the British Empire in 1934. While the Roaring 20s had swept the cities of Europe and America with a post-war exuberance for high and wild living, life in the Antipodes was still mainly agrarian and ultra-conservative. The fact that the Pyjama Girl had sported bobbed hair, dyed platinum blonde, and had been wearing silk pyjamas rather than, say, a woollen nightgown suggested that she had been a "flapper" – a good-time girl, more used to dancing and drinking than church attendance and housework. Stern parents and preachers across the country pointed to her grim death as a morality tale made flesh. She had evidently lived the high life, and had paid for it with a brutal death. If annoyed youngsters hoped that the solution of the case would end the lectures, they were to be disappointed. Many, in fact, lived to lecture their own children before the case was apparently closed.

RATTENBURY AND STONER

The Rattenburys had come to England from Canada in 1928, and bought a house at Manor Road, Bournemouth, called the Villa Madeira.

They made an odd pair. Francis Rattenbury, a retired architect, was 61 and looked it, particularly when he was somnolent from his generous intake of whisky. Alma was 36, and was still pretty. She had two sons from a previous marriage, and a baby from her present one, and was intelligent, lively and artistic – she had once written song lyrics for a living.

She tended the house and garden and her husband with kindness and good humour, and seemed the ideal wife. She also employed a companion-help, Miss Irene Riggs, who was devoted to her.

In recent years, Francis and Alma had ceased to have sex, and they now slept in separate bedrooms.

In September 1934, Francis Rattenbury, who was now 67,

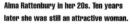

Alma Rattenbury in her 20s. Ten years later she was still an attractive woman.

The Rattenbury family, Alma, her architect husband Francis – 25 years her senior – and their son, at the seaside. Irene Riggs is in background. It was her third marriage, and the couple had ceased to sleep together. Francis Rattenbury was apparently broad-minded enough to accept that his wife might need to take a lover.

advertised in the local paper for a handyman and chauffeur, having decided to give up driving. This brought George Stoner into the household, claiming to be 22. In fact, he was 17, but so big that he looked older. He was neither handsome nor particularly intelligent, but he soon shared Irene Riggs's devotion to Mrs Rattenbury. As for the lively

Alma Rattenbury leaving court after her discharge, escorted by a doctor.

sharing the same bed, Stoner was insanely jealousy.

At 9.30 Alma Rattenbury retired to bed to read. An hour later, the companion Mrs Riggs was woken by Alma's voice screaming her name. She rushed downstairs to find Alma shaking her husband, who was limp. Mrs Riggs thought it was a heart attack until she looked closely and saw his head was covered in blood and he had a black eye. She telephoned his medical attendant, Dr O'Donnell, who found that Francis Rattenbury was still alive. In a local hospital, it was discovered that he had been badly battered on the top of his head, and the police were called immediately.

> ## " YOU HAVE GOT YOURSELF INTO THIS MESS THROUGH TALKING TOO MUCH. "
> ### George Stoner

Back at the Villa Madeira, Alma was not behaving like an anxious wife, but was drunk, and flirting outrageously with the policemen, even kissing them. Beneath the façade of the competent house-wife there obviously dwelt a party-going, good-time girl.

In the garden, a policeman found a mallet sticky with blood and hair. On being shown the weapon, Alma immediately confessed to attacking her husband. The police assumed she was drunk and hysterical, so Dr O'Donnell gave her some sedatives and sent her to bed. However, when she woke up the next morning, she repeated her confession and was taken to the police station. She then appeared before a magistrate, and was remanded to

and sex-starved Alma, she treated George Stoner at first like her son, then decided it would do no harm to introduce him to the pleasures of sex. Once he was allowed to "board in", and moved into the bedroom opposite hers, he simply spent the night in her bed. If her husband knew, he was unconcerned.

Alma was horrified when George confessed to her that

he had just turned 18, and she wanted to break off the affair. He became stubborn and determined, and bullied her into changing her mind. The power she had granted him seemed to have gone to his head, and he became bossy, even telling her that she ought to drink fewer cocktails.

In March 1935, under the pretext of going to town for a surgical operation, Mrs

Rattenbury took Stoner up to London where they stayed for three days at the Kensington Palace Hotel, and Alma bought him new clothes.

Not surprisingly, Stoner was feverishly in love, and when, upon returning to Bournemouth, he learned that Alma was to take her husband to see a friend in Bridport the next day, Monday, March 25, and that they would be

Villa Madeira, Manor Road, Bournemouth, where the murder occurred.

George Percy Stoner, the illiterate 17 year-old youth hired as a chauffeur-handy-man, who became Alma Rattenbury's lover.

Holloway prison in London. As she was being taken out of the house by police, George Stoner said: "You have got yourself into this mess through talking too much."

Alma was in Holloway when her husband finally died on March 28, and on the same day

Stoner admitted to the killing, saying, "Do you know Mrs Rattenbury had nothing to do with this? When I did the job, I believed he was asleep. I hit him and then came upstairs and told Mrs Rattenbury." He admitted to borrowing the mallet from his grandparents "to put up a tent".

Alma Rattenbury and George Stoner faced a joint

trial on a charge of murdering Francis Rattenbury; the proceedings took place at the Old Bailey on May 27 to 31, 1935. The prosecution argued that the murder was the result of a plot cooked up between the two accused, but it was obvious that this was entirely untrue. The jury eventually found Alma

Rattenbury not guilty and she was discharged. But the verdict on George Stoner was a foregone conclusion. As her lover was condemned to death, Alma Rattenbury was heard to moan: "Oh no."

Alma's last cigarette

In fact, the home secretary took Stoner's youth into account and commuted his death sentence to life imprisonment. But Alma Rattenbury was unaware of this. Three days after her acquittal, she put a knife in her handbag and walked along the banks of the River Avon near Christchurch. Then, after smoking a last cigarette, she stabbed herself in the chest six times, and threw herself into the river.

THE RUXTON CASE

The 1930s equivalent of the Crippen murder was the Ruxton case, which filled the British public with just the same combination of morbid fascination and physical nausea. The mystery also had its equivalent of Sir Bernard Spilsbury in the brilliant Scots pathologist John Glaister.

On a cool autumn day, September 29, 1935, a young lady noticed a bundle jammed against a boulder in a stream called the Gardenholme Linn, near the Scottish border. Something that looked like a human arm was sticking out of it.

The police soon discovered two human heads on the bank, as well as four more bundles. Each proved to contain human remains – thigh bones, legs, pieces of flesh, and an armless torso. One sheet of newspaper wrapped round two upper arms proved to be the *Sunday Graphic* for September 15, 1935.

The following day, Professor John Glaister – author of the classic *Medical Jurisprudence and Toxicology* – arrived with his colleague, Dr Gilbert Millar. He quickly realized that this killing was not the work of some terrified amateur; the murderer had taken care to cover his tracks. He had not only dismembered the bodies, but

Bridge over the Annan where dismembered bodies were found in September 1935.

removed the skin from the heads, to make the faces unrecognizable, and cut off the fingertips to make fingerprint identification impossible.

Glaister took the remains to the anatomy department of the University of Edinburgh, and there "pickled" them in a formalin solution.

The first task was to sort the pieces into two separate bodies, and this was made easier by the fact that one was six inches shorter than the other. When it was finally done, Glaister found that they had one almost complete body, the taller one, and one that was minus a trunk.

What could be deduced about the murderer? First, that he was almost certainly a medical man. The skill used in dismembering the body showed a thorough knowledge of anatomy. He had also removed the teeth, knowing that they could lead to identification by a dentist.

Fortunately, the murderer had either lost his nerve or been interrupted, for he had left a pair of hands with their fingertips intact. After soaking them in hot water, Glaister was able to get an excellent set of prints. And the discovery that the assorted pieces of flesh included three breasts also made it clear that both bodies were of women.

The next problem was the age of the bodies. Glaister determined this by means of the skull sutures. Sutures are "joining lines" in the skull, and they seal themselves over the years; they are usually closed completely by the age of 40. In one of the two skulls, the smaller of the two, the sutures were unclosed; in the other,

they were almost closed. This indicated that one body was that of a woman of about 40; the other was certainly under 30. X-rays of the jaw-bone of the younger woman showed

> **AND THE DISCOVERY THAT THE ASSORTED PIECES OF FLESH INCLUDED THREE BREASTS ALSO MADE IT CLEAR THAT BOTH BODIES WERE OF WOMEN.**

that the wisdom teeth had still not pushed through, which meant she was probably in her early 20s.

As to the cause of death, this was fairly clear. The taller woman had five stab wounds in the chest, several broken bones, and many bruises. The hyoid bone in the neck was broken, indicating strangulation before the other injuries

had been inflicted. The swollen and bruised tongue confirmed this. Glaister reasoned that a murderer who strangled and beat his victim before stabbing her would probably be in the grip of jealous rage. As to the other body, the signs were that she had been battered with some blunt instrument. It hardly needed Sherlock Holmes to infer that she had been killed as an afterthought, probably to keep her silent. The fact that the murderer had taken less trouble to conceal her identity supported this.

Meanwhile, the police were working on their own clues. The *Sunday Graphic* was a special local edition, printed for the Morecambe and Lancaster area. And the clothes in which some of the remains had been wrapped were also distinctive: the head of the younger woman had been wrapped in a pair of child's rompers, and another

bundle had been wrapped in a blouse with a patch under the arm.

In Lancaster, a Persian doctor named Buck Ruxton had already attracted the suspicions of the local police. Five days before the remains were found in the Linn, Ruxton – a small, rather good-looking man with an excitable manner – had called on the police and mentioned that his wife had deserted him. The police were investigating the murder of a lady called Mrs Smalley, whose body had been found a year earlier, and in the course of routine investigations, had questioned a domestic in Ruxton's household; he wanted to protest about this harassment. So when he spoke of his wife's disappearance, they were not in the least surprised; they knew that the relations between the two were stormy. Two years before, Mrs Isabella Ruxton had come to the

View from bridge of spots where parcels containing human remains were found.

police station to protest that her husband was beating her, and Ruxton had made wild accusations of infidelity against her.

The parents of Mrs Ruxton's maid, Mary Rogerson, were not only surprised but incredulous when Ruxton came and told them that their daughter had got herself pregnant by the laundry boy, and that his wife had taken her away for an abortion. Nothing was less likely; Mary was a plain girl, with a cast in one eye, who loved her home and her parents, and spent all her spare time with them; she was as unlikely to get herself pregnant as to rob a bank. In spite of Ruxton's feverish protests, they reported it to the police. On the evening of October 9, 1935, 10 days after the remains had been found in the Linn, Ruxton came to the police and burst into tears. People were saying that he had murdered his wife and thrown her into the Linn; they must help him find her. They soothed him and sent him away.

But, in fact, Ruxton had been the chief suspect since earlier that day. The Scottish police had been to see the Rogersons, and had shown them the patched blouse. As soon as they saw it, they knew their daughter was dead; Mary had bought it at a jumble sale and patched it under the arm. They were unable to identify the rompers, but suggested that the police show them to Mrs Holme, with whom Mary and the three Ruxton children had spent a holiday earlier that year. And Mrs Holme recognized the rompers as a pair she had given to Mary for the children.

The police then spoke to the Ruxtons' charlady, Mrs Oxley.

Dr Buck Ruxton (Bukhtyar Rustomji Ratanji Hakim), the violently jealous husband who murdered his wife, and was forced to kill the maid who heard it.

She told them that on the day Mrs Ruxton and Mary Rogerson had disappeared – Sunday, September 15, 1935 – Mr Ruxton had arrived early at her house and explained that it was unnecessary for her to come to work that day as he was taking the children away to Morecambe, and his wife had gone to Edinburgh. The following morning, she turned up to find the Ruxtons' house – at 2 Dalton Square – in a state of utter chaos, with carpets removed, the bath full of yellow stains, and a pile of burnt material in the yard. A neighbour told the police that Ruxton had persuaded her to come and

February 21, 1985   Hospital Doctor   13

=FORENSIC MEDICINE=

Grim 'jigsaw' solved murders

Prof Bernard Knight looks at a classic example of how the expertise of medical professors brought a doctor to the gallows

ONE of the classic exercises in anatomical reconstruction was perhaps appropriately made in a double murder committed by a medical practitioner.

A woman out for a stroll one Sunday in 1935 was shocked to see a human arm sticking from a parcel thrown into a small stream just over the Scottish border, on the Carlisle-Edinburgh road.

After a police search, no less than 70 fragments of human remains were recovered, wrapped clumsily in newspaper and cloth.

Within the next two months, more pieces of limb were found scattered around the country-side.

The mutilated parts were taken to Glasgow, where they were examined by John Glaister, professor of forensic medicine, and J. C. Brash, professor of anatomy. They were later assisted by Professor Sydney Smith from Edinburgh.

They had to deal with two

The photograph of Mrs Ruxton used by detectives in the first recorded 'photo-fit' experiment

The photograph negative of Mrs Ruxton's skull which police fitted perfectly over her photograph

heads, two incomplete trunks, seven sections of arms and hands, four legs with only two feet and a large mass of flesh including three female breasts, genitalia and a uterus.

It was obvious that a deliberate effort had been made to render identification imposs-ible, as the facial elements such as eyes, lips, noses and ears were missing and all teeth had been ex-tracted after death, as had the finger-pads carrying prints.

Painstaking work was done to assemble as much as possible, when it became evident that two female bodies were represented.

One was a young woman bet-ween 18 and 25, about 4ft 11in, with an appendix scar, eight teeth missing before death and chronic tonsillitis.

The other was an older woman, probably in her thirties, 5ft 3in, having borne children and suffered from a bunion.

While the doctors had been working, the police had also been active. Among the wrappings of the grisly parcels was a copy of the *Sunday Graphic* for September 15. This contained a report of the crowning of a car-nival queen in Morecambe.

Detectives soon found this was a special local edition for the Lancaster area.

At about the same time the chief constable of Dumfries recalled reading a newspaper report that the housemaid of a Lancaster doctor had gone miss-ing. When the Lancashire police made inquiries, they found that the doctor's wife was also missing.

The doctor in question was an Indian, Bukhtyar Rustomji Hakim, a Parsee family practi-tioner, who had qualified in

clean up his house to prepare it for the decorators, claiming that he had cut his hand badly on a tin of peaches. She and her husband had obligingly scrubbed out the house. And Ruxton had given them some bloodstained carpets and a blue suit that was also stained with blood.

> ## AS SOON AS THEY SAW [THE BLOUSE] THEY KNEW THEIR DAUGHTER WAS DEAD.

On October 12, the police questioned Ruxton all night, and at 7.20 the next morn-ing he was charged with the murder of Mary Rogerson.

In spite of Ruxton's attempts to cover his tracks, and to per-suade various witnesses to of-fer him false alibis, the truth soon became plain. Ruxton was pathologically jealous, but there was no evidence that his "wife" - they were, in fact, not married - had ever been unfaithful. A week before the murder, Mrs Ruxton had

gone to visit her sister in Ed-inburgh, with a family named Edmondson, close friends of the Ruxtons. Mrs Ruxton and the Edmondsons booked into separate rooms; Ruxton, however, was convinced she had spent the night in the bed of Robert Edmondson, an assistant solicitor in the town hall. Ruxton had driven to Edinburgh to spy on them.

The following Saturday, Isabella Ruxton had gone to spend the afternoon and evening with two of her sisters in Blackpool. Convinced she was in a hotel room with a man, Ruxton had worked him-self into a frenzy, and when she came back far later than expected, he began to beat her - perhaps in an attempt to make her confess - then throttled her unconscious and stabbed her. Mary Rogerson had probably heard the screams and come in to see what was happening; Ruxton believed she was his wife's confidante in her infidelities, and killed her too.

He had spent the next day dismembering the bodies and

packing them in straw; that night, he made his first trip north to dispose of them...

The "photofit" picture of Isabella Ruxton imposed on the skull that was found under the bridge.

Photo finish

Ruxton's counsel, Norman Birkett, must have known that his client did not stand a ghost of a chance. His line of defence was that the bodies found in the Linn were not those of Isabella Ruxton and Mary Rogerson, but of some other persons. But when the medical experts – Glaister, Millar, and Professor Sydney Smith – gave their evidence, it was obvious that the identity of the bodies had been established beyond all possible doubt. One photograph, which has subsequently been used in every account of the case, superimposed the larger of the two skulls on a photograph of Mrs Ruxton. She had a rather long, horsey face, and it was obvious that the two fitted together with gruesome exactitude.

Ruxton, however, seemed determined to trap himself in a web of lies and evasions. The result was a unanimous verdict of guilty, arrived at in only one hour. He was hanged at Strangeways jail, Manchester, on May 12, 1936.

1938

THE KILLING OF PERCY CASSERLEY

At 9.10, on the evening of Wednesday, March 23, 1938, a hysterical woman rushed out of 35 Lindisfarne Road in Wimbledon, and hammered on the nearest front door. She was Georgina May Casserley, wife of the managing director of a local brewery. She told her neighbours, the Burchells, that she had just returned from a walk to find the house burgled and her husband bleeding on the floor.

Mr Burchell and his son hurried next door to investigate, and found Percy Casserley lying on the floor of the disordered lounge. He had been shot in the head and neck and was breathing with a choking gurgle. The police arrived within minutes, but Casserley died soon after.

Surveying the crime scene, detectives found obvious signs of a break-in. The burglars appeared to have entered the house through the French windows in the dining-room, breaking the glass from the outside to reach the catch. The coat-stand in the hall had been upset and silverware was scattered across the dining-room floor. Other items of silverware were lying on the blood-spattered lounge floor. By the door to the lounge was the fawn button of a mackintosh that had been ripped off the coat so fiercely, it had taken a patch of cloth with it. At first sight, it seemed to be a straightforward case of a burglary that had gone wrong, but investigation into the Casserleys' background soon raised some doubts.

Percy had spent a month of the winter of 1937 in a nursing home for alcoholics. On his return, Ena had told him that she was pregnant. Since they had not had marital relations since he had undergone an operation in 1936, he understandably took the news badly. Questioning the couple's maid, Lydia Scott, the police discovered that the father was a builder's foreman called Edward Royal Chaplin.

Chaplin, a muscular, handsome man of 35, was undoubtedly more attractive than tall, 58-year-old Casserley. Ted, as Chaplin was known, had been working on a house being erected on a neighbouring plot of land. One day, while Percy was at the clinic,

Marital difficulties

Percy Arthur Casserley had married Georgina, nicknamed "Ena", some 11 years previously. She was 20 years his junior and there had been some marital difficulties of late. Percy, due to retire in a year's time, was a serious alcoholic, drinking an average of a bottle-and-a-half of whisky every evening. As a result, he was often irritable, moody and anti-social. Moreover, Ena Casserley, now 38, was known by the neighbours to be desperate to start a family, but her husband had apparently vetoed the idea.

Lydia Scott, the Casserley's maid and Georgina Casserley's confidante. Lydia told Ted Chaplin that Percy Casserley had threatened Georgina with a gun: did that drive him to murder the older man?

Ena had asked him in for a cup of tea. The relationship had quickly developed to the point where he had stayed overnight at Lindisfarne Road and she had visited him at his flat in Morden. By the time Casserley returned from the nursing home, Ena had already missed a period.

Following his wife's shock announcement, Percy Casserley had a minor nervous breakdown, and returned to the nursing home for a fortnight, from March 8 to 22. During this time, Ted and Ena saw each other regularly. The pair appear to have been genuinely in love. When Chaplin heard of Ena's condition, he insisted that she should divorce her husband and marry him. Ena was by no means averse to the idea. Unfortunately, it seemed certain that Casserley would block divorce proceedings. Under British law at the time, a court would be very unlikely to allow a woman a divorce from an unwilling husband who had not himself committed adultery.

On the night following Percy Casserley's second return from the nursing home, Ena and the maid Lydia had planned to go to the cinema. At the last minute, Ena was forced to drop the plan. She explained to the maid that when she had told her husband she was going out, he had become enraged and threatened to shoot her. Lydia later told the police that Mrs Casserley had seemed genuinely frightened and upset.

As the maid was leaving, Ena had asked her to pass a message on to Ted. If he came to the back door, she said, she would be able to see him for a couple of minutes, but no more. Lydia gave him the message, and also told him about the shooting threat. What effect such information had on him is easy to guess.

The police investigation had by now turned up several pieces of evidence that did not concur with Ena Casserley's burglary story. Microscopic examination of the pane of glass broken out of the French window showed that it had been smashed from inside the house, and the autopsy, conducted by Sir Bernard Spilsbury, revealed that Casserley had been beaten about the head and back, and that the killing shot to the head had been fired from point-blank range. Why, thought investigators, would burglars have beaten then executed a householder they had accidentally surprised?

On March 29, detectives visited Ted Chaplin on a building site in Epsom. They

> **"I'VE CALLED TO SEE WHAT THE TROUBLE IS BETWEEN YOU AND MRS CASSERLEY. I'VE JUST LEFT HER AND SHE'S TERRIBLY UPSET. YOU KNOW ABOUT HER CONDITION. I'M RESPONSIBLE FOR IT. I WANT TO SUGGEST TO YOU THAT EITHER SHE COMES AWAY WITH ME TONIGHT OR I'LL PHONE AND GET HER POLICE PROTECTION, AS I UNDERSTAND YOU'VE THREATENED MRS CASSERLEY."**
> Edward Chaplin

Georgina Casserley, six-months-pregnant with Ted Chaplin's baby, arrives at the Old Bailey to stand trial with her lover.

asked him to accompany them to the police station. He asked if he might get his coat first. On his return he was wearing a fawn-coloured raincoat with a button missing.

Chaplin initially denied being at Lindisfarne Road on the night Casserley had been shot. Then, after being told that his denial might further implicate Ena Casserley, he decided to confess.

He admitted going to the Casserley house that evening, after having spoken to Lydia Scott. He had arrived just after 7.30 p.m. and met Ena coming out of the front door in tears. They had walked to an off-licence together to buy a fresh bottle of whisky for Percy, which was Ena's excuse for leaving the house. Chaplin said that she had plainly been terrified by her husband's threats, and he had decided to settle matters there and then.

On their return to number 35, they conferred in the scullery for a few moments. Chaplin, still in his raincoat and hat, had said: "You had better leave this to me" and, after sending Ena upstairs, went into the lounge to confront his lover's husband.

According to Chaplin's statement, Casserley was dozing in an armchair by the fire when he entered. "Good evening," said the younger man. Casserley, surprised, got up, dropping his spectacles on the floor. "I've called to see what the trouble is between you and Mrs Casserley," Chaplin had continued. "I've just left her and she's terribly upset. You know about her condition. I'm responsible for it. I want to suggest to you that either she comes away with me tonight or I'll phone and get her police protection, as I understand you've threatened Mrs Casserley."

Percy Casserley looked stunned. "Oh, so it's you, you swine," Chaplin said he exclaimed, then the old man appeared to be overcome with grief. Casserley, head in hands, staggered drunkenly to the writing-bureau and slumped into a chair.

Then, according to Chaplin, Percy had suddenly whipped open a drawer and pulled out a .25 automatic pistol. Chaplin, taken off guard,

Crowds outside Wimbledon Police Court strain to catch a glimpse of infamous lovers.

made a leap and grabbed Casserley's right forearm, twisting it until he dropped the gun. The older man leant against him heavily, as if passing out, then unexpectedly dropped to one side and grabbed the gun in his left hand. Chaplin caught both the other man's wrists and the two fought in a face-to-face struggle, both trying to force the gun away from themselves. Then the gun went off.

According to Chaplin, the bullet entered and exited Casserley's neck, making a superficial but frightening wound. Chaplin was shocked

and let go of the other's right wrist. He then tried to grab Casserley round the waist to throw him to the floor. The older man – still in possession of the gun – half-turned, doubled-up and grabbed Chaplin's testicles with his free hand. In agony, Chaplin snatched an electric torch from the top of the bureau and belaboured the stooped man on the back and head. Casserley let go of Chaplin's testicles, but maintained his desperate grip on the automatic. Chaplin, still holding the other's left wrist, tried to throw him again. Casserley fell backwards, dragging the young man down

on top of him. They lay face pressed against face, Casserley, now with both hands on the gun, trying to level it at his assailant. Chaplin heard two clicks from the automatic, then Casserley went limp and said: "All right, I give in."

Chaplin let go and began to stand up, then he heard another click and saw that Casserley was aiming the gun at him with both hands. He leaped forward, forcing the older man's arms upwards. Then the automatic went off a second time. The shot entered Casserley's head, just in front of the left ear. He collapsed and lay still.

Chaplin told the police that his first impulse was to call for medical aid. Then, realizing that this would compromise Ena, he decided to make it look like a bungled burglary. Ena Casserley .was horrified when he went upstairs and told her what had happened, but fell in with his plan. Percy was still breathing; if she hurried for help, it might not be too late…

Following the signing of his statement, Edward Chaplin was formally arrested. He gave every appearance of wanting to assist the authorities, even offering to lead them to the half-completed house in which he had hidden Casserley's automatic and cartridges, saying: "I'll show you where the gun is, you'll never find it on your own."

Searching Chaplin's flat in Morden, the police found Percy Casserley's diamond ring, and a life-preserver (a long-handled cosh). Chaplin said the cosh was a gift for his aged father, but freely admitted that he had washed blood off it recently. It had been in the drawer in which he had temporarily stored the pistol, he said, and some of the blood had rubbed off on it.

Percy Casserley was buried the day Chaplin was arrested. Three days later, on April 1, Georgina Casserley was also arrested and charged with being an accessory after the fact.

Edward Chaplin's trial opened at the Old Bailey on Tuesday, May 24, 1938. The prosecution's case, put by G. B. McClure, KC, was that Chaplin had deliberately murdered Percy Casserley, and his "confession" was a lie. Chaplin, he said, had stayed in the Casserleys' house while Percy was at the clinic. During that period he would have had ample time to discover where the automatic pistol was kept. Indeed, it might have been as early as this that Chaplin hatched his plan to kill his lover's husband.

Specifically, the Crown believed that Chaplin had gone to Lindisfarne Road on the evening of March 23, armed with the cosh and a murderous intent. He had attacked and beaten the older man, then cold-bloodedly shot him. If there had been any fight at all, Casserley had only been trying to protect himself, not attack a younger and fitter man. Chaplin had then, by his own admission, faked the burglary to throw the authorities off the track.

McClure asked why, if his story of accidental shooting were true, had Chaplin not called a doctor? He knew that there was a telephone in the house. Chaplin claimed he had panicked, and had only thought of protecting Ena However, Percy Casserley's diamond ring had been found in Chaplin's flat. If he was in a panic, why had he paused to acquire this grim memento?

The Crown's main witness was Sir Bernard Spilsbury, who had conducted the autopsy on Casserley. He told the court that he had found 17 separate bruises on the victim's head and back. All of these might easily have been caused by a cosh. By comparison, the court was told, Edward Chaplin had been totally unmarked when he was examined following his arrest, less than a week later.

Spilsbury went on to state that the shot which had caused the neck wound, since there were no powder burns to the skin, had been fired from more than 12 inches away. This was quite a distance, considering the two men were supposed to be struggling hand-to-hand at the time. And a pistol, pointing upwards and forced more than a foot from the body, tends to point away from the combatants. On the other hand, the shot to the head had been fired with the weapon pressed against Casserley's temple, execution-style.

McClure went on to point out that Percy Casserley was right-handed; as indeed was his assailant. Yet, according to Chaplin's statement, he had picked up the weapon with his left hand and, despite several opportunities to change hands during the fight, had never done so. Chaplin claimed that the gun had been in Casserley's left hand each time it went off, thus causing the wounds to the left side of his neck and head. But wasn't it more likely, asked the prosecutor, that the gun had been in *Chaplin's* right hand as he stood confronting his victim, thus wounding Casserley's left side?

Chaplin was defended by the masterful Norman Birkett, arguably one of the best defence advocates of the twentieth century. He pointed out that his client had freely admitted to beating Casserley's back with the torch while the latter gripped "a portion of his body". However, Sir Bernard Spilsbury had found no bruises to the front of the corpse. Surely, he said, if Chaplin had launched an unprovoked attack, he would have struck at Casserley's face?

Chaplin had another stroke of luck, in that Casserley's .25 Webley and Scott automatic was found to have a defective reloading mechanism. Weapons expert Robert Churchill told the court that after the first shot, the pistol would invariably jam for a few trigger pulls. This tied in with Chaplin's description of the clicks the automatic had made as Casserley tried to shoot him.

In his summing-up, Mr Justice Humphreys told the jury that if they believed that Casserley had been shot "in

An unlikely story

The most unlikely aspect of Chaplin's story, said McClure, was the length of the fight. Percy Casserley was 58 and sickly. Edward Chaplin was 35 and, as the court could see, strongly built and at the peak of physical fitness. Was it conceivable, the prosecutor asked, that the younger man could have had so much trouble overcoming his infirm rival? After disarming Casserley's stronger hand in a matter of seconds, why had Chaplin had so much trouble with his left arm? Finally there was the matter of the fatal shot to the temple. At the end of his summing-up, McClure confronted the jury: "Chaplin was holding the hand that was holding the pistol. Whose was the force that was pressing that pistol against the skin? The man [Casserley] was flat on his back..."

Mr Justice Birkett (left) the presiding judge on the Chaplin-Casserley trial, had no sympathy for the heavily pregnant Georgina: "I'm not going to treat you with lenience, because I think that there is nothing in particular in your condition that calls for it.".

the heat of passion in the course of a quarrel so serious that the accused lost complete control of himself" they might convict Chaplin of manslaughter, but not murder. Considering the largely circumstantial nature of the Crown's evidence, it was not surprising that the jury took this course. Edward Chaplin was convicted of man-slaughter and sentenced to 12 years' imprisonment.

Outside, the six-months-pregnant Georgina Casserley fainted when she was told the sentence. Her trial, as an accessory after the fact, took place just half-an-hour later. She pleaded guilty and wept uncontrollably throughout.

Before passing sentence, the judge spoke his mind candidly. "The less said about your part in this case the better," he said. "I'm not going to treat you with lenience because I think there is nothing in particular in your condition that calls for it. Your case has aroused the most ridiculous nonsense. A great many people have treated you as though you were some sort of heroine. You were a participator in a vulgar and sordid intrigue." He then condemned her to 11 days' imprisonment; a fate less severe than her public humiliation in the courtroom.

Edward Chaplin was finally released, after eight years in prison, on May 17, 1946. Ena Casserley was waiting at the prison gate and they were married the same day.

1940s

THE DEATH OF LORD ERROLL

One of the most active seducers in the part of Kenya known as the "Happy Valley" was a handsome — if slightly overweight — aristocrat named Josslyn Hay, who was the 22nd Earl of Erroll. He was believed to have slept with every attractive woman for miles around.

In November 1940, two more Britons joined the expatriate community: Sir Henry–"Jock"–Delves Brough -ton, and his lovely wife Diana. Broughton was 35 years her senior, a rather dour and unpopular man who had divorced his first wife in 1939, and lost no time in proposing to the aristocratic Diana Caldwell. He had assured her that if she fell in love with a younger man, he would not only grant her a divorce, but would provide her with an income of £5,000 a year.

At a ball at the Muthaiga Country Club while her husband was away, Diana met Lord Erroll, and by the time Broughton returned, his wife was in love with the younger man. Unfortunately, Broughton no longer had the cash to make good his original promise of a £5,000-a-year allowance.

Nevertheless, Broughton seemed to be taking it all very well. On January 23, 1941, he invited his wife, Lord Erroll and a friend named June Carberry to a "farewell dinner" at the Muthaiga Club, and toasted the "happy couple".

Pretty blonde Diana Delves Broughton had married a man who was 35 years her senior.

Sir Jock Delves (pronounced Deeves) Broughton, racehorse owner and big game hunter, was, in fact, almost bankrupt.

The Muthaiga Country Club, Nairobi, where Erroll ate his last meal.

Erroll and Diana left to go dancing; he brought her home by 2.30 a.m., walked her to the front door, then drove off.

Half an hour later, two local men driving a milk truck saw a car tilted over at an angle in a drainage trench. They peered in through the window and saw a man who was obviously dead.

The police were called, and the dead man was identified as Lord Erroll. At the mortuary it was recognized that he had been shot in the left ear by a .32 bullet.

The obvious suspect was Broughton. He claimed to have spent the night in bed, except for two occasions – at 2 a.m. and 3.30 a.m. – when he knocked on the bedroom door of June Carberry "to check that she was all right". Obviously, he could have left

"Joss" Erroll was a member of Oswald Mosley's British Union of Fascists, and a dedicated seducer of other men's wives.

the house between these two visits, but there was no evidence that he had.

When Arthur Poppy, Superintendent in charge of the case, heard that Broughton had been engaged in target practice at a nearby farm, he located the .32 bullets that matched the one found in Erroll's brain, and another discovered in the car. Poppy's theory was that Broughton had sneaked out of the house while Erroll was saying good-bye to Diana, and hidden in his car. He had waited until Erroll slowed down, then shot him in the ear, hanging on to the safety straps – which were torn out – as the car crashed into the ditch. Then he had returned home and climbed in through a window.

On the morning after the murder, Broughton had set fire to the rubbish in the rubbish pit in his garden, sprinkling it with petrol; later, the remains of a golf stocking, with traces of what looked like blood, were found in the pit. Poppy also found a pair of burnt

gym shoes, and theorized that Broughton had worn these to do the murder. He suspected that the crime was premeditated, since Broughton had reported the theft of two .32 Colt revolvers three days before Erroll's death.

Broughton was arrested on March 10, 1941, and his trial began on May 26. But although the prosecution case looked watertight, it foundered on the fact that the gun that had killed Erroll had five right-hand grooves and a black powder propellant, while the stolen Colts would have had six grooves. The bullets found at the firing range failed to strengthen the case, since the gun that fired them could not be produced.

So on July 1, 1941, Sir Jock Delves Broughton was found not guilty. But life stubbornly refused to return to normal.

June Carberry, a major witness at the trial.

Ostracized by his neighbours, Broughton decided to go to Ceylon; reluctantly, Diana went with him. Their relationship became increasingly strained, and she frequently accused him of Erroll's murder; finally they separated.

Final admission

Broughton returned to England in 1942, and was immediately arrested by the Fraud Squad. The charge was that he had organized two mysterious robberies which had brought him large (and much needed) sums of money. The charges could not be made to stick. But his son Evelyn had by now discovered that Broughton had defrauded the estate and cheated him out of the bulk of his inheritance. On December 2, 1942, Broughton committed suicide at the Adelphi Hotel in Liverpool with a lethal dose of Medinal.

In 1979, June Carberry's daughter Juanita, who had been 15 at the time of the murder, admitted that Broughton had confessed to her on the day after the murder, and told her that, after killing Joss Erroll, he had thrown the gun into the Thika Falls. But his claim that the murder had been unpremeditated was almost certainly yet another of this devious man's countless lies.

THE CORPSE IN THE CHAPEL

It was over a year since the end of the Blitz, which had seen intensive aerial bombing across Britain, but victims were still being unearthed from bomb-shattered ruins. On July 17, 1942, workmen were demolishing a bombed Baptist chapel on Vauxhall Road, south London. One of the men, digging through the rubble and earth that had seeped down into the vestry cellar, hooked his pick under a heavy stone slab and hauled it up. Underneath he found a scorched human body; now little more than a skeleton hung with a few rags of flesh.

Despite the havoc caused by the bombing, official procedure was still adhered to when a body was found. The police were informed, and Inspectors Keeling and Hatton duly arrived to examine the corpse. The remains consisted of a torso and a severed head. The arms were missing from the elbow and the legs from the knee. The skull was bare of flesh and the lower jaw was also missing. The inspectors knew that the chapel had been built on an old cemetery some 50 years before. Yet the body did not look old enough to be left over from that period. On the other hand, if this was a bomb victim, how had he or she come to be buried under a stone slab in a cellar some distance from the nearest bomb crater?

The remains were wrapped in brown paper and taken to Southwark public mortuary. The next morning, the Home Office pathologist Dr Keith Simpson arrived to inspect them. Simpson's workload had increased dramatically since the start of the Blitz; he had to examine many hundreds of bomb victims in addition to his normal, crime-related work. In a state of chronic overwork, it would

> **WHOEVER THE VICTIM WAS, HE OR SHE HAD NOT BEEN BLOWN APART, BUT DISSECTED.**

not have been surprising if he had simply concluded that the burned skeleton was yet another casualty of the war. But on close examination he noticed several interesting anomalies. The head had not been broken off when the workman lifted the torso out of the grave; it had been neatly severed. The same was true of the missing forearms and legs. Whoever the victim was, he or she had not been blown

Police photographs of the chapel cellar, the remains as they looked when they were discovered (centre), and the remains after forensic cleaning (bottom).

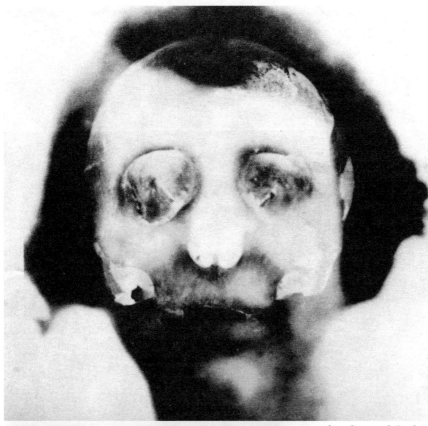

Simpson noted two additional clues. The first was a yellowish powder, which was found on the earth where the body had been buried. The second was a wooden chest, just under five feet long. Since the box did not belong to the chapel, it was guessed that it had been used by the murderer to transport the body to the cellar. The yellow powder Simpson recognized as corresponding to a yellow stain to the victim's head and neck. When analysed at Guy's Hospital, the substance was found to be slaked lime.

This proved to be important for two reasons. First, it

> 66 – IT IS QUICKLIME, NOT SLAKED LIME, THAT GENERATES HEAT IN THE PRESENCE OF MOISTURE AND CAUSES FLESH TO DISSOLVE. [THE STUFF] HAD ACTUALLY DISCOURAGED MAGGOTS FROM EATING THE FLESH, AND SO HAD ACTED AS A PRESERVATIVE. 99

showed that the murderer was ignorant of elementary chemistry. If he hoped for decomposition he had chosen the wrong substance – it is quicklime, not slaked lime, that generates heat in the presence of moisture and causes flesh to dissolve. Instead, the slaked lime had actually discouraged maggots from eating the flesh, and so had acted as a preservative.

Grisly remains

Simpson had the remains removed to his laboratory at Guy's Hospital. On close examination, it seemed clear that the murderer had gone to great effort to conceal the identity of his victim. Some attempts had been made to incinerate the body, although fortunately not much damage had been done. The flaying of the head and the removal of the eyes was obviously intended to prevent facial identification. The arms had plainly been removed to confound attempts at fingerprint identification. Finally, the removal of the lower jaw could be a half-hearted attempt to confound dental identification; fortunately, most of the upper set of teeth had survived.

apart, but dissected. Studying the skull, he noted that the face and scalp had neither rotted away nor been burned off; the head had in fact been flayed. All the evidence pointed to murder.

He was able to tell the police that the victim was a woman – the remains of the womb were still visible in the decayed trunk. She had been dead about a year to 18 months, judging by the deterioration of the soft tissue. This ruled out the possibility that she was a leftover from the old graveyard, and it also ruled out the possibility that she had been killed when the chapel was bombed, since that had taken place almost two years previously.

The second interesting point was why the killer had chosen to coat the neck as well as the head. Was it especially important to him to eradicate this area as well? When Simpson dissected the victim's voice box he found that the right horn of the thyroid cartilage had been broken. A blood-clot around it showed that the injury had been sustained while the woman was still alive. It was a sure sign of strangulation, since that form of injury occurs in no other way. A bruise on the back of the head suggested that the woman might have been throttled while having her head beaten against some hard surface.

Simpson now began to piece together a physical description of the victim. Despite the removal of the scalp, he managed to find a small piece of skin the killer had missed. Under a microscope the hairs from this area proved to be dark brown, turning to grey. This supported his estimate of her age. The sutures of the skull – the joins between the skull plates – gradually seal up as a person ages. Judging from the victim's skull, Dr Simpson guessed that she was between 40 and 50.

Despite the absence of the lower jaw, Simpson found several identifying features in what remained. Three of the four molars had been capped, there were marks showing that a denture had replaced the front teeth, the palate was high, and there was a marked thickening of the bone in the region of the back teeth. If the victim's dentist had kept accurate records, these details could be as revealing as a set of fingerprints.

Rachel and Harry Dobkin on their wedding day in September 1920. They then found that they disliked each other so much, they separated permanently just three days later.

Inspector Keeling was delighted with these findings. He had learned that the wife of a fire-watcher in the Baptist Chapel had gone missing at about the right time, and Simpson's description fitted her perfectly. Her name was Rachel Dobkin, aged 47, and she had not been seen since April 11, 1941.

Mrs Dobkin had not been living with her husband at the time – in fact they had been separated for over 20 years. Harry Dobkin was a short, balding, heavy-set man with a bullish demeanour. Born of Jewish parents in Russia in 1891, he had been taken to England when he was only a

several occasions, the courts imprisoned him for defaulting, but the experience left him just as unreliable. Rachel was reduced to badgering him in the street for money, and the ensuing rows were explosive. She had him summoned for assault on four occasions, but each time the magistrate dismissed the charge.

On the afternoon of April 11, 1941, the pair had tea in a café in Dalston. Harry had just landed a job as fire-warden – a special Blitz night-watchman whose job was to spot any fires starting in a set area – and Rachel was doubtless keen to share his good fortune. They left at 6.30 p.m. and this was the last time Rachel Dobkin was ever seen alive. Rachel's sister, Polly Dubinski, became alarmed when she failed to reappear by the following afternoon and reported her disappearance to the police However, with so many unrecorded deaths due to the Blitz, the authorities were sceptical of Polly's assurance that Rachel had been murdered by her husband.

Harry Dobkin was eventually interviewed on April 16, 1941, but denied knowing anything about his wife's disappearance or her present whereabouts. He told the police that when they had parted company, Rachel had told him that she was not feeling well and was going to her mother's to listen to the wireless. That was the last he had seen of her.

On August 26, 1942, after the discovery of the body in the chapel, Inspector Hatton asked Dobkin to accompany him to the Baptist Chapel "to assist the police with their enquiries". Since no reports had yet appeared in the press it should have been impos-sible for Dobkin to know how the victim had died. Yet, on being shown the grave in the cellar, he protested: "I wouldn't strangle a woman! I wouldn't hit a woman! Some men might, but I wouldn't. I didn't know the cellar was here, and I've certainly never been down here in my life." The inspector formally charged him with the murder of his wife, and took him into custody.

> ❝ I WOULDN'T STRANGLE A WOMAN! I WOULDN'T HIT A WOMAN! SOME MEN MIGHT, BUT I WOULDN'T. I DIDN'T KNOW THE CELLAR WAS HERE, AND I'VE CERTAINLY NEVER BEEN DOWN HERE IN MY LIFE. ❞
> Harry Dobkin

The trial took place in the Old Bailey on November 17, 1942. Dobkin's only real hope was that the defence counsel, F. H. Lawton, could undermine the medical identification of the victim as his wife. However, as the trial continued, this hope dwindled away. Lawton cross-examined the prosecution's witnesses with great expertise, but argument was all but useless against the fact that Rachel Dobkin's dental records matched the skeleton's mouth exactly.

The jury took 20 minutes to find Harry Dobkin guilty, after which judge Wrottesley sentenced him to death. Shortly before he was hanged, Dobkin confessed to the murder. In his book *Forty Years of Murder*, Dr Simpson mentions, with perhaps justified smugness, that it was his duty to do Dobkin's post mortem following the execution.

few months old. Rachel and he had been introduced, in the traditional Jewish fashion, via a marriage-broker. After the wedding, in September 1920, they took such an intense dislike to each other that they separated, after only three days. Long enough, however, to conceive a son.

In 1923, Rachel obtained a maintenance order of £1 per week, but Dobkin proved reluctant to meet the obligation. He made a precarious living by alternating work as a ship's steward and cook with minor jobs in the tailoring trade, and his payments were both irregular and infrequent. On

MURDER IN THE WOODS

On October 7, 1942, a unit of marines was engaged in battle training on the beautiful, but windy, slopes of Hankley Common, near Godalming in Surrey. Two marines climbed to the summit of a heather-covered ridge and noticed something strange protruding from a mound of sandy earth. It was brown and desiccated yet looked disturbingly like a human hand. Closer inspection revealed that it was a decomposed human forearm, including hand, with the thumb and two fingers missing. Protruding from the mound there was a second lump of desiccated flesh. By its shape and position the marines guessed that it was part of the leg. Abandoning their exercise the men alerted the rest of their unit, and the Surrey police were called by field telephone.

Acting for the coroner, Dr Eric Gardner was the first medical man to arrive, at around noon the next day. While awaiting the arrival of Dr Keith Simpson, medico-legal adviser to the Surrey police, Gardner made a preliminary inspection of the surface details. The missing thumb and fingers of the hand seemed to have been gnawed off by vermin, probably rats. Carefully examining the texture of the earth, Gardner found that there was an inverted piece of turf near the top. Turning this over revealed a clump of heather that, although shrivelled, had evidently still been green and flowering when the sod was cut. Gardner knew that in this region heather finished flowering at the beginning of September, so the corpse must have been buried about a month before it was found. Without even examining the body a likely time of death had been established.

By the time that Keith Simpson arrived, the site was crowded with police officers. An official photographer was at work recording the scene, and Detective Inspector Ted Greeno of Scotland Yard had also been called in.

With the earth removed from the corpse, a thick smell of putrefaction filled the air. The doctors worked on unperturbed. It soon became clear that the body was that of a woman. She was buried shallowly, lying face down in the earth with arms and legs outstretched. The right arm in particular stuck straight out, as though pointing. She had been wearing a green and white summer dress with a lace collar, a head-scarf knotted around her neck, a slip, bra and panties. The underwear was neatly in place, showing no signs of the tearing normally associated

The unearthed and badly decayed corpse of a young woman was discovered buried in a shallow mound of earth on Hankley Common, Surrey.

with a sexual assault. The scarf was knotted tightly, but was loose on the neck, and so was unlikely to have been used as a ligature. The cause of death seemed to be obvious: the back of the skull was smashed in, evidently from a heavy blow or blows from a blunt instrument. Owing to the extensive damage and the action of vermin, the head was on the point of losing its shape completely.

The pathologists' job was made doubly difficult by the fact that the body was infested with maggots. Despite the freezing cold and drizzle, the two doctors found that the heat generated by the decomposition of the body made it necessary to remove their jackets. Although the infestation of blowfly larvae hindered the pathologists' investigation of the body's wounds, and made the job of excavation even more unpleasant, it did reveal one thing: the body had remained uncovered and in the open before its burial, possibly for up to two days. This would have allowed time for the extensive laying of blowfly eggs.

The victim had been wearing socks, but no shoes. Examining her feet, Dr Simpson found that one of the socks was torn, and that both feet had suffered grazing and lacerations. This seemed to point to the body having been dragged some distance, with the heels scraping along the ground. The pointing gesture of the right arm could mean that this was the limb by which she was dragged.

Simpson and Gardner realized that no proper medical examination of the corpse could take place until the blowfly larvae and other beetles were killed off. This

was achieved by leaving the infested body in a vat of lysol until the creatures died, a process that took two days.

Meanwhile, Detective Inspector Greeno had ordered his men to search the common for the murder weapon, and also for the dead woman's shoes or other personal effects that might have been lost either during the attack or in the body's journey to its makeshift grave.

At the end of two days, Dr Gardner joined Simpson at Guy's Hospital in London to conduct a full autopsy. on the body Superintendent Webb of Surrey police was also present. The woman's face had all but been eradicated, so a description for identification purposes would have to be built up from other details. She was aged about 19 or 20, 5 feet 4 inches tall, with small hands and feet. Although her two front teeth seemed to have been knocked out, they had evidently been prominent and overlapping. Her hair was sandy-brown, cut in a bob and had been bleached shortly before death.

She had suffered three stab wounds to the front of the head and another, single wound under the right elbow. The flesh of the right arm showed "vital reaction" to the wound, meaning that from the shape of the puncture it could be seen that it had been sustained while the victim was alive. It looked like a classic "defence wound" – one sustained as the woman had tried to shield her head from attack. The weapon used to make the stab wounds seemed to have been hooked at the end, Simpson observed, because when it had been pulled from the victim's right arm it had drawn out the ends

Maggots held the clue

As to the time of death, the original estimate of about a month before the discovery seemed to be thrown into doubt by the advanced state of decomposition. Much of the corpse's fat had turned to adipocere, a greasy, white substance that usually takes at least five weeks to form in the outdoor British climate. That anomaly could be resolved, however, by taking into account the raised temperature created by the maggot infestation. Under those conditions the original estimate could easily be correct.

of some severed tendons.

The physical description compiled by Simpson and Gardner was enough to nudge Superintendent Webb's memory. Something about the green and white dress had seemed familiar to him at the excavation, and now, aided by the other particulars determined by the pathologists, he completed the picture.

The woman's name was Joan Pearl Wolfe. Webb had met her six or seven weeks before the discovery of her body, a fortnight before she died. The police in the area knew her because they were concerned about her lifestyle: she lived in the woods in a makeshift hut made from leaves and branches. She was friendly with the soldiers stationed nearby but wasn't a prostitute, and gossip had it that she was living rough because she had run away from home.

For days Greeno's men continued to painstakingly search Hankley Common. Their care was rewarded periodically: Pearl Wolfe's shoes were found, separately, both some distance from her grave on the ridge. Lying near

one of the shoes, police found a bag containing a rosary. This very probably belonged to Wolfe; she was a devout Roman Catholic. In the same area, by a small stream, there was also a military tripwire. Could she have run on to the wire while being pursued, knocking out her two front teeth as she fell? This seemed to become a more likely scenario when police located a heavy birch stake near the stream. Stuck on its surface were brown, bleached hairs.

Meanwhile, other officers were making enquiries about Joan Pearl Wolfe among the local community. Several people reported seeing her with a Canadian private named August Sangret. It was this soldier who, according to locals, had built the wigwam-like home for her in the woods. When she had been admitted to hospital earlier that year, she had kept a photo of the Canadian by her bed. Pearl had apparently been seen knitting baby-clothes early in September. An abandoned cricket pavilion was said to be one of their meeting places, and when police examined the building

they found it covered in their graffiti, including Sangret's home address in Canada, and the address of Joan, Pearl Wolfe's mother. Also pencilled on the wall was a prayer:"O holy Virgin in the midst of all thy glory we implore thee not to forget the sorrows of this world."

It was now fairly certain that it was the wooden stake that had delivered the killing blow. Simpson found that the hairs clinging to it belonged to Joan Pearl Wolfe. There was little else that the stake could tell police: it bore no bloodstains and its bark would not retain fingerprints. As the search of Hankley Common continued, this time looking specifically for the knife, Greeno headed

for the Canadian army base, Witley Camp.

From Sangret's commanding officer, Greeno's men discovered that Sangret had asked for a marriage request form, but had never returned it completed. It transpired that Sangret had reported Pearl Wolfe missing to his provost sergeant, telling him that if she was found he wanted nothing more to do with her. To his fellow soldiers Sangret had apparently explained her disappearance in a number of ways: to one he had said that she was in hospital, to another that she had run out of clothes and gone home.

Greeno telephoned the base and asked them to confine Sangret until his

arrival. Then he took him to Godalming police station. Sangret was a saturnine, good-looking man of medium height, half French-Canadian and half Cree Indian. His native American ancestry was evident in his face, straight features and bronze-coloured skin. As Greeno laid out the victim's clothes before him, he looked grim.

These clothes, Sangret admitted calmly, belonged to Joan Pearl Wolfe, and the last time that he had seen her had been on September 14. He had no idea where she might have been since then. Sangret did not ask if anything had happened to her, and Greeno decided not to say that she was dead. If Sangret knew anything of the crime, he might incriminate himself. Yet Sangret admitted nothing.

As Greeno interviewed his chief suspect, his officers were making other discoveries on Hankley Common. In and around a small dell on the ridge-side, above the stream where the stake had been found, the searchers found a number of interesting items. Pearl Wolfe's identity card, revealing her to have been 19 years old, was found in the undergrowth together with a green purse, a white elephant good-luck charm, a crucifix and the marriage

request form that Sangret's CO had issued to him. Even more revealingly, police discovered a letter written by Pearl and addressed to Sangret. It was a love-letter written from hospital and dated August 25. In it she explained to Sangret, whom she addressed as "my darling", that she was pregnant and looking forward to their coming marriage.

While no one doubted that Sangret had murdered Pearl, there was not enough evidence for Greeno to arrest him, and the slow work of enquiry continued. A friend of Sangret's on the army base told police that he wrote letters for him because Sangret himself was illiterate. As well as writing letters to Pearl Wolfe for Sangret, he had also transcribed love-letters to a woman in Glasgow. Sangret was evidently an enthusiastic ladies' man.

More significantly, a Private Crowle told police that while out blackberrying one day he had seen a knife like the one described by Simpson stuck into a tree near the wigwam in the woods. He had taken it to the provost back at camp, who had in turn given the knife to Sangret via a corporal named Harding. According to both Crowle and Harding, the knife was British Army issue, black-handled with a hooked point. Yet it was not among Sangret's possessions when the police searched them.

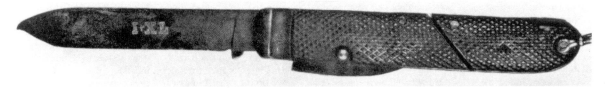

The Crown case

The Crown's accusation centred around a reconstructed version of events agreed upon by Simpson and Greeno. The scenario was this: Sangret, unwilling to marry Pearl Wolfe, argues violently with her at the dell near Hankley Common. Sangret becomes so angry that he pulls out the black-handled knife and stabs at her head. She shields herself from the blows with her crooked right arm, then runs away from her attacker, spilling the contents of her handbag as she flees. Pursued by Sangret, and probably screaming for help, she falls over the tripwire by the stream and crashes down, knocking out her front teeth. Sangret, perhaps in an effort to silence her, beats in her head with a stake. The body is concealed in a blanket for one or two days in the open, before Sangret returns and drags it to the ridge-top, where he buries her shallowly in a mound of sandy earth.

Where had it gone?

The answer soon presented itself. One of the toilets in the wash-house attached to the Witley Camp guardroom was found to be blocked, and a private named Brown was detailed to clear the obstruction. After grabbing two handfuls of damp paper and cigarette butts, Brown felt something hard. Pulling the object free, he found that it was a black-handled knife with a hooked point.

How had the knife ended up stuck in a U-bend? Sangret had been locked in the guard-room on Greeno's request when he was on his way to question him. The soldiers guarding him remembered that just before Greeno had arrived, Sangret had requested to go to the toilet. If Sangret had done it to dispose of the knife, as seemed

likely, it could only be because he knew about its connection to Greeno's visit. This was certainly incriminating.

Sangret was once again called in for questioning. Beginning with a few casual enquiries, Greeno then matter-of-factly asked Sangret why he had not mentioned the hook-pointed knife before. Foolishly Sangret admitted knowledge of the knife, saying that it had belonged to Pearl's previous boyfriend. He explained that he had not seen it after the provost had got hold of it, denying that it had been returned to him. This statement was enough for Greeno, and he asked the Surrey police to arrest August Sangret and charge

A photograph of one of the wounds that directly linked Pearl's murder to the hook-ended knife.

him with the murder of Joan Pearl Wolfe. Sangret was in custody for five months before his trial was held at Kingston Assizes.

The knife formed the centrepiece of the prosecution's evidence. The police had Sangret's statement admitting he had owned it. They also had further circumstantial evidence that Sangret had tried to hide it when he thought he was suspected of the crime. This is why the defence decided to concentrate upon Dr Simpson's medical evidence, trying to introduce an element of uncertainty.

It was during this trial that, for the first time in a British court, a forensic scientist brought the skull of a murder victim into court to demonstrate his findings. With the knife and the heavily wired and riveted skull, Simpson showed how he believed the wounds were made. Linton

Thorpe, the defence counsel, demanded to know whether the black-handled knife was the only implement that could have caused such holes, and whether indeed the wounds might not have been made by any knife. Dr Simpson stuck to his findings, repeating them again and again. During this evidence the defendant remained totally impassive.

Taking the knife and the skull with them, the jury retired. In two hours they were back. Their verdict was that August Sangret was guilty of murder. They accompanied their finding with a strong recommendation for mercy.

In spite of this recommendation, Sangret was hanged at Wandsworth jail a week later. When Dr Simpson performed the routine autopsy upon him, he found that the soldier had a tattoo on his arm: the name "Pearl".

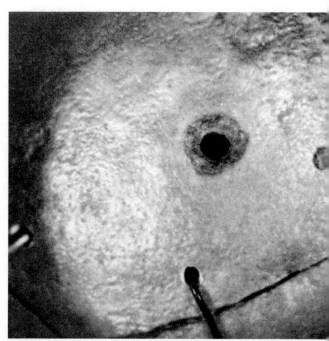

WHO WAS THE WOMAN IN SACKCLOTH?

On Friday, November 19, 1943, two sewage workers were testing the depth of the River Lea as it ran through the outskirts of the Bedfordshire town of Luton. Despite the lateness of the year, the river was running shallow. The men noticed a large, cloth-bound bundle floating in the water – or rather, beached on the mud in six inches of water. As they approached it they saw the pale pink of human flesh peeping through rips in the cloth. They ran for the police.

When the sacks – four of them – were stripped away, the police found themselves looking at the naked body of a fairly young woman, with the legs doubled-up and held in place by a cord; the ankles were also tied together. The face was so battered as to be unrecognizable. The flesh to the lower left side of her face was torn open and the lower and upper jawbones beneath had been broken. Even her tongue was split open. All her teeth were missing, although evidently as a result of dentistry rather than the damage to her head. Her whole face was swollen and black with bruises, and there were more bruises on her throat – apparently finger indentations from a powerful right hand. Given the damage to the victim's head, it was hardly surprising that the first doctor to examine her decided that she had died from a shotgun blast.

The corpse was fresh and had apparently been dumped in the river during the night; the sewage workers had been past the spot at four o'clock the previous afternoon and were certain it had not been there then. The Bedfordshire chief constable decided to ask for help from Scotland Yard, and Chief Inspector William Chapman arrived the next day, accompanied by the famous pathologist, Dr Keith Simpson.

It took Simpson very little time to determine that the woman – who was in her mid-30s – had not died of a gunshot wound, but from several very heavy blows with a blunt object. Whoever had undressed her and trussed her up like an oven-ready chicken, had presumably been aware that she was still breathing. The development of bruises under the ropes on her ankles indicated that she had died some 40 minutes after being tied up.

The degree of *rigor mortis* revealed that she had been attacked and died sometime on the afternoon of November 18. The cause of death was a

Sir Keith Simpson: the brilliant pathologist who earned a reputation as the Sherlock Holmes of the medical profession.

massive brain haemorrhage. She had borne at least one child, and had died five months pregnant with another. There were no signs of rape or sexual attack.

The Luton mortuary rebuilt the dead woman's face until it looked more or less human again. A photograph was taken, which was shown in local cinemas, with a notice: "Police are still anxious to establish the identity of this unfortunate woman..." It was discovered later that the dead woman's 17-year-old daughter had seen the photograph, and had failed to recognize it. Her two sons, aged 14 and 15, did tell their father that a photograph they had seen in a shop-window resembled their mother, but he told them that that was impossible.

Inspector Chapman spent unproductive weeks in pursuing every possible lead. A search was instituted for every missing woman in the Luton area – an astounding 404, thanks to the chaos of the war – but all were eventually accounted for. Thirty-nine members of the public went to view the body in the mortuary, and four of them thought they knew the dead woman's identity, but proved to be mistaken.

The months dragged on – December, January and February – and the enquiry seemed to have reached a dead end. Unable to think of any new possibilities, the detectives decided to review all the evidence they already had. Among the backlog was a black coat found on a rubbish dump, from which apparently random areas had been cut: a waste of cloth that, at a time of clothes rationing, automatically aroused suspicion. A dyer's tag was found inside the garment. The shop was traced and the records showed that the coat had belonged to a Mrs Rene Manton, who lived at 14 Regent Street, Luton.

Inspector Chapman went to the house, and the door was opened by a 10-year-old girl who identified herself as Sheila Manton. For the first time in weeks, Chapman experienced a flash of optimism. Sheila undoubtedly bore a resemblance to the dead

Bertie Manton in his wartime National Fire Service uniform.

woman. She explained that her mummy had left home some time ago; she had gone to stay with her mother, then with a brother in Grantham. Chapman asked if he could see a photograph of Sheila's mother. The picture the little girl gave him convinced him he had cracked the case: the woman in sackcloth was Rene Manton.

According to Sheila, her granny – Rene Manton's mother – lived nearby. Chapman went to visit Mrs Bavister and she turned out to be a half-blind old lady who flatly denied that her daughter had come to stay with her after leaving her husband. She had received four letters from her daughter since last November, all sent from an address in Hampstead. Chapman noticed that the letters had a number of spelling mistakes, which included "Hampstead" spelt as Londoners pronounce the word: without the "p".

Rene Manton's husband Bertie proved to be a member of the National Fire Service who had once been a light-weight boxer – someone strong enough to beat a woman to death. Chapman went to see him at the fire station. Manton admitted that he and his wife – whom he married in 1926 – often had violent quarrels. She had left him once before, and he suspected that she had been unfaithful to him with soldiers. Manton also admitted that Rene objected to a certain barmaid of his acquaintance.

Manton said his wife had "slung her hook" after a quarrel last November – he gave the date as November 25, six days after the finding of the body – and had gone to stay with her mother. He remembered the date she left

home because it was the last day of his annual leave. He said that his wife had been home since then to collect her clothes, and he identified the letters received by her mother as being in his wife's handwriting. When he was shown the photograph of the body he said flatly: "That's nothing like her. I wouldn't do a thing like that."

Manton eventually and grudgingly provided the name of Rene's dentist. When he was shown the photograph of the dead woman, the dentist instantly recognized her. After all, he had removed all of Rene's teeth – this was a common procedure before the invention of antibiotics, even for young people; false teeth were considered a better option than a dozen or so, potentially

life-threatening toothaches in the patient's later life. The dentist's records were precise, and the plaster cast of the victim's jaws matched them point-for-point.

Manton's story was unravelling fast. He had given the last day of his annual leave as the day Rene had left him. Enquiries with the fire brigade revealed that Manton's leave had ended not on November 25, as he had told investigators, but on the 18th – the day of the murder.

Asked to note down various addresses for the police, Manton spelled Hampstead without the "p". And when these samples were compared to the letters sent to his mother-in-law, it was obvious that the handwriting of the correspondence was his, not his wife's.

One more thing was needed to confirm that Rene Manton was indeed the dead woman. The Yard's chief fingerprint expert Fred Cherrill was called to Luton to try to find a fingerprint that matched those of the corpse. After searching the Manton house for hours, he began to think that it was hopeless; someone had polished every cup,

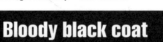

Bloody black coat

Manton's story was that he and Rene had quarrelled around midday on November 18. He said that she had flung a cup of hot tea in his face with the words: "I hope it blinds you." He had grabbed a heavy wooden stool and hit her several time with it. She hit the floor with her face a broken mess.

Convinced she was dead or dying, he undressed her, tied her knees, cut open four sacks, wrapped her in them, then hid her body in the cellar. He cleaned up the blood before their four children returned home, and when they had gone to bed that night, he balanced the corpse on his bicycle and wheeled it to the river – unaware just how shallow it was flowing. The next day he had burned her bloody clothes and false teeth. But he had overlooked Rene's black coat, and later made an attempt to cut out the dried bloodstains before he threw it on a rubbish dump: his key mistake in what Chapman called "a nearly perfect murder".

plate, cupboard-door and shelf. But finally, in the stair cupboard, he found a shelf of jam jars and bottles. Cherrill tested them one after another, and again had to admit that they had been cleaned very thoroughly. Finally, only one bottle was left, lurking in a dark corner – a pickle jar. The layer of dust on its neck revealed that it had not been cleaned. This jar yielded a thumbprint, which proved to be that of the dead woman.

Chapman arrested Manton and charged him with the murder. Manton immediately broke down and admitted: "I killed her, but it was only because I lost my temper. I didn't intend to."

Manton's story was clearly designed to convince a jury that he was guilty only of manslaughter – of losing his temper and striking out at Rene. But the marks on her throat showed that he had throttled her after knocking her down. This suggested that he had intended to kill her.

Bertie Manton was found guilty of the murder and sentenced to death. His appeal was turned down, but a petition organized by his children and fellow workers collected over 26,000 signatures. His death sentence was reprieved, but he died of cancer in Parkhurst prison three years later.

Bertie Manton's 16-year-old son collects signatures on a petition, asking that his father's death sentence for killing his mother is reprieved.

LEY AND SMITH

This is the story of a lunatic who was able to persuade dupes to pander to his madness. In all the history of British justice there has never been a stranger case.

On the afternoon of November 30, 1946, a man walking home along Slines Road, near Woldingham, in Surrey, noticed what looked like a bundle of rags lying inside the entrance to a chalk pit. When he looked more closely he realized it was a man's body.

A policeman who was summoned observed that the corpse was lying in a shallow trench, like a half-dug grave. There was a loosely tied rope round the neck outside an overcoat that covered the body. When he opened the coat, he found tied round the throat a length of rope and a piece of cloth.

A quick glance revealed that it was not a natural death or suicide. The ground was wet and muddy but, although the dead man's clothes were stained with mud, the soles of the shoes were perfectly clean. He must have been carried there. It looked as if he had met his death elsewhere, then been dumped at the chalk pit. A muddy pickaxe lying nearby could have been used to dig the trench. The green rag round the throat gave off a distinct smell of polish.

A pathologist from Weybridge Hospital confirmed that the man had been strangled and dumped before *rigor mortis* had had time to set in – which usually happens in four or five hours, although in cases of asphyxia it can take more. Since the *rigor mortis* was just starting to relax, it looked as if the man had been dead about 48 hours.

Moreover, it was clear that whoever killed him must have hated him, for he had been beaten up before he was killed. Haemorrhages on the heart and lungs also revealed that this had been done slowly.

A visiting card in the man's pocket bore the name John McMain Mudie. A 35-year-old barman of that name had been missing from the Reigate Hill Hotel for two days. The corpse was soon identified as Mudie. He had last been seen going out to serve cocktails at a private party on November 28, two days before.

Enquiries revealed that he was pleasant, polite and had no known enemies. No one could suggest who might have wanted him dead.

The previous Wednesday, the day before Mudie vanished, two gardeners had been walking past the chalk pit when they saw a man standing near the bank. When he saw them, he turned and ran behind some trees and jumped into a car, which then drove past them at speed. They were curious enough to note the car number plate, although by the time they came forward they could only recall that it contained the numbers 101. But they said it was a Ford 8, dark blue or black in colour. Patient detective work revealed that a dark blue Ford 8, number FGP

101, had been rented from a Knightsbridge car hire firm on Wednesday November 27, the day before Mudie disappeared, and returned on Saturday November 30, the day the body was found. It had been hired by a carpenter named John Smith. When asked why an ordinary working man should hire an expensive car for three days, he gave no satisfactory reply.

Smith was at present working for a man named Thomas

Ley, who owned a large house in Beaufort Gardens, Knightsbridge, and his work entailed French polishing. Recalling that the rag around Mudie's throat smelt of French polish, the police felt they had an obvious suspect. They put Smith into an identity parade, and one of the two witnesses

of the car at the chalk pit seemed reasonably certain that this was the man who had been driving the car.

A search of Mudie's room at the Reigate Hill Hotel revealed another clue – some correspondence with Thomas Ley. It was apparently based on a misunderstanding. Ley

seemed to have sent Mudie two cheques and asked him if he would forward them to someone called Maggie Brook for a second signature. Mudie, baffled, had said that he had no idea where Maggie Brook was now. She had lived for a time in the same block of Wimbledon flats as himself,

looking after her son-in-law while his wife was in hospital. But Mudie hardly knew her. So he returned the cheques to Ley.

Surely it was hardly co-incidence that this Thomas Ley, for whom the suspected murderer worked, had also been in touch with the victim?

Further investigation of the case revealed that Ley seemed to be subject to obsessive jealousy. Evidently, he had talked to the landlady of the Wimbledon flats, Mrs Evans, and explained that Mrs Brook had asked him to take her away from the place because she was being pestered by the men in the house. He asked for the names of the male lodgers, and the landlady gave them to him. The list of names included John Mudie. Mrs Evans assured Ley that it was unlikely Mudie had slept with Mrs Brook. Later, Ley called again, saying he wanted to apologize to Mudie, so Mrs Evans gave him Mudie's new address, the Reigate Hill Hotel.

So Ley suspected Mudie of having an affair with Maggie Brook, who was Ley's mistress. Could that be the motive behind the murder?

The next clue led the police to the Royal Hotel in Woburn Place, near Ley's home. They learned that Ley had approached the head waiter there, and asked if he knew a car-hirer who would do a highly paid job and keep his mouth shut. It was not illegal, Ley assured him. The head waiter then recommended a man called John Buckingham, an army

Thomas John Ley: respected former Minister for Justice in New South Wales, rich businessman and insane murderer.

Justice minister of dubious legality

Who was this Thomas Ley? Before he retired to England in 1929, he had been the Hon. Thomas Ley, Minister for Justice in New South Wales. But a charge of bribery, and two suspicious deaths – of business associates who were in his way – brought an end to his Australian political career. His vast fortune, it was said, had been made through activities of dubious legality. Everything indicated that he was brutal, ruthless, and totally determined to get his own way.

Maggie Brook, the widow of a Perth JP, had been his mistress since 1922, but they had ceased to have sex 10 years before the murder of John Mudie.

Top: The Right Honourable Thomas Ley in 1925, aged 45. This was around the time that several scandals forced him to retire from Australian politics.

Above: John Williams Buckingham, who agreed to assist Ley and Smith under the false belief that they were merely frightening off a blackmailer.

The blackmailer was a barman named John Mudie. What was needed, explained Ley, was a woman who was willing to pose as a wealthy lady wanting to hire a barman for a house party in Knightsbridge. Buckingham knew just the person – an old friend called Lil Bruce.

Dressed up, Bruce, would call at the Reigate Hill Hotel with her chauffeur, and get to know Mudie. She would profess herself so pleased with his services that she would ask if he ever took on commissions for private parties, and whether, in that case, he would come and serve drinks to politicians and celebrities at her house…

All went as planned. On the Sunday before Mudie was due to be kidnapped, Lil Bruce was driven in her chauffeured limousine to the Reigate Hill Hotel, went into the bar, ordered a large martini and a light ale for her chauffeur (the uniformed chauffeur was, in fact, Buckingham's son), then invited him to come and serve drinks at her home the following Thursday evening.

On Wednesday John Smith drove down to look at the chalk pit. His motive in getting involved was that he wanted to emigrate to South Africa, and

deserter who ran a car-hire company in Knightsbridge.

So the police went to Buckingham – and found they had the solution to the case.

What they learned was that Ley had claimed he wanted to kidnap a blackmailer, and was willing to pay well.

was hoping to make enough money to do it in style. But he lost his nerve when spotted by the two gardeners, and fled. This costly error led to the tracing of the car and the trapping of the conspirators.

The following day, the kidnapping of the innocent Mudie went smoothly. Mudie was picked up in the chauffeured limousine by Mrs Bruce and Buckingham's son, and taken to 5 Beaufort Gardens, Knightsbridge. Inside, he was grabbed from behind in a dark passage by Smith and Buckingham, and gagged. Then he was taken to the basement, and tied to a chair. Buckingham was then paid £200 – £30 of it for Lil Bruce – and left. The unfortunate Mudie was left to be beaten and slowly strangled by Ley. (Buckingham was later told by Ley that Mudie had been made to sign an agreement never to bother Maggie Brook again, and given £500 to leave the country.) Finally, Smith drove the body to the chalk pit and dumped it.

Rather than be charged with conspiracy to kidnap, Buckingham turned King's Evidence. And Ley and his accomplice Smith were soon under arrest, and charged with murder.

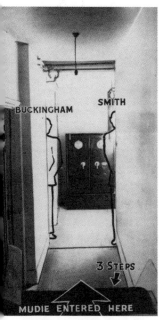

BUCKINGHAM   SMITH

3 STEPS

MUDIE ENTERED HERE

The police reconstruction of what John Mudie would have seen moments before Buckingham and Smith kidnapped him.

The trial opened at the Old Bailey on March 19, 1947, before Lord Goddard. Ley, a grossly fat man, blustered and did his best to confuse with irrelevancies. An ex-convict named Robert Cruikshank (bribed, according to the judge's summing-up) also tried to introduce a note of doubt by claiming that he had broken into Ley's house on the evening of the murder, found a man tied to a chair in the unlit basement, and tried to free him in the dark, but fled without succeeding (the implication being that he might have strangled Mudie accidentally by pulling on the ropes).

This feeble attempt at extenuation failed, and Ley and Smith were sentenced to death. But on May 5, Ley was

Emily Ley arrives from Australia to see her husband convicted for murder.

examined by three specialists and declared insane; he was sent to Broadmoor, where he died of a brain haemorrhage a month later.

Was Ley insane? Undoubtedly. His madness took the form of paranoid jealousy, and had even been directed at Maggie Brook's son-in-law and another male resident of the Wimbledon flats before it fixed on Mudie. After Ley's death, Smith's sentence was commuted to life imprisonment.

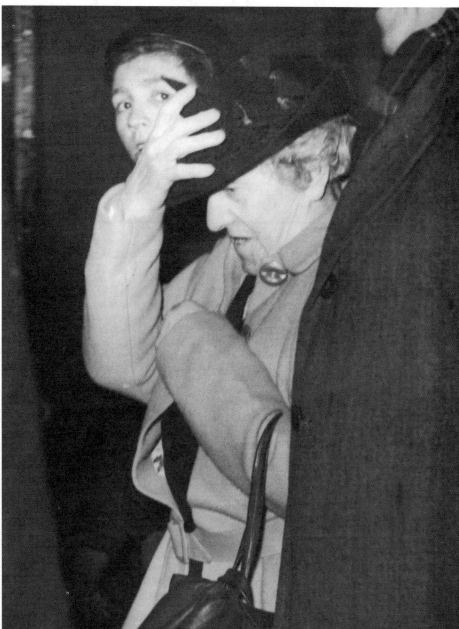

1947

THE ACTRESS AND THE STEWARD

Gay Gibson, a 21-year-old actress who had been working in South Africa, embarked from Cape Town on the liner *Durban Castle* for Southampton on October 10, 1947. Eight days later, when the liner was 147 miles off the coast of Africa, a stewardess knocked on her cabin door with the morning orange juice, and found it unlocked and the cabin empty. The ship's loudspeaker broadcast an appeal to her, but brought no result. Captain Patey decided to turn the ship around, hoping she might still be recovered from the shark-infested waters. But they failed to find any sign of her.

The watchman, Fred Steer, told the captain that at 3 o'clock that morning he had been summoned to her cabin by a long buzz on the electric bell and that, when there was no answer to his knock, he started to open the door. Inside he saw the steward James Camb, who said "It's all right", and pushed the door shut in his face.

It meant dismissal for a deck steward to be in the cabin of a female passenger at night, but Steer decided to do nothing. Although married with a child, the handsome Camb had a reputation as a ladies' man, and the watchman had covered for him before.

Questioned by the captain, Camb simply denied that he had been near Gay Gibson's cabin. But it was noticed that he was wearing a long-sleeved uniform rather than the usual light tropical singlet. Asked to remove it, it was seen that he had a number of scratches down his right arm and near the shoulder, which looked

as if they had been made by long nails. Camb explained this was heat rash.

At Southampton the police came aboard. Camb now decided to admit that he had been in Gay Gibson's cabin at 3 a.m., but claimed it was only to ask if she wanted a lemonade. Police Sergeant Quinlan told Camb that if he had any better explanation, he had better produce it now. Thereupon, Camb made the incriminating comment: "You mean that Miss Gibson might have died from a cause other than being murdered – she might have had a heart attack or something?"

He went on to say that Gay Gibson had invited him to her cabin, and that while in the act of sexual intercourse she had suddenly had a fit, foamed at the mouth, and died: "I tried artificial respiration on her. While doing this, the night-watchman knocked at the door and attempted to open it. I shut the door ... I panicked ... I did

not want to be found in such a compromising position ... I could not find any sign of life...After a struggle with the limp body I managed to lift her to the porthole and push her through ... I cannot offer any explanation as to how the bell came to be rung…"

Camb was thereupon charged with the murder of Gay Gibson.

At his trial, which began at Winchester Assizes on March 20, 1948, before Mr Justice Hilbery, Camb insisted that he had gone to Cabin 126 at 2 a.m. at the actress's invitation, and that she had greeted him wearing nothing but her yellow dressing-gown. The objection to that was that her black pyjamas were missing, suggesting she was wearing them when she was pushed out of the porthole.

Pathologist Dr Donald Teare, for the Crown, said that blood, saliva and urine stains on the bed-sheets were indicative of strangulation. Defence pathologists Dr

Dennis Hocking and Professor James Webster claimed that these stains were equally indicative of a fit.

Dr Griffiths, the ship's surgeon, spoke of examining Camb's scratches, and remarked that they looked like the mark of fingernails.

Camb could not explain why he had not summoned medical assistance to the girl, and – more important, if his story of accidental death was true – why he had disposed so hurriedly of the only evidence which could have substantiated that story.

On March 23, Camb was found guilty. But he escaped capital punishment because the "no-hanging" clause was then under discussion in Parliament as part of the Criminal Justice Bill, and he was released on licence in September 1959.

Gay Gibson, a beautiful and promising young actress, was murdered and her body crammed out of a porthole to be left to the tender mercies of the sharks.

She said no

Was Camb guilty of Gay Gibson's murder? Fairly certainly, but it may not have been the planned rape the prosecution suggested. He had been on friendly terms with her, and had been heard saying "I've got a bone to pick with you", which suggests a certain familiarity. When he went to her cabin, he was hoping that she would be ready to yield. However, the fact that her contraceptives were still in her case makes it clear that she said no. This probably led to a struggle that ended in her death.

Camb was to go back to prison in 1967 for indecently assaulting minors, and his licence was revoked so he had to complete the life sentence. Released in 1978, he died of heart failure in July 1979.

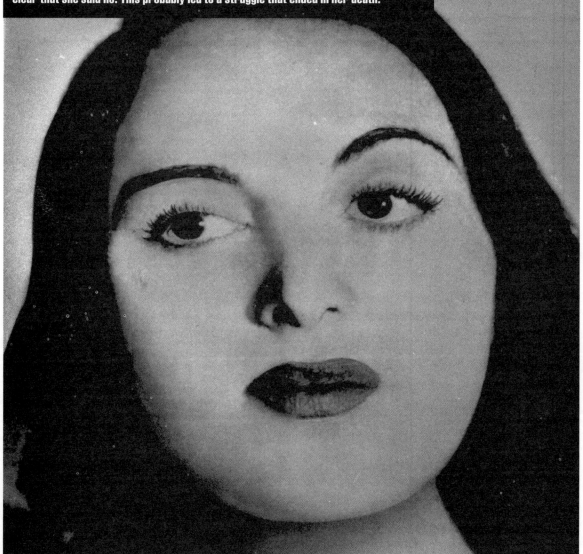

THE GUAY CASE

On September 9, 1949, a Quebec Airways Dakota DC-3 on a flight from Montreal to Seven Islands exploded in mid-air, only minutes after take-off. The plane dived into inaccessible forest near Sault-au-Cochon, 40 miles north-east of Quebec. All 23 on board, including four children, were killed. Since witnesses noticed that the engines were still running as it crashed, engine failure was clearly not the cause of the disaster.

The plane had taken off from Quebec five minutes late. If it had been on time, it would have been over the St Lawrence River estuary when it crashed, and forensics would almost certainly have failed to find the cause of the explosion. As it was, the metal of the baggage compartment showed traces of an explosion, and chemical analysis revealed the cause to be dynamite.

A careful check of every item of freight against the company's list revealed that only one seemed to be missing, a "religious statuette" weighing 26 lbs. But there was no record of its sender; all the receptionist could remember was that it was delivered by a woman dressed in black.

An appeal through the news media failed to trace her. Ten days later, a taxi driver named Pelletier came to the police to say that he had picked up a woman of this description on the day of the explosion – and he could also remember the address. This proved to be the home of a woman named Marie Pitre. But when the police tried to call on her, they learned that she was in hospital, recovering from the effects of a large overdose of sleeping tablets.

As soon as she was able to give an interview, Marie Pitre told them how she had come to take the parcel to the Ancienne Lorrette Airport. It seemed she had been performing an errand for her employer, a jeweller named Joseph Albert Guay, who was married. In the past she had been his mistress,

though that was now over. But she owed him money, and he offered to cancel some of the debt by way of payment for the errand.

It seemed their affair had ended when he met a beautiful teenage cigarette girl named Marie-Ange Robitaille in a nightclub, and had set her up in an apartment. Then his wife Rita found out, and confronted Marie-Ange.

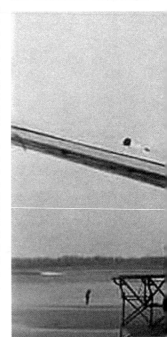

Rita Guay was one of those killed in the airline crash. Just to achieve her death, her killer had been willing to murder 19 other adults and four children.

Devastated by the betrayal, the girl left him. But he had persuaded her to return by assuring her that they *would* be married soon.

Then Marie Pitre dropped her bombshell. "I didn't know his wife would be on that flight." And she went on to describe how, some weeks before, Guay had asked her to purchase 10 pounds of dynamite, which he needed for landscape gardening.

Assuming this dynamite had blown up the Dakota, how had it been detonated? It would need a timing mechanism. And Marie, the police discovered, had a crippled brother named Genereux Ruest, who was an expert clock repairer. Soon, Ruest admitted that he had made the timing mechanism; Guay, he said, had told him that he needed it for exploding the dynamite to blow some rocks out of the ground.

Joseph Albert Guay: a man willing to commit an atrocity to achieve his own selfish ends.

Albert Guay, a thin-faced man of 32 with a pencil-line moustache, was arrested, and the newspapers headlined the "love bomb murder" – since it was by now plain that he had decided to kill his wife Rita in order to marry the pretty cigarette girl. Moreover, it was at his urging that Marie Pitre had taken the overdose.

At the trial in March 1950, the defence had an impossible task, since Guay was so clearly guilty. Moreover, his friend Lucien Carreau described how, as they were driving back to Guay's house for a drink, the jeweller had offered him $500 to give Rita a dose of poisoned cherry brandy.

A Douglas Dakota DC-3, of the type that was bombed out of the air on 9 September, 1949 over Montreal.

1949

Cigarette girl

Guay, it emerged, had been an extremely spoilt child who would stop at nothing to get his own way. During the Second World War he had worked in an arsenal, and had married a beautiful dark-haired girl named Rita Morel. All went well until they had a daughter, whereupon the egocentric Guay began to feel unappreciated, and took Marie Pitre as a mistress. Finally he became wildly infatuated with the cigarette girl, and had no trouble seducing her. Although she was only 16, he was not her first lover.

Joseph and Rita Guay in happier times. Following Rita's discovery of his extra-marital affairs, Guay decided that Rita would be better off dead. The fact that she was insured for $410,000 must have helped his decision.

Joseph Guay in the dock. His plot to kill his wife eventually led him and two others to the gallows. If his wife's flight had not been delayed by five minutes, his ruthless plan might have gone undetected.

It also emerged that Guay had worked out the time of the explosion to happen when the Dakota was over water, but had been foiled by the late take-off.

This, and the evidence of Marie Pitre and her brother, guaranteed that Guay would be found guilty. At this point, the narcissistic schemer determined to take them down with him, and alleged that they took part in Rita's murder knowingly.

This, in fact, was perfectly feasible. Would not the watch-maker have been a little suspicious that Guay needed a timing mechanism just to blow up rocks – what was wrong with wires and a detonator? And did not Marie Pitre recognize that the heavy parcel was more than a religious statuette?

Which is why, after Guay had been sentenced to death, the two also faced separate trials for complicity, and followed him to the gallows.

> ❝ **AT LEAST I DIE FAMOUS.** ❞
> Albert Guay

Guay, who was hanged before Marie Pitre, remarked typically, "At least I die famous."

THE SHOOTING OF THE BASEBALL STAR

The shooting of baseball star Eddie Waitkus – first baseman of the Philadelphia "Phillies" baseball team – by lovesick fan Ruth Steinhagen made headlines all over America, and seemed doubly bizarre because the two were not even acquainted.

Waitkus, a handsome bachelor, was a favourite of feature writers because, apart from being one of America's best baseball players, he was intelligent, spoke four languages and loved opera. He had also fought with distinction in the war in the Pacific.

On June 15, 1949, Waitkus had played a brilliant game at Chicago's Wrigley Field against his old team, the Cubs, and the Phillies won an easy victory. After the game, and an evening of drinks and dinner, a short taxi ride took Waitkus and his teammate "Swish" Nicholson to the Edgewater Beach Hotel, on the shores of Lake Michigan, one of the best hotels in Chicago. They arrived at 11.30 p.m.

A bellhop approached the players and told Waitkus that a lady had asked him to deliver a note. The writer said that she had something of great importance to communicate to him, and begged him to come to her room: 1297-A.

Puzzled, but intrigued, Waitkus enquired at the desk who was in room 1297-A, and was told that it was a Miss Ruth Anne Burns from Portland Street in Boston. Waitkus felt curiously uneasy. He knew the address – he had lived there as a child. He showed the note to two team-

Waitcus in his Phillies baseball uniform. Despite being shot at close range with a rifle, he recovered his fitness and continued his sporting career.

mates whom he joined for a drink. They advised him to give her a call before going. He did, and the girl told him to come up in half an hour, to give her time to get out of bed and get dressed.

He found room 97 on the 12th floor and knocked. The dark-haired girl who opened it was attractive, but nearly as tall as Waitkus himself - six

Eddie Waitkus, one of the most famous American sporting stars of his day, was an attractive bachelor with thousands of fans nationwide. Unfortunately, one of those fans wanted to kill him.

feet – (he was an inch taller) and her rather long face might have been described as horsey. She invited him in, then said: "I've a surprise for you". As he sat down, she went to a cupboard, then turned round holding a rifle, which she pointed at him. He asked with astonishment: "Is this some kind of joke? What have I done?" Then she fired, hitting him in the right lung. After which Ruth Steinhagen – her real name – knelt by his side as he collapsed, and held his hand in her lap. She then told the hotel operator to call a doctor.

Waitkus had been lucky; the small-calibre bullet had slipped between two ribs. A larger calibre would have probably knocked a broken rib into his lung or heart, killing him. In the hospital, his condition stabilized early in the morning so his life was no longer in danger.

Ruth Steinhagen, 19 years old, was arrested, and just over two weeks later, on June 30, appeared in court. By that time, she had explained to her court-appointed psychiatrist that she had been planning to shoot Waitkus for two years. "As time went on I just became nuttier and nuttier about the guy. I knew I would never get to know him in a normal way, so I kept thinking I will never get him, and if I can't have him nobody else can. Then I decided I would kill him."

After the trial

Regaining his health was a long fight for 30-year-old Waitkus, but he knew all America was behind him, and his popularity was enormous. He did daily runs along the beach of the Edgewater, and there met a pretty 20-year-old blonde named Carol Webel, whom he married — they had three children. In 1950 he returned to baseball, playing as well as ever, and led the Phillies to win the World Series.

At 36, he was thinking of retirement. He accepted a job in a New Jersey firm, Eastern Freightways, where his celebrity made him the ideal sales manager.

But the transition proved harder than he expected and he was soon hating the job, and drinking heavily. His marriage slowly broke down, and in 1961 he suffered a nervous collapse and had to be hospitalized. In 1967, however, when he became a permanent member of the teaching staff at a baseball sanctuary, the Ted Williams Camp, he finally found the peace he had been seeking. He eventually died in September 1972 of cancer of the oesophagus.

Together with other fans she would wait for hours outside the baseball park in order just to see him leave. Yet when he finally emerged, she always hid away. Her fantasy had built up so much psychic energy that she was unable to endure even the least contact with reality.

After a three-hour hearing, with the slowly recovering Waitkus in court, she was found guilty, and committed to the Kankakee State Hospital, in effect judged insane.

Ruth Steinhagen awaits trial: she worshipped Eddie Waitcus so much that she decided to kill him.

Ruth Steinhagen spent three years in the Kankakee State Hospital, diagnosed as schizophrenic with paranoid tendencies. She then returned to North Chicago to live with her family, and when her parents died in the early 90s, she and her younger sister Rita continued to live in the same house, leading a reclusive existence.

1950s

THE RESISTANCE HERO AND HIS WIFE

The case of Yvonne Chevallier is memorable because, although she was plainly guilty of murder, the jury acquitted her because it found the dead man's mistress so irritating.

Many people must have wondered why the brilliant and popular Pierre Chevallier, hero of the Resistance, married the dowdy, and socially inept Yvonne. The answer was simply because they seemed made for making love together.

When Pierre Chevallier, a recently qualified doctor, met the country midwife Yvonne Rousseau in 1935, both were 24, and they clapped together like two magnets. She was from a peasant background and he was from one of the oldest families in Orléans, but that was unimportant. Yvonne gave up her country practice and moved into his flat. His family were horrified, since she was plain, homely, and incapable of intelligent conversation. But their physical passion made them oblivious to all other considerations. For four years they were ecstatically happy.

Then came the Nazi invasion, and Dr Chevallier went off to fight. He won the Légion d'Honneur for tending the wounded under fire, and after the capitulation in June 1940 returned home to join the Resistance. He soon became its local leader, and when saboteurs were parachuted in from England, it was Chevallier who received and hid them. He was so well-organized that when the Germans began their retreat in 1944, Chevallier's men went on the attack and drove them out of Orléans before the Allies arrived. He was elected the city's first post-war mayor virtually without opposition. He gave up doctoring, and devoted his time to the reconstruction of Orléans, which all agreed to be a masterpiece of civic architecture.

But while an ideal doctor's wife, Yvonne was not a lady mayoress; she was too withdrawn and modest. And his enormous protectiveness, which had held together their marriage so far, now began to fade. Yvonne suffered torments because of her social ineptitude. She even learned book reviews by heart so as to have something to say at dinner parties.

As their relationship deteriorated, she went on her knees before him. He said irritably: "The only thing you know how to do properly is cry."

Yvonne Chevallier stands trial for the murder of her Cabinet Minister husband, Pierre. A plain-faced, unintellectual and shy woman, she found life as the spouse of a philandering politician intolerable.

One day she went through his pockets and found a love letter signed "Jeanette". Could this be the beautiful redhead Jeanette Perreau, the wife of a department store owner, 15 years younger than Yvonne? She went and confronted her, accusing her of being Pierre's mistress. Disdainfully, Jeanette denied it. So did Pierre – with furious brutality he told her to mind her own business.

In the general election of 1951, Pierre gained the seat by a huge lead. During the party that followed, Jeanette and Pierre stood holding hands. Yvonne caused a scene. After that, her husband told her he had had enough of her, and asked for a divorce. Sobbing, she refused.

She made an unsuccessful suicide attempt, but only made herself ill. She decided to visit Jeanette's husband to tell him about the affair. To her amazement, he told her he knew.

On the evening Pierre was made a minister, they had a particularly nasty quarrel. She seized an automatic she kept in her wardrobe and told him she was going to kill herself. He replied: "Good, but wait until I've gone."

It was the last straw. In fury, she fired four shots into him, the last through his head.

Despite the general public's detestation of Yvonne Chevallier for killing a popular war hero, the judge at her trial was sympathetic from the start: an opinion that was also shared by the public by the end of the trial.

Downstairs her little son began to cry. She went down and asked the cook to take care of him, then went back and shot Pierre once more as he lay on the floor.

It was that last shot that might have cost her her life, for it showed deliberation.

Yvonne was suddenly the most unpopular woman in Orléans, indeed in the whole of France, as her husband was widely admired. So strong was the feeling against her that the trial was moved from Orléans to Rheims.

On November 7, 1952, she listened to the opening statement from the judge, Raymond Jadin, and he was obviously moved by her plight. His presentation sounded more like a sympathetic summing-up.

When Leon Perreau, Jeanette's complaisant husband, was questioned, he made it quite clear that he did not mind his wife's infidelity,

which she had been honest about from the beginning.

Then Jeanette Perreau entered the box, looking beautiful, cool and self-possessed. Things began to go against her when she told how she and Pierre had begun their affair when they were on a train going to Paris:"And you became his mistress? Oh no, I made him wait…"

That hint of playing hard-to-get made her sound

Yvonne Chevallier is congratulated on her acquittal for murder. But she apparently couldn't forgive herself, and unofficially sentenced herself and her children to exile on Devil's Island.

calculating. And when she implied that her love life was her own business, hostility became stronger, until it finally exploded into boos. Her response was to stride disdainfully out of the box, without permission.

When the evening newspapers appeared that day, it was Jeanette Perreau who was the most unpopular woman in France. So no one was surprised when, after being out for only 40 minutes, the jury found Yvonne not guilty of every charge.

Together with her children, Yvonne Chevallier moved to Saint-Laurent-du-Moroni, part of the South American penal colony that used to be called Devil's Island. No one doubted this was her attempt to expiate her crime. Yvonne Chevallier eventually died, in obscurity, in the 1970s.

Jeanette Prerreau – "the other woman". Her self-possessed arrogance on the witness stand angered the jury and all but brought about the aquittal of Yvonne Chevallier.

Devil's Island

When Yvonne Chevallier flew out to French Guiana with her two children in 1953, the infamous penal colony had not been used for five years, and its buildings were in ruins. The island itself, which is part of the penal colony, has an area of 34.6 acres and is 25 miles long, much of it jungle. It has six months of tropical rain followed by six months of blazing heat, and its discomforts include mosquitoes and vampire bats. The only convict who was still there was the executioner Moucheboeuf, who had despatched dozens of his fellow convicts, and did not dare to return to France.

Established as a penal colony in 1852, it was used for political prisoners and the worst thieves and murderers, because it was virtually escape-proof, and most of them died there. One of the few who survived and returned was Alfred Dreyfus, the army captain who had been accused of spying for Germany and found guilty on trumped-up evidence. He was able to return to France after four years and, although only 39, had a white beard and looked like an old man.

PAULINE DUBUISSON

On the morning of March 17, 1951, a young man named Bernard Mougeot got stuck in a traffic jam on the north bank of the Seine, and his taxi arrived at his destination five minutes late. That five minutes cost the life of his best friend, Félix Bailly, for when Mougeot arrived, Félix was lying dead on the floor with three bullets in him, and his killer, an attractive brunette named Pauline Dubuisson, was lying unconscious on the floor, a gas pipe from the stove in her mouth. The fire brigade was called and she was revived with oxygen.

Even since she was 13, in 1940, Pauline Dubuisson had enjoyed an eventful love life. At 14 she was expelled from school for immorality with German soldiers; at 16 she was the mistress of 55-year-old Colonel Von Domnick, director of the German Hospital at Dunkirk. After the Liberation in 1945 she was punished by having her hair shorn (along with other "collaborators") in the main square at Dunkirk. In 1946 she studied medicine at the medical faculty of Lille University ("she is well-balanced, but haughty, provoking and a flirt" said one of her reports). She also embarked upon a study of erotic techniques, recording the names, along with the respective sexual preferences, of her many lovers – a project that played its part in stirring up public hostility to her during her trial.

Félix Bailly, a fellow student, was one of many with whom she had an affair. It lasted for two years, and his name duly figured on her list, along with the names of others of whose existence Félix Bailly was wholly unaware. He was naturally disillusioned by the discovery of her serial infidelity and, in November 1949, Bailly ignored her pleas

and transferred his studies from Lille University to Paris.

The two were not to meet again until March 1951; in the meantime many more names were added to the list. Pauline Dubuisson subsequently explained her mode of life with the remark: "I wanted to force myself to love other people, in order to persuade myself I was capable of having lasting sentiments for him." But the fact remains that she never, during the 18 months they spent apart, made any attempt to contact Bailly or visit him in Paris.

Meanwhile, Bailly had fallen in love with another, less volatile, girl, Monique Lombard, and received the consent of her parents to their engagement. When seeing a mutual acquaintance, he asked after Pauline, adding, "Is she still as loose as ever?"

Pauline learned of Félix Bailly's engagement, and at the beginning of March 1951 met her ex-lover in Paris; according to her testimony their old relationship was resumed. On March 10, she bought a .25-calibre automatic pistol, explaining to the

Pauline Dubuisson in the dock, aged 24. A sexual predator, she had had numerous lovers since she was just 13 years old.

police (who had to grant her a certificate of purchase) that she often had to travel late at night alone.

On March 15, she left her lodgings after leaving a note for her landlady expressing her intention of shooting

Félix Bailly's grieving relatives at the trial of Pauline Dubuisson. They had been warned that Pauline intended to kill Félix, but neither they nor Félix's friends managed to protect him.

Félix Bailly, then herself; the landlady sent telegrams of warning to both Bailly and his parents. That day Pauline visited Félix Bailly at his flat to try to persuade him to break his engagement, and was rebuffed. As a result of that encounter, Bailly asked some of his student-friends to act as bodyguards, and slept elsewhere that night.

On the evening of March 16 he returned cautiously to his flat, where he kept the outside door on a chain. On the following morning, he answered the door to Pauline, apparently thinking she was his friend Bernard Mougeot, at that moment hastening across Paris, but delayed by traffic. Mougeot would find Félix Bailly dead, shot through the forehead, back and behind one ear; Pauline Dubuisson lay unconscious by the stove.

In custody, awaiting trial on a charge of assassination (which could mean the death penalty) she again attempted suicide by slashing her wrists, but finally stood trial on November 18, 1953, at the Assizes of the Seine before the presiding judge M. Raymond Jadin. Her icy self-control earned her the newspaper nickname "Mask of Pride"; she claimed that after sleeping with Bailly one night in March he had unaccountably rejected her: "... he kissed me, everything was just as it used to be ... I felt I was coming out of a night-

Press photographers jockey to get pictures of the young *femme fatale*.

mare ... then, in the morning, he threw me out ... life didn't mean anything any more to me ... it was at that moment I decided to kill us both".

It is still uncertain whether Dubuisson was motivated by humiliation or jealousy, or even by a grinding and genuine regret for a lost passion. The jury found her guilty of murder, not of assassination – largely, it is believed, through the influence of the sole female juror. The prisoner was sentenced to penal servitude for life, possibly 20 years. Still cold and imperturbable, she was led out of court.

She served her sentence in Haguenau prison in Alsace, working as a hospital nurse, and was released in 1959.

Master and slave?

Why Pauline Dubuisson murdered the lover from whom she had been separated for two years is a mystery to which she never chose to give an answer. But a paragraph in Derick Goodman's *Crimes of Passion* may offer the solution. The prosecutor Maitre Floriot spoke of Pauline's private diary, her "carnet", in which she recorded her highly involved love life, and declared:

"She meets Félix Bailly and once she has definitely conquered him, when she knows he is in a position from which he is incapable of extricating himself, she takes a sadistic pleasure in seeing him come to cry on her shoulder, to groan, to plead with her, to give in to her every whim. For a proud being such as Pauline Dubuisson, the satisfaction is without parallel.

"One day he understands, and flees..." That is to say, Pauline is the dominant partner, the master, in the relationship, and to be deserted by her "slave", to know that he is to marry another, is intolerable. So the master executes the slave without remorse.

THE EMMETT-DUNNE CASE

The British Army sergeant Frederick Emmett-Dunne devised an ingenious plot to murder a fellow NCO so he could marry the man's wife, and very nearly got away with it.

At 3 a.m. on the morning of December 1, 1953, the body of Sergeant Reginald Watters was found hanging from banisters at Glamorgan Barracks at Duisburg, Germany, by his friend Emmett-Dunne. His death caused dismay among the men, for the pleasant and easygoing Watters was greatly liked, whereas Emmett-Dunne was regarded as untrustworthy and abrasive. However, a young and inexperienced doctor who examined the body found throat injuries consistent with hanging, and at an Army inquest a verdict of suicide was returned.

That might have been the end of it if it had not been for the suspicions of one man, Sergeant Frank Walters of the Rhine Army Special Investigation Branch, who was appointed to look into the death. While making inquiries he heard barrack rumours that Emmett-Dunne had been having an affair with Watters' German wife Mia, an ex-nightclub singer. Moreover, the guard-room log book had been altered, providing Emmett-Dunne with an alibi for the time Watters died. But the suicide verdict meant that the investigation foundered.

Walters returned to England and joined the Metropolitan Police. There, he happened to learn that Emmett-Dunne

and Mia Watters had married in Leeds on June 3, 1954, only seven months after the death of Reg Watters. He contacted the Special Investigation Branch in Germany who posted detectives, disguised as craftsmen and drivers, in the barracks. What they learned was basically that Emmett-Dunne had been having secret meetings with Mia Watters for about a year before Watters' death.

The resulting dossier was sent to Scotland Yard, and Superintendent Colin McDougal went to Germany to investigate further.

It was this that led to the decision to exhume the dead

sergeant. The Home Office pathologist Francis Camps came from England to examine the body, particularly the neck, to see if his death was due to hanging. He concluded that death had been due to a karate chop to the Adam's apple, the kind taught to commandos. Watters had been dead before he was hanged.

Emmett-Dunne and his wife were living in married quarters at Taunton, Somerset, when they were visited by the police. Emmett-Dunne naturally denied everything. He and Mia, he claimed, had met by pure chance in a pub in Leeds, where she was staying with Watters' sister, the landlady. "My only crime was marrying before the proper lapse of time prescribed by Victorian morality."

Taken to Bow Street and charged with the murder of Sergeant Watters, Emmett-Dunne protested that, as he was a citizen of Eire, a British court could not try him for a crime committed in a foreign country. Since this was true, he was handed over to the military police, taken

The victim, Sergeant Watters, sits on the far right of the picture. His wife, Mia, the reason Sergeant Emmett-Dunne murdered him, is the second woman from the left.

to Germany and charged on April 15, 1955, with murder.

The trial began in Düsseldorf on June 27, 1955. Emmett-Dunne chose the only defence open to him: that he had killed Watters in self-defence because Watters was pointing a loaded gun at him.

The question was: would the court believe Emmett-Dunne's story of the jealous Watters pointing a gun at

him – he even claimed to be able to see the bullet in the barrel – and having to kill him in self-defence?

The answer was no. Emmett-Dunne was found guilty of the murder of Sergeant Watters, but since the killing had occurred in Germany where there was no death penalty, he was sentenced to life imprisonment, to be served in England.

The truth behind the killing

The story that emerged was that at 7 o'clock on the evening of the murder, Emmett-Dunne had driven from the barracks to a nearby hotel to collect Watters and take him to meet a major who was interested in buying a car Watters had for sale. Some time over the next quarter of an hour, he killed Watters with a blow to the throat with the side of his hand, which he had learned in commando training.

He drove to Block 4 of the barracks, with the body wrapped in a long waterproof cape (Watters was only just over five feet tall) and placed it inside near the entrance. When a corporal tried to go in, Emmett-Dunne told him that Sergeant Watters had given orders that this entrance was not to be used.

It so happened that Emmett-Dunne's half-brother Ronald Emmett was also serving in Duisburg. Deciding he needed help, Emmett-Dunne went and found him, and explained that he had been forced to kill Watters to avoid being killed by him. Then he asked his brother to help him hang the body to make it appear he had committed suicide. Private Emmett was horrified and refused, but Emmett-Dunne reminded him they were brothers, so he finally agreed.

Ronald Emmett fetched a bucket, whereupon Emmett-Dunne himself hoisted the body up by a rope from the banisters, leaving the bucket lying on its side, as if kicked over by Watters as he hanged himself.

1954

DENISE LABBÉ AND JACQUES ALGARRON

The Denise Labbé case, perhaps one of the most sinister crimes of passion on record, will inevitably remind British readers of the Moors murders of Ian Brady and Myra Hindley. Fortunately, these killers claimed only one victim.

Denise Labbé was born into a poor family near Rennes in mid-western France. Through study at evening classes she became a secretary in Rennes when she was 20. Since Rennes is a university town, she began at once having affairs with students, often several at a time, as if to make up for the dreary years she had spent escaping her background. Some wanted to marry her, but were put off by her infidelity. One young doctor made her pregnant, and she gave birth to a daughter named Catherine. Denise found a nurse for her own children, and paid a quarter of her small salary to maintain her. In spite of her nymphomania, she was a devoted mother.

She was 28 when, in May 1954, she met an officer-cadet named Jacques Algarron, a good-looking young man four years her junior, who already had two illegitimate daughters and many mistresses. Denise's daughter Catherine was then two and a half.

They met at a Saturday dance, and Algarron suggested they meet again the following week. Something had "clicked" between them – based on the fact that he was an intellectual control-freak, while there was a deeply masochistic element in her personality that made him recognize her as a potential slave.

Before they met again, he had written to her telling her, in cold and precise terms, that although he had no intention of falling in love with her, and that she was certainly not the girl of his dreams, he nevertheless intended to make her his mistress next time they met.

The following Saturday she surrendered immediately. He enjoyed biting her, and making her back bleed from his scratches. And she enjoyed it so much that she would sit on the beach with her lacerated back visible to all passers-by, as if to say "I am a slave whose master beats her."

In Paris, where Denise and he moved separately, he took her to a café opposite Notre Dame cathedral, and asked her, "If I asked you to murder your daughter for me, would you do it?" She tried to avoid

Denise Labbé arrives at court under Gendarme escort: when her lover had demanded that she kill her two-year-old daughter, she agreed.

his piercing eyes, then finally whispered: "Yes". As they parted, he said: "If your daughter dies within a week, I will see you next weekend."

She started to say: "We have no right…", but his threatening look silenced her.

The next evening she made her first attempt to kill Catherine. Alone with her child in her mother's room,

Philosophy of murder

Algarron, at 24, was a child of post-war existentialist philosophy as propounded by Camus and Sartre. Man was free because he lived in a godless universe, and could do as he liked without fear of hell. This philosophy took for granted Nietzsche's assertion "God is dead". Nietzsche's corollary was that man must have the strength to strive to become a "superman".

Algarron explained to Denise his own concept of an "extraordinary couple" who would be "capable of committing any act whatsoever for each other, [let us say] to the point of killing a taxi driver".

she picked her up and, in spite of her screams, thrust her out of the window, two storeys up. But as she held her suspended above the pavement, she found she was unable to go through with it.

When Algarron telephoned her the next day to ask if she had done it, she told him she'd tried but failed.

When he came to Rennes that weekend, his reaction to her disobedience was to make her go into a phone booth with him while he phoned another mistress and arranged to spend the night with her. The next night he slept with yet another.

Before he left Denise, he took her for a walk by the Saint-Martin canal, pointed to a narrow suspension bridge,

> ## IF I ASKED YOU TO MURDER YOUR DAUGHTER FOR ME, WOULD YOU DO IT?
> Jacques Algarron

and said: "That is where you must drown your daughter."

The following day, September 30, she took Catherine there and threw her into the water. But maternal instinct made her scream for help. The lock-keeper jumped in and pulled the child out.

It was two weeks before she tried again to kill the child. On October 16 she threw Catherine into the river. Back indoors she was asked what had happened to the child, and deliberately led the search in the opposite direction. But the river was shallow, and the child's cries were heard in time. She was pulled out, blue with cold, and wrapped in a blanket.

Three weeks later, on

Jacques Algarron, a coldly ruthless army lieutenant who was quite prepared to have a little girl murdered to bind her mother to him as his love slave.

November 8, Denise Labbé drowned her own daughter, Catherine, in a stone wash basin in the yard, holding her head under until she stopped breathing.

The child's foster-mother, Madame Laurent, thought that all these accidents were too much of a coincidence, and reported her suspicions to the police. Finally, under their questioning, Denise broke down and confessed.

She and her lover were tried in May 1956. The horrific story of the murder stunned all of France. Denise was spared the death sentence, but received life imprisonment. Algarron was sent to prison for 20 years.

PAULINE PARKER AND JULIET HULME

On the afternoon of June 23, 1954, two girls ran into a tea-shop in Victoria Park, Christchurch, New Zealand, covered in blood and in a state of hysteria. "Please help us. Mummy's been hurt. She fell and hit her head on a brick, and it kept bumping, bumping, bumping…"

Police and doctors who rushed to the scene found the body of Mrs Honora Parker lying across a path in the park, her head brutally lacerated. The girls, 16-year-old Pauline Parker and 15-year-old Juliet Hulme, claimed she had fallen and banged her head, but that was absurd when she had obviously been hit repeatedly, while bruises on her throat suggested someone had also tried to strangle her. A bloodstained brick in a sock lay beside the body. It would have been obvious, even to the dimmest policeman, that she had been beaten to death. Taken in for questioning, the schoolgirls quickly admitted being responsible.

The story that slowly emerged was of one of those feverishly intense schoolgirl friendships that have lesbian overtones. Until 15-year-old Juliet came to her school, Pauline had been a rather passive, unco-operative pupil, with a poor academic record. Physically, they were opposites: Juliet, the daughter of a physicist, was tall, slim and blonde, Pauline dark, plump and several inches shorter. So far, their mental lives had consisted entirely of fantasy. Now they blended their fantasies, and their main object in life was to be together. They slept together when they could (mostly at Juliet's home), took baths together, talked about sex together, and started to write novels together, assuming the "identities" of their characters, Charles II, Emperor of Borovia, his mistress, Deborah, and Lancelot Trelawny, a Cornish soldier of fortune.

Convinced that they were both geniuses, they planned to go to New York, find a publisher for their novels, then go to Hollywood and perhaps become actresses.

At first delighted that their lonely daughters had found friendship, their parents began to feel alarmed at the morbid intensity of the relationship, and were soon inclined to think the worst. Nor were they entirely wrong. An entry in Pauline's diary on June 12, 1954, 10 days before the murder, recorded that she

and Juliet had invented saints and then "…we enacted how each saint would make love in bed. We felt exhausted but very satisfied."

Both sets of parents now began to consider how they might put an end to the friendship – an insensitive idea, certain to arouse powerful resistance. The Hulmes

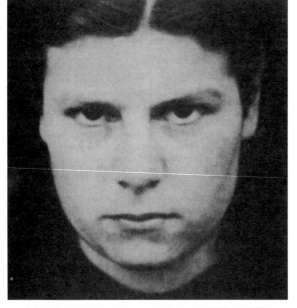

Pauline Parker, the older of the two girls but the most introverted. She became convinced that the death of her mother would solve all her problems.

Juliet Hulme (left) and Pauline Parker (right): their teenage infatuation with each other and the fantasy world they had constructed was enough to drive them to murder.

most of the days before the Hulmes were due to sail. But this was only pretence. Both believed that if Mrs Parker was out of the way, Pauline could also sail for South Africa.

As killers, they were pathetically incompetent. Their idea was to lure Pauline's mother on a walk to the park, strike her down with one heavy blow, then claim she had tripped and hit her head.

In the actual event, Juliet walked ahead and Pauline found an excuse to drop behind. She then hit her mother with the improvised cosh. Mrs Parker fell to the ground, but was clearly not dead. As both girls beat her and tried to strangle her, their plan of making it seem an accident became increasingly unworkable. In truth, it must have been one of the most incompetent murders ever.

At their trial in Christchurch, which opened on August 23, 1954, both girls appeared unrepentant, and pleaded not guilty; their defence submitted a plea of insanity. This convinced no one, and six days later the jury returned a verdict of guilty. Because both were juveniles, they were not hanged, but sentenced to be detained "until Her Majesty's pleasure be made known". Both were released in 1958.

decided that the solution might be to go on a long visit to relatives in South Africa and take Juliet with them.

The girls became frantic as the day of their separation drew closer. Pauline was now obsessed with the idea of going with them, and the Hulmes did not seem entirely unsympathetic. But the strong-minded Mrs Parker felt this would be an admission that all their efforts had been wasted, and firmly opposed it. Naturally, she became the chief target of their hatred. Pauline committed her thoughts to her diary:

"February 13th. Why could not mother die? Dozens of people, thousands of people, are dying every day. So why not mother, and father too?"

"June 20th. We discussed our plans for moidering mother and made them a little clearer. I want it to appear either a natural or an accidental death."

On the morning of the day of the crime, the diary entry read: "I felt very excited and the night before Christmassy last night. I did not have pleasant dreams, though."

They had lulled Honora Parker's suspicions by appearing to accept that separation was inevitable. As a concession they were allowed to spend together

What Juliet did next

Oddly enough, Juliet finally achieved her aim of becoming a successful writer. She moved to Scotland and, under the name of Anne Perry, wrote a series of detective novels set in Victorian England. In 2005 an interviewer asked how the murder had affected her life. She replied: "I hope it has made me wiser and a lot less quick to judge... In order to come to terms with something like that, you have to go into yourself. You learn that you may well be punished for the things you do wrong. When you've done something you know is ugly, it doesn't matter what anybody on the outside says to you — what you have done to yourself is the worst thing. You also know you will never, ever, do that again."

The murder case was the basis of the film *Heavenly Creatures*, in which Kate Winslet played the Juliet Hulme character. Perry said she hadn't seen the film and didn't want to: "If I were to say that one part wasn't true, then I'd be saying the rest is."

THE BORED HOUSEWIFE

The 1950s were a time when bored American couples discovered the pleasures of wife-swapping parties. One method was for the husbands to toss their house-keys on to the floor, and for the women to scramble for them. They would then accompany the man thus acquired to the nearest bedroom. This greatly enlivened social life in the suburbs of Boston.

In early 1954, a pretty housewife named Lorraine Clark was enraptured by this new diversion. She was 28 and, having been married since she was 18, felt she deserved a break from child-rearing (she had three) and housework. Her husband Melvin, 29, a hard-working foreman in an electronics firm, gave her nothing to complain about except that she found him dull, and possibly undersexed. He seemed content to spend his days at work and his weekends running a boat-rental business on Lake Attitash, near the town of Amesbury. Lorraine, who worked as a waitress in a local diner, felt life was slipping away from her. This discovery of sexual variety gave her life a new kind of excitement.

Her husband was apparently unaware of what was going on until he returned home – probably for something he had forgotten – on the evening of April 10, 1954, after leaving to work a night shift. He found Lorraine in bed with a lover and the man withdrew apologetically, leaving the couple to exchange furious words. The thought of giving up adultery apparently filled Lorraine with rage, and she grabbed the nearest weapon, two very sharp knitting needles, and stabbed Melvin twice in the chest with both. Then she went and got the .32 pistol they kept, and made

sure he was dead by shooting him twice in the head.

It was now necessary for her to consider her next move. Common sense told her that claiming self-defence was no solution, since she had shot as well as stabbed him. In her later confession she described how it had taken her three hours to decide that her best chance of getting away with it would be to dispose of the body. She finally bound the corpse with wire, and took him to the nearest river – the Merrimack, six miles away. The problem of how to prevent it from floating was solved by taking three 15lb anchors from the boat shed. Then she drove home, and settled down to the problem of removing the bloodstains before the children returned. (It is not clear where they were at the time, but probably staying with grandparents.)

Explaining her husband's disappearance was solved by telling her friends that Melvin had walked out on her after a quarrel, and those who knew about her recent love-life had no difficulty understanding his reaction. A week after the murder she instituted divorce proceedings, alleging "cruel and abusive treatment".

She had hoped that the river would carry her husband out to sea. Unfortunately, heavy rains swelled the Merrimack, causing it to spill over its banks.

So instead of ending in Ipswich Bay, the body was deposited in marshes beside the estuary, where it was noticed by a bird-watcher on June 2. Although the body was too badly decomposed to be recognizable, and the dental plates had been removed to render identification more difficult, Melvin Clark was finally identified by his fingerprints. Three weeks later, after a seven-hour grilling at the office of the district attorney, Lorraine made a full confession, admitting that she had committed the murder alone and had no accomplice.

On September 17, 1954, at Salem, Massachusetts, Lorraine

Clark was indicted for first-degree murder. The Boston public, primed for scandal by hints of wife-swapping, was disappointed when the district attorney merely referred to her "uncontrollable infatuation for other men". They were further deprived when Lorraine Clark pleaded guilty, so no trial took place. On November 29, 1954, her plea of "murder two" – manslaughter in the UK – having been accepted, Superior Court Judge Charles Fairhurst sentenced her to life imprisonment in the women's reformatory at Framingham, where she would become eligible for parole in 15 years.

A meal before bed

At least the public learned the name of the man Lorraine Clark was in bed with on the night of the murder. It was 23-year-old Arthur G. Jackson, apparently a close friend of the dead man; in fact, he and his wife Shirley had been seeing a great deal of the Clarks. It even emerged that after Jackson's separation from Shirley, Melvin Clark had helped him move into an apartment in Newburyport where, while her husband was working late, Lorraine had cooked meals for him before they went to bed. It is an interesting commentary on the old-fashioned Puritanism of Massachusetts in the 1950s that the day after she was sentenced, Jackson was put on trial for adultery with Lorraine Clark and sentenced to three years.

THE RUTH ELLIS CASE

The case of Ruth Ellis, the last woman to be hanged in England, still arouses intense controversy, many condemning it as judicial murder. As a friend of someone intimately involved in the case, author Colin Wilson knows the inside story and does not share their feelings.

This was Clive Gunnell, who in 1955 was a car salesman. On the evening of Easter Sunday, April 10, 1955, Clive and his friend David Blakely emerged from the Magdala public house in Hampstead. As Blakely fumbled for his car keys, a small peroxide blonde woman approached. As she pointed a revolver at him, Blakely gave a cry of alarm and ran towards the rear of the car. Two shots hit him in the back. Even as he lay on the pavement, with Clive Gunnell bending over him, the woman went on firing over Clive's shoulder. When the hammer clicked on an empty chamber, she turned and said unemotionally: "Go and call the police." By the time the ambulance arrived, David Blakely was dead.

The killer was 28-year-old Ruth Ellis. She and Blakely had been lovers for two years, ever since they met at a London club. Blakely was

David Blakely and Ruth Ellis. Blakely was an immature philanderer and Ellis was insecure and needed constant attention from a lover. Their relationship was very stormy.

66 **I HOPE I NEVER SEE THAT SHIT AGAIN.** 99
Ruth Ellis on first meeting Blakely

something of a playboy; he had a well-paid job, and an allowance from his stepfather. His passion was racing cars.

Their relationship had been stormy. Both were emotionally unstable. Ruth hungered for constant flattery and attention; Blakely was immature, and inclined to become so rude when drunk that he drove away many regular customers at the Little Club, where Ruth was the hostess. Eventually, the proprietor fired Ruth, largely because of her relationship with Blakely. A businessman named Desmond Cussen took her – and her two small children – into his flat in Devonshire Place and financed her; he was so devoted to her that he even made no objection to her sleeping with Blakely.

Born into a relatively poor family in Rhyl, North Wales, Ruth Neilson had left school at 15 and worked as a machinist in a factory and as a Woolworth's shopgirl. At 17 she had become a photographer's assistant, and soon fell in love with a French Canadian soldier named Clare. She learned she was pregnant soon after Christmas 1944. Clare had promised to marry her, but a letter to his CO revealed that he already had a wife and children in Canada. A son was born in 1945.

Ruth became a photographer's model and often posed in the nude. In a Mayfair club she met vice-boss Morris Conley, who was soon sleeping with her, and persuaded her to work for him

Ruth Ellis worked as a nightclub hostess, a role somewhere between barmaid and deputy manager. She was not expected to sleep with customers, but nobody stopped her either.

as a hostess in the Court Club. She did not have to sleep with customers, but it helped her pay. In November that year she married a recently divorced dentist, George Ellis – another customer – who was an alcoholic. He was 41, she 24. A daughter was born in 1951, but by then her husband's alcoholism had become worse, and they separated. She returned to being a club

hostess for Morris Conley, and in 1953 he made her manageress of the Little Club in Brompton Road, Knightsbridge. She received £25 a week and a rent-free flat. One client even gave her £400 for going on holiday with him.

Her first meeting with the weakly handsome David

Blakely was not a success – she remarked afterwards, "I hope I never see that little shit again." Blakely had just become engaged to an heiress, but he was an incorrigible philanderer. Since Ruth made a habit of being available to customers of her choice, it was not too difficult to persuade her to let him sleep with her. He understood that he was not her "lover" – merely a customer who was being allowed to spend nights in her bed. And, according to Ruth, she was not particularly in love with him either. Nevertheless, Blakely was soon sleeping regularly in her flat. They became lovers almost as a matter of habit. It was also a matter of vanity; Ruth liked the idea of having an affair with this ex-public schoolboy with his private income and racing car, and he liked the idea of having a sexy blonde mistress whose bed was right above the club.

In February 1954, she had an abortion – this time Blakely's baby. But while Blakely was away racing at Le Mans, she slept with her devoted admirer, Desmond Cussen. He lent her money and pressed her to marry him. Ruth was not interested – not because she preferred Blakely, for both of them slept with other people, but because she was not deeply attracted to Cussen. She may also have preferred Cussen as an adoring swain rather than a husband who might take her for granted. Cussen even arranged to send her son Andy to a private school.

Ruth and Blakely quarrelled after she noticed scratches on his back. He was the one who made it up, and the affair continued. Both of them were now drinking much more heavily. He often hit her when he lost his temper, on one occasion knocking her down the stairs. One night, she went back home with a man who had picked her up, and took off all her clothes to reveal bruises all over her body. Profits at the club were slumping, and when Conley finally fired her at the end of 1954, she moved in with Desmond Cussen. But she often spent the night in a hotel with Blakely.

It was clear to friends like Clive Gunnell that the couple were bad for one another. Blakely was aggressive when drunk, and he was drunk much of the time. Ruth was less aggressive but could give as good as she got. They often quarrelled, but always made up in bed. Even when she knew he was having an affair with a married woman in Penn, she continued to let him sleep with her.

Towards the end of January 1955, they went on a nine-day drinking spree that ended with quarrels and hysteria. On another occasion Ruth hid Blakely's car keys, and when Clive Gunnell and a friend arrived to pick him up, Ruth had a black eye and bruises. There was another hysterical scene when Blakely found his keys and tried to drive off. Yet after more bitter recriminations, he sent her red carnations with a note: "Sorry darling. I love you. David."

David Blakey was a moderately successful racing car driver, but was also a spoiled brat. His disinclination to treat Ruth's tantrums seriously cost him his life.

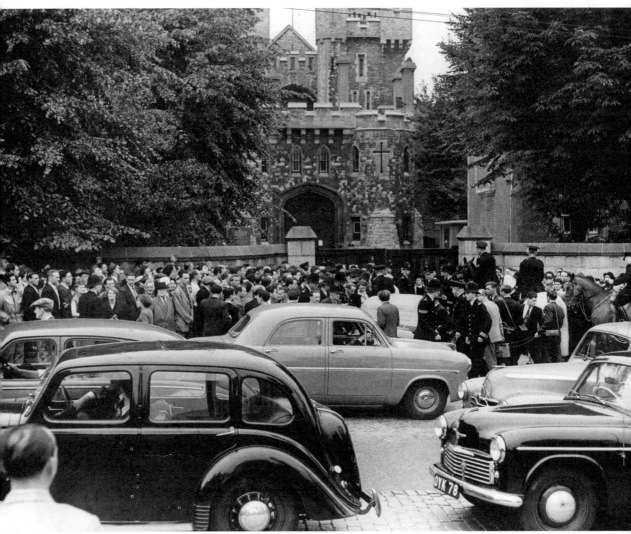

When she decided to leave Cussen's flat, the faithful admirer lent her the money to rent a new one in Kensington. Blakely told her he had broken off his affair with the married woman, and she allowed him to stay there with her. She then got Cussen to take her down to a pub in Penn, and found Blakely in there with the married woman. Back in Kensington, after another violent quarrel,

he hit her in the stomach and caused a miscarriage.

In spite of this, they spent the night before Good Friday, 1955, in her flat. Ruth had become extremely sexually demanding, and Blakely was taking amyl nitrate, a sexual stimulant. He left the flat early because he found her son (now 10) too noisy. Later that day he told friends – a married couple named Findlater – that he couldn't

stand it any longer, and had to get away.

Carole Findlater, who had once been Blakely's girlfriend, was glad to hear it; she disliked Ruth intensely. She persuaded Blakely to come home for lunch, and that night he stood Ruth up and went out with them. Late at night, Ruth repeatedly rang the Findlaters demanding to talk to him. When they refused she drove around to

Crowds gather outside Holloway Prison to wait for the news of Ruth Ellis's execution. Many were there as protestors against the death penalty.

their flat and smashed in all the windows of Blakely's car. The police arrived, and Ruth was finally driven back home by Desmond Cussen.

The following day – Saturday – was spent unsuccessfully pursuing Blakely. Ruth was now convinced he was making love to the nursemaid of the Findlaters. Until late that night she hung around opposite the Findlaters' flat.

On Sunday, there was a party at the Findlaters', after a lunchtime drink at the Magdala public house. At nine that evening, Carole Findlater ran out of cigarettes, and asked Blakely to go and get her some. Blakely decided they also needed more beer, and asked Clive Gunnell to go with him to the Magdala public house...

According to Ruth Ellis - speaking shortly before her execution - she had been pouring out her fury to Desmond Cussen when he had handed her a loaded revolver. He had then driven her to woodland where she practised shooting. And later, she alleged, he drove her to the Magdala public house.

She arrived minutes before David Blakely came out with Clive Gunnell. Soon after that, David Blakely lay dead on the pavement and Ruth Ellis was taken into custody.

On Monday, June 20, 1955, Ruth Ellis stood in the dock at the Old Bailey. When she told the prosecuting QC, Christmas Humphreys, that she had intended to kill Blakely, the judge told the jury that only one verdict was possible: murder. They took only 14 minutes to arrive at a guilty verdict.

On July 13, 1955, she drank a hot brandy, then walked firmly to the execution shed. Ten years later, in 1965, capital punishment was abolished in Britain.

The official notices, announcing the completed execution of Ruth Ellis, the last woman to be hanged in Great Britain.

Ruth's "suicide"

Clive Gunnell had a nervous breakdown after witnessing the murder. He told me (CW) that he rejected the idea that Ruth killed David Blakely because she was so much in love with him. He felt she was an exhibitionist who craved attention, and that the murder was a theatrical performance as much as a crime of passion. Years of drunken parties and prostitution (for she was basically a high-class call girl) had led to states of depression and boredom when she needed emotional stimulants. She killed Blakely because she was infuriated at his refusal to speak to her or see her after their last lovemaking session on Good Friday; there may also have been an element of self-disgust contributing to her decision to make the break final by killing him. Her death, Clive argued, was a spectacular form of suicide.

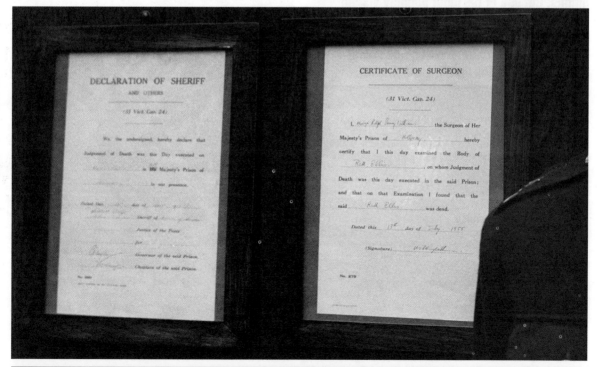

THE LANA TURNER SCANDAL

The Hollywood movie industry and the American Mafia have had plenty of conflicts, off screen as well as on. While actors like Edward G. Robinson, Jimmy Cagney and Humphrey Bogart were portraying mob thugs on the screen, real gangsters were pressuring the studios for "protection" money, providing drugs for dissolute stars, blackmailing those same stars and even illegally controlling sections of the industry, like the teamsters' and the extras' unions. But one of the most publicly visible conflicts involving these two behemoths came about through a love affair between a petty gangster, Johnny Stompanato, and one of Hollywood's leading lights, Lana Turner.

Turner had been talent-spotted while serving as a counter girl in a soda fountain on Sunset Boulevard. Appearing in a minor role in the 1939 movie, *They Won't Forget*, the 16-year-old Turner, dressed in a tight sweater, was the most memorable thing about the film. The studio press office labelled her "the sweater girl" – a title she naturally hated – and Lana was soon starring in hit movies.

But off screen Lana Turner's private life was often unhappy. She ran through four marriages in two decades, gaining little, but bad, memories and a daughter, Cheryl Crane, who rowed continuously with her. Cheryl later said that she resented her "life in the fish bowl": the continuous press spotlight on her as well as her mother. By the time she was 14, Cheryl had tried to run away both from home, and from the Catholic boarding school that her mother had hoped would curb her rebellious streak.

On top of the family rows Lana was, by the late 1950s, getting worried about her career. She was approaching middle age, and could hardly pass as "the sweater girl" any more. Her acting career was beginning to look as if it was levelling off, and she feared that she might soon be slipping into the relative obscurity of the has-been star. Then, in 1957, she got the sort of ego boost she must have felt she needed. Out of the blue, a man called John Steele started to send her flowers every day, along with gushing compliments and a gentlemanly request to meet for a drink some time. Lana had no idea who the man was, but the adulation was welcome – coming, as it did, in the recent wake of her fourth divorce.

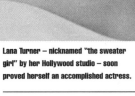

Lana Turner – nicknamed "the sweater girl" by her Hollywood studio – soon proved herself an accomplished actress.

She met with Steele and found him both fascinating and attractive. A wavy-haired, saturnine man of distinctly good looks, John told her thrilling tales of his war years in the US Marines, of his post-war life as a club-owner in pre-revolution China and of his conversion to Islam following his – now ended –

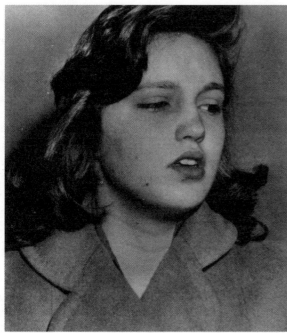

Left: Cheryl Crane, Lana Turner's daughter. Life as a starlet's daughter made her both miserable and rebellious.

marriage to a Turkish beauty. Turner was swept off her feet and was soon swept into Steele's bed.

In fact Steele was lying about key aspects of his background. He was actually called Johnny Stompanato, was five years younger than Lana (not, as he claimed, five years older) and had very firm connections with the Mafia. It was true that he had served with distinction in the US Marines, but he had been a dull bureaucrat in China, not a dashing club-owner. Arriving in California in 1948, Stompanato had initially funded himself by black-mailing a British aristocrat with a drugs habit. He had then joined the Californian branch of the national Mafia syndicate (derisively called the "Mickey Mouse Mafia" by mobsters elsewhere in the country). His charm and military training soon won him a job as occasional body-

Right: Johnny Stompanato – a professional gigolo with strong mafia connections. Was he actually a blackmail plant by mob boss Mickey Cohen?

guard to Mickey Cohen – boss of the "Mickey Mouse Mafia".

But Stompanato's favourite way of earning money was as a gigolo. He'd find a rich, older woman, charm her into bed, then spend her money until there was none left; then he'd go looking for a new victim. In picking on Lana Turner, however, Stompa-nato was well out of his usual league. The Hollywood studios were famously protective of their starlets' wholesome im-ages – sleeping with mob-sters was a definite no-no. The LA police would have been delighted to throw him in jail at the slightest complaint, from either Lana or her studio.

According to Turner, Johnny soon became bored with being a star's flunky and res-entful that, after discovering

that he was in the Mafia, she refused to be seen in public with him. Matters came to a head while Lana was filming *Another Time, Another Place* in England with an unknown young co-star called Sean Connery. Stompanato is said to have jealously threatened Connery with a gun. Connery, brought up in the slums of Glasgow, punched him to the ground with embarrass-ing ease. It was perhaps this humiliation that caused Johnny to hit Lana during a later argument in her hotel room.

Turner had Johnny thrown out of Britain, revealing to the authorities that he was travelling under a false passport. She tried to avoid him by flying to Mexico

rather than California after finishing the movie with Connery. But Johnny was waiting at the airport at Acapulco with a bevy of pressmen when she got off the plane. Almost certainly, Mickey Cohen had used his connections to discover Lana's secret travelling plans.

Turner later admitted that she should have stuck to her guns and not taken Stompanato back, but he was a "forbidden fruit" that she couldn't resist. Yet, according to Lana, Johnny just couldn't control his resentful and violent streak. He was furious when she refused to take him to the 1958 Academy Awards – where Lana had been nominated for her role in

Peyton Place. He was doubly furious when she didn't win and, when she returned home, he beat her about the face with his fists. Lana kept the abuse secret, she later admitted, but Cheryl saw her bruised face the following day and guessed that Johnny had hit her mother.

The relationship staggered on to the following Easter, when Lana finally decided to throw Johnny out. The result was, unsurprisingly, a massive row, but Johnny didn't use violence. After much shouting and screaming he agreed to leave, took some suits out of Lana's wardrobe and started for the door with them slung over his shoulder. At that moment Lana unlocked the bedroom door and her daughter rushed in. Cheryl later claimed that, as Johnny moved to walk around her mother, she had seen his upraised right hand holding something (his suits as it turned out) and thought he was about to brain Lana. The 14-year-old stepped up to him and hit him in the stomach. Lana was startled to see the big man crumple to the ground moaning: "My God, Cheryl. What have you

A policeman examines Stompanato's corpse. The killing wound had severed a major artery in his stomach, yet there was no blood splashed over Lana's pristine bedroom. Neither are the suits visible, that Johnny was said to be carrying over his shoulder when Cheryl stabbed him.

Right: The knife that killed Stompanato. An inadequate forensic examination failed to identify mystery fibres found on the blade.

done?" Then Lana saw the bloody carving knife in her daughter's fist.

Panicking, Lana lost precious minutes calling her mother rather than an ambulance. Johnny, with a major artery in his stomach severed, bled to death before Lana's mother arrived with a doctor. The police, anxious not to appear to be giving a star's daughter preferential treatment, questioned Cheryl then locked her up in Juvenile Hall.

It was now that the Mickey Mouse Mafia went publicly head-to-head with Hollywood (in this case in the form of Lana Turner and her famous lawyer, Jerry Geisler). Mickey Cohen moved quickly to scotch suggestions that Stompanato was an unwel-

come guest in the Turner household. "I can't understand it," he told pressmen, "I thought she liked him very much. We were happy – Cheryl and Johnny and me. We used to go horseback riding together." The suggestion that Lana's family mixed not just with small-time hoods, like Johnny, but with big fish like Cohen must have horrified the studio press office. Cohen then "obtained" and published Johnny and Lana's letters to each other, showing them to have been on very loving terms.

Turner and Geisler later claimed that, at this time, they found evidence that Johnny meant to blackmail Lana: negatives of her sleeping naked,

and pictures of Johnny having sex with another woman. Presumably, they said, he intended to doctor the images to make blackmail photos. They burned all the pictures, which was perhaps foolish because, aside from Lana and Cheryl's claims that he was violent, there was no evidence against Johnny's conduct.

Cheryl Crane was not immediately charged with murder. A jury at a coroner's inquest had first to decide if the killing had been justifiable homicide. Lana, as star witness, gave a bravura performance to the court and to the courtroom television cameras. She painted a vivid picture of Stompanato as a violent gigolo, and of the fear that

1958

Despite Cheryl's famous mother, the police offered her no preferential treatment.

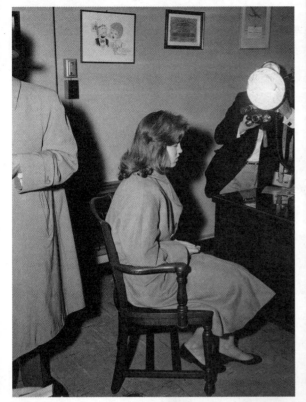

"Lies! All lies!"

In the face of the jury's decision, the LA prosecutor chose not to press charges against Cheryl. This was perhaps a shame, as certain anomalies that came out during the inquest might have been cleared up during a full trial. For example: why were there no fingerprints on the carving knife? Why was there no blood on the floor where Johnny was said to have bled to death? What were the unidentified "light and dark fibres or hairs" found on the knife? And why did an anonymous man stand up at the end of the inquest to shout, "Lies! All lies! This mother and daughter were both in love with Stompanato! Johnny was a gentleman!"?

Rumours have thus continued to circulate that it was actually Lana who killed Johnny, having discovered that he had seduced Cheryl. She then, the rumours say, wiped the knife clean of her fingerprints, moved his body (for some reason) to her bedroom and then persuaded her daughter to take the blame because, being a minor, she would be very unlikely to be charged with murder.

had driven her daughter to stab him. The jury were clearly moved, and took only half-an-hour to decide that Cheryl had been right to use lethal force to protect herself and her mother.

Lana Turner's career was given a big boost by the publicity and her inquest performance, but Cheryl immediately went to live with her grandmother and refused even to speak to her mother for some years. Mickey Cohen said disgustedly of the inquest verdict: "It's the first time in my life I've ever seen a dead man convicted of his own murder."

Lana's show-stopping performance on the witness stand.

135

1960s

ELIZABETH DUNCAN

For those who would like to believe that female criminals are never as bad as their male counterparts, Elizabeth Duncan is the most convincing refutation. She was an egomaniac, a pathological liar and a lifelong petty swindler who, until her arrest for hiring two hitmen to get rid of her daughter-in-law, managed to give the impression of being a hyper-respectable middle-class American matron. Considering how many times she had married bigamously, and how many dud cheques she had written, it was amazing that she had never been in jail.

Her son Frank, on whom she doted, was born in 1928, when she was in her mid-twenties. In view of the fact that his mother was so neurotic, possessive and domineering, he managed to grow up relatively unscathed, studied law, and eventually practised it successfully in California. His mother went to all his court appearances, and applauded noisily when he won. His friends and colleagues felt that the sooner he found a wife and escaped his mother, the better. But she had no intention of losing him to another woman.

At 59, she had managed to keep her son unmarried by means of hysterics and emotional blackmail – for example, when they had quarrelled about her plan to purchase a beauty parlour for which she did not have the funds, and he ordered her out of his apartment, she took an overdose of sleeping tablets.

This proved to be her worst mistake so far. In the cottage hospital where was recovering, one of the nurses was a charming, pretty girl named Olga Kupczyk, 29, from Vancouver. Her son came to visit, and he and the nurse were instantly attracted. Within months Olga was pregnant. When Frank told his mother, she exploded with fury, and told the girl, "I'll kill you if you marry my son." She meant it.

Frank thereupon married Olga secretly. His mother soon found out, and her first shot in the battle to separate them was an advertisement in a local newspaper, signed in Frank's name, declaring that he would not be responsible for any debts except those of his mother. She then visited Olga and launched into a screaming tirade that ended only when Olga's landlady persuaded her to go away.

She confided to her best friend and admirer, Mrs Emma Short, that she was planning to disfigure Olga with acid, then decided it might be better for Mrs Short to invite Olga to her apartment, where the avenging mother would leap out of a cupboard and strangle her. Mrs Short gently pointed out the plan's many defects, such as getting rid of the body...

Finally, Mrs Duncan hit upon what seemed a simple and workable plan. She would hire killers with a promise of $6,000 (which she did not possess) and get them to bury Olga where she would never be found.

Mrs Short accompanied her friend to a seedy beer joint run by an illegal Mexican immigrant named Marciano Esquivel, who had been charged with receiving stolen property and was being represented by Frank

Elizabeth Duncan – mother-in-law from Hell. When confronted on the witness stand with evidence of her bigamy, numerous dud cheques and a ruthless murder, she was unrepentant.

The highest-scoring bigamist

Elizabeth Duncan was probably the highest-scoring bigamist in criminal history. Even she did not know how many times she had been married. Her biographer Peter Wyden estimates between 11 and 20.

At 14 she was married to Mr Dewy Tessier, by whom she had three children (soon placed in an orphanage). But even before that she seems to have been married to a Mr Mitchell.

In 1927 she married an Edward Lynchberg, but in 1928 was wed to Frank Low, the father of her adored son. Mr Low already had a wife, so the marriage was finally annulled on those grounds.

The next husband was Mr Duncan, whose name she kept. While still "married" to him she married one Frank Craig, largely because he had an excellent credit rating, and for this reason she continued to use his name on business documents for many years. She also married a Mr Jacob Gold.

Asked in court, "Do you mean to convey that it is a normal relationship for a wife to go out and marry somebody else during the time of the marriage?", she replied cheerfully: "I don't know what it is, but, anyway, I did it."

Elizabeth casually regards her son's misery as the prosecutor describes the strangulation of his wife by his mother's hired assassins.

Duncan. She explained to his wife Esperanza that she was being blackmailed by her son's wife, and needed someone to quietly remove her. Mrs Esquivel, anxious to please, recommended two Mexican boys named Luis Moya, 21, and Gus Boldonado, 26. These young men met with Mrs Duncan, were much impressed that a lady of her social status was willing to employ them, and agreed to kill Olga. Mrs Duncan gave them an advance of $175.

The young men hired a Chevrolet for $25, borrowed a .22 pistol, and drove to the apartment building where Olga lived. Moya knocked on her door and, when she appeared in a housecoat, explained that he had driven her husband home from a bar, and that he was drunk in the back of the car. He needed help to bring him up.

When Olga stuck her head in to look at the prostrate body in the back seat, Moya hit her on the head with the pistol, while Boldonado straightened up and dragged her into the car. As they drove away, Olga began to scream. She was silenced with several more violent blows.

Thirty miles down the road, they pulled in at a roadside culvert, and tried to shoot her. But the gun jammed, and Boldonado had to strangle her. Then they buried her in a makeshift grave.

Two days later, Moya rang Mrs Duncan and asked for the rest of the money. She gave them $120 and promised the remainder later. Enraged at this betrayal, they began a campaign of pestering her.

Then Elizabeth Duncan made her greatest mistake. She went to the police and told them she was being blackmailed. Moya and Boldonado were arrested, and promptly told them the full story. The result was that all three stood side by side in court, and were sentenced to death.

Frank Duncan did his best to save his mother, launching many appeals. All his efforts failed, and on August 8, 1962, Elizabeth Duncan and her two dupes died in the San Quentin gas chamber.

Despite everything, Frank Duncan stood by his mother to the very end.

SHARON KINNE

When Sharon and James Kinne married in Independence, Missouri, in October 1950, she was a pretty 16-year-old and was pregnant. It was not an ideal match, for she was an imaginative and dominant girl who dreamed of a more exciting life than being married to an electronics engineer. Soon after the marriage she miscarried, but it was too late to change her mind. Instead, she carried on an affair with a youth she had known at school, John Boldizs. In 1958 she gave birth to a daughter named Danna.

Her husband suspected her infidelity, and on the afternoon of March 19, 1960, told her he was filing for divorce. That evening, the police received a call from Sharon saying that her husband had been shot dead.

James Kinne was lying in bed with a bullet in his head. Nearby was a well-oiled .22 revolver. Sharon's story was that she had been in the bathroom when she heard Danna saying: "How does this thing work, daddy?" Then there was a bang. James was a gun enthusiast who, it seemed, often left weapons around. Danna was allowed to play with them.

The police were not suspicious, otherwise they would have tested the child's hands, and her mother's, with paraffin for powder blowback. And after the funeral, Sharon received a sizeable insurance payment and bought herself something she had always longed for – a blue Ford Thunderbird. She was charmed by the man who sold it to her – Walter Jones. Soon they were having an affair.

When Sharon returned from a trip to the north-west, she told Walter she was pregnant and suggested marriage. He pointed out that this was impossible since he was already married.

Two days later, on May 27, 1960, Sharon reported to the police that she and John Boldizs had discovered the body of Walter Jones's wife Patricia in a car in a lovers' lane. She had been shot four times in the head with a .22. According to Sharon, they had gone out to search for Patricia at her husband's request after she had gone missing.

When the police learned that Sharon had persuaded a male co-worker to buy a .22 for her, and register it in another name, they charged her with murder. The case collapsed, however, when ballistics evidence showed her gun was not the one that had fired the fatal bullets.

But she was immediately re-arrested. The murder of Patricia Jones had made the police decide to re-examine her husband's death, and an expert had stated that a two-year-old child could not pull the trigger of a .22. In 1962 she was tried again and sentenced to life.

She fought the verdict, but at her re-trial was again found guilty. In the Tipton Women's Prison, she quickly established herself as the most dominant woman on her block. Then, in March 1963, the Superior Court overturned the verdict and granted her another trial. For technical legal reasons, this ended in a mistrial. In a fourth trial the jury could not agree, and a fifth trial was ordered for October 1964. Released on bond, she moved to Kansas City where she slept with a number of members of the local Mafia. One of her lovers, Sam Puglise, became her regular boyfriend.

Before the new trial could take place, she and Puglise went on a trip to Mexico City. The fact that she signed a number of dud cheques before they left suggests she did not intend to return.

Four days later, on September 18, 1964, after a quarrel

Sharon Kinne. Her first possible murder, that of her husband using her small daughter to take the blame, might have come straight out of a novel: exactly the same ploy is described in Dashell Hammett's book, The Dain Curse.

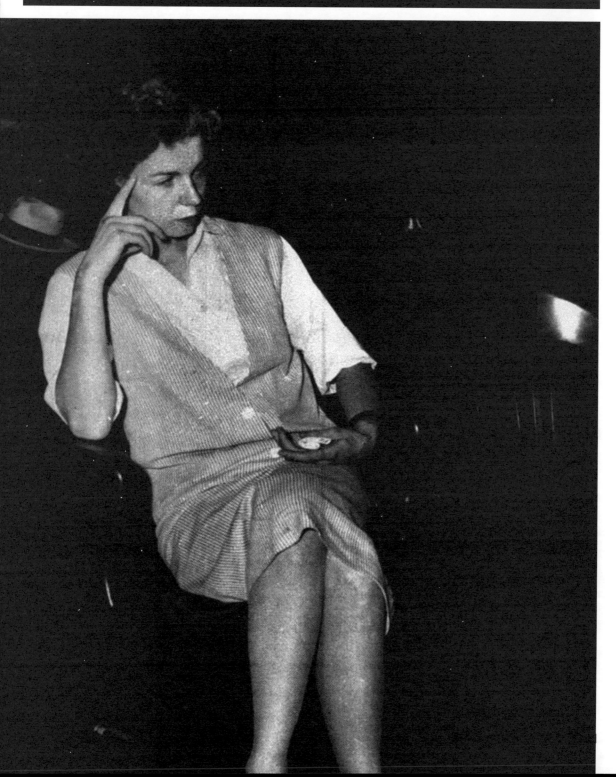

Patricia Jones was shot four times in the head. Her body was "discovered" by Sharon Kinne.

with Puglise, Sharon went out alone to a bar, and there met a radio announcer named Francisco Parades Ordonoz. She left with him and they went to a motel, where they registered as man and wife.

Several hours later, the manager, Enrique Rueda, went to investigate after he heard shots. He found the couple on the floor, wrestling for control of a gun. Sharon won, and shot Ordonoz twice in the heart, killing him. When Rueda tried to wrest the gun from her she shot him in the shoulder. But he seized the gun and held her until the police arrived.

Her story was that Ordonoz had attacked her, and she had shot him in self-defence. The Mexican newspapers nicknamed her "*La Pistolera*". When someone from the US Embassy came to see her, she unconcernedly told him: "I've shot men before and managed to get out of it."

Her comment leaked out and was reported by the press; it was virtually a challenge to the Mexican legal system. When she went on trial a year later, she was found guilty and sentenced to 10 years. She appealed, and three years were added to her sentence.

Ordonoz's murder had an interesting postscript. In the motel room occupied by Sharon and Puglise, the police found a .22 pistol, which was the same one that had killed Patricia Jones. However, under the law of double jeopardy she could not be tried a second time.

Top right: Police scour the area where Patricia Jones was found shot.

Right: Walter Jones: his affair with Sharon Kinne probably cost his wife her life.

Far right: Sharon Kinne under arrest for murder in Mexico City.

Not the end of the story

On December 7, 1969, Sharon Kinne escaped from Ixtapalapa women's prison, and has never been seen since. Strangely enough, although her absence was discovered at nine in the evening, it was not reported until two o'clock the following morning, giving her five hours or more to disappear.

She clearly received help in escaping – probably someone waiting for her with transport to take her to the nearest border, with Guatemala.

When a book about her, *Just an Ordinary Girl* (the words she had used to a reporter) by James Hays, was published in 1997, there was a renewal of interest in her story, and a section of a TV programme about fugitives from justice was devoted to her. But the search came to nothing.

She was 29 when she vanished – still pretty, and capable of arousing both desire and loyalty. She had also, no doubt, had time to reflect on the incompetence of her criminal exploits so far, and how this had led her to spend around three years behind bars. Probably she took this into account in planning her future career.

1967

THE DEATH OF JOE ORTON

On the morning of August 9, 1967, one of Britain's most gifted playwrights, Joe Orton, was battered to death by his homosexual lover, Kenneth Halliwell, who then killed himself with an overdose of sedatives. It was the end of a short and dazzling career.

Orton had been born in Leicester in January 1933, the son of a factory worker. The driving force in the family was his mother Elsie, who was a musician and singer, and she was determined that her eldest son John would rise in the world. She pawned her wedding ring so that he could take a business course in Clark's College.

Kenneth Halliwell, on the other hand, was the son of middle-class parents from the Wirral, Liverpool, whose father was chief cashier at the Cammell Laird shipyard. His mother, whom he adored, died when he was 11, planting the seed of a lifelong habit of self-pity, and the low self-esteem that went with it.

John Orton's heart was not in business, but in the theatre. At 17 he achieved a place at the Royal Academy of Dramatic Art (RADA) in London. He was just 18 when he came to the capital in May 1951, with a grant from the Leicester Educational Committee. He and two others shared a basement flat close to RADA. Halliwell came to RADA at the same time and found a flat in West Hampstead. When, a month later, Orton and his flatmates had to move out, they accepted Halliwell's offer to move in with him.

On the day they moved in, Orton wrote in his diary "Well!", on the next day "Well!!", and on the third day "Well!!!" – the exclamation marks probably recording his initiation into homosexuality.

Halliwell, who had a legacy (his father had also died), could offer Orton security. The downside of their relationship was that he was deeply and morbidly possessive, so that he glared at other students who even spoke to Orton.

After the RADA course, each went his separate way for a while, Halliwell to a small repertory company in Wales and Orton to an assistant stage manager's job in Ipswich. Soon both decided they had no future in the theatre, and moved back to share a flat in London and try to write novels. Where Halliwell was concerned, this was a shame. As an actor he could release emotions and aggressions, otherwise bottled up.

At this stage Halliwell was very much the master and Orton the pupil. Orton did not want to become a writer, but found that as he went on he gradually began to enjoy it. The discipline of working with the obsessive Halliwell was good for him. But as Halliwell's legacy ran out, cash became scarce and they had to economize on electricity,

getting up at daylight and going to bed at dusk. They aimed to live on £5 a week. In 1957 they went to work in Cadbury's chocolate factory to make the money to buy a new flat. This they finally did, in Noel Road, Islington.

By way of making their own small anarchist protest against a society they perceived as riddled with hypocrisy, they amused themselves by stealing books from the local library, making small but outrageous changes in the covers and blurbs, and then returning them unobserved, enjoying the puzzled or shocked expressions of old ladies who took them off the shelves. For example, in a book by the actress Dame Sybil Thorndike, in which an illustration showed her looking soulfully towards heaven, Orton pasted part of a photograph of a Greek statue, so she was gazing at mammoth genitalia, while the caption read: "I was working from dawn to dusk to serve… thousands of soldiers, sailors and airmen."

They did this from 1959 to 1963; then nemesis caught up with them. The librarian came to suspect them, and needed an example of their typewriter face. So he wrote them an official letter complaining about a van parked outside their flat. They wrote back a tart reply,

Joe Orton in his flat in Islington, North London.

using the typewriter on which they had been writing the indecent blurbs. Halliwell and Orton were arrested, and each given six months and a £262 fine, which cleaned out their savings.

As unpleasant as this sounds, it was, in a sense, the making of Orton the playwright. He wrote: "Before prison I had been vaguely conscious of something rotten somewhere: prison crystallized this. The old whore society really lifted up her skirts and the stench was pretty foul…" It had turned him into a Swiftian satirist. On Halliwell the effect was less fortunate, increasing his tendency to self-pity. A year after release he tried to commit suicide by slitting his wrists.

Rejection and isolation

Their novels, with titles like *The Last Days of Sodom* and *Priapus in the Shrubbery*, continued to be rejected. One publisher, Charles Monteith of Faber, thought they had promise and even gave a party for the authors. It was a failure – they sat on a settee and talked to no one but each other.

But they rather enjoyed isolation. They read a lot, and Orton learned something about style from the novelist Ronald Firbank, whose cool, civilized prose is full of demure sexual innuendos ("And how is your young grandchild's erotomania, Mrs Tooke?").

The two now began to collaborate on a play, *The Boy Hairdresser*, influenced by the theatre of the absurd and, in particular, Harold Pinter. It was about a man whose brother has been killed in a road accident by a careless driver – he provokes the driver to kill him so he will go to prison. This is presented with grotesque humour. The BBC liked it, and it was finally broadcast in August 1964 as *The Ruffian on the Stairs* (meaning death).

Orton became famous overnight, but Halliwell, who regarded himself as the architect of Orton's success, found himself regarded as nothing more than Orton's live-in partner, a mere appendage – and, moreover, a disagreeable appendage, since he was neurotic and self-assertive. (He refered to Orton's plays as "our plays".) Orton now began to daydream of getting rid of him and being allowed to pursue his new celebrity lifestyle alone.

The next play, *Loot*, was even more anarchic. Hal and Dennis, teenage homosexuals, tip the corpse of Hal's mother out of its coffin to hide the proceeds of a bank robbery. They conceal the corpse, bandaged like a mummy, in the wardrobe. Authority is represented by the absurdly conceited Inspector Truscott, convinced that he is a great detective. *Loot* is a brilliant farce that was an immense success, but this only made Halliwell more withdrawn and tense. He took to wearing sunglasses all the time and stopped greeting acquaintances. Halliwell was headed for a breakdown.

Orton failed to recognize what was happening – or if he did, only felt impatient about it. One friend later remarked: "Joe's real love was himself."

In May 1967, they went to Tangier, Morocco, where both slept with Arab boys. Orton wrote in his diary:"To be young, good-looking, healthy, famous, comparatively rich and happy is surely going against nature … I hope no doom strikes." But they had violent quarrels, one of which ended with Halliwell saying: "When I get back to England, we're through." Orton undoubtedly hoped he meant it.

Back in London, Orton spent much of his free time "cottaging" (picking up men for sex in public lavatories). He wrote about it in his journals, which he left around for Halliwell to read. Walking on the beach at Brighton, he records, he felt enraged at the sight of young boys in bathing costumes, whose bodies were forbidden to him.

While Orton was on a visit to Leicester, Halliwell went to the theatre where *Loot* was playing, met an actress who was in it, and confided to her that he was on the verge of a serious breakdown and had been in touch with the Samaritans – who take calls from would-be suicides.

On August 9, 1967, Halliwell snapped. As Orton lay asleep, he took a hammer and hit him nine times on the right side of the head. Then he took an overdose of sleeping tablets.

When a chauffeur called at 11.40 the next morning to take Orton to lunch with a producer, there was no reply to his knock on the door of the top flat. He peered through the letter-box and saw the bald head of Kenneth Halliwell on the floor.

On a desk the police found a note: "If you read his diary all will be explained. K.H."

Success at last

By the time the BBC accepted *The Ruffian on the Stairs*, Orton had decided to call himself Joe rather than John, because he was afraid people might confuse him with the "Angry Young Man" John Osborne. And, encouraged by the acceptance by the BBC, he went on to write a play, *Entertaining Mr Sloane*, in which a young man takes a room in the house of a respectable middle-aged brother and sister, who quickly set about seducing him. He is only looking for a free meal ticket, but when he loses his temper with the old grandfather and kills him, he suddenly finds himself entrapped. His host and hostess will not send for the police if he agrees to become their sex-slave.

Orton had found himself an agent, Peggy Ramsay, and she found a producer, Michael Codron, who had taken the small Arts Theatre for two years. Presented in May 1964, *Entertaining Mr Sloane* impressed many critics, but still lost money. Oddly enough, it was the playwright Terence Rattigan, whose own more conventional plays were now regarded as passé, who arranged for its transfer to the West End, where it ran for months.

1968

THE MAX GARVIE CASE

On May 19, 1968, Mrs Hilda Kerr went to the police station at Laurencekirk, Scotland, to report that her brother Max Garvie was missing. His disappearance, and the story behind it, would turn into one of the most memorable scandals of the 1960s, complete with wife-swapping, sexual perversion and murder.

axwell Garvie owned a 200-acre farm near Carnbeg, in Kincardineshire, and his beautiful wife Sheila was three years his junior. When she married him in 1955 she was 20, and within 10 years they had three children. He had founded a local flying club and gave it the use of a twin-seat Bolkow Junior, which he often used for flights to London, Hamburg, Amsterdam and Rotterdam. Later it would be remarked that these cities all have many sex clubs.

But all was not well. For Garvie was, to put it crudely, a sex maniac, whose wife began to complain to close friends about his sexual demands, which included sodomy. He became keenly interested in nudism, and founded a club in Aberdeenshire that soon became known locally as "Kinky Cottage". It was also observed that he spent a great deal of time with young men.

At a Scottish National Party meeting they met a young schoolteacher named Brian Tevendale, 22, who began to help out at the farm at weekends. He introduced the Garvies to his sister Trudy, married to a policeman, Alfred Birse. Soon Trudy and Max Garvie began to be seen drinking together at local hotels, while Brian and Sheila

Garvie also seemed to form a couple. Trudy's husband Fred seemed to accept the situation, particularly when Max Garvie gave a party and presented him with a hired lady.

If anyone doubted that they were engaged in wife-swapping, this ceased to be in doubt when Sheila Garvie disappeared to Bradford with Brian Tevendale. Sheila's mother, Edith Watson, moved in to look after the house and children. It became obvious to Garvie's friends that he badly wanted Sheila back. Finally, he persuaded her to go to London, where he flew to collect her. Suddenly it looked as if the game of sexual musical-chairs was over. It was said that Garvie had paid to have Tevendale beaten up twice.

Then, on May 14, 1968, Max Garvie disappeared. And once again, Sheila Garvie and Brian Tevendale began to be seen together. On July 26 they attended the wedding of Tevendale's friend Alan Peters in Aberdeen.

Meanwhile, an extensive police search had failed to turn up any sign of Max Garvie. His car was found parked across the runway at the flying club. The police began digging around the farm, dredged old wells, and directed enquiries to nudist clubs abroad.

Brian Tevendale was Sheila Garvie's lover, with the full compliance and encouragement of her husband, Max. However, when Brian and Sheila ran off together, Max became less understanding.

Then, on August 16, Sheila Garvie's mother went to the police at Laurencekirk, and told them that her daughter had admitted being involved in the murder of her husband, whose body was now in an underground tunnel at Lauriston Castle, near St Cyrus. It seemed that Sheila had confessed simply because she wanted her mother to share her secret. But Edith Watson was a churchgoer, and she

wrestled with her conscience for three months before she decided that she had to go to the police.

Sheila Garvie and Brian Tevendale were arrested; so was Tevendale's friend Alan Peters. The body of Max Garvie was found in the tunnel, covered with stones. He had been struck on the head, then shot with a rifle.

The two men were alleged to have gone to Garvie's farm-

Sheila Garvie (pictured above) found it difficult to keep up and comply with her husband's bizarre sexual demands.

house on the evening of May 14, while he was at a Scottish National Party meeting. They hid until he came home and went to bed, then went into his bedroom, where Peters struck him on the head with an iron bar to knock him unconscious, then Tevendale shot him through the head with a rifle. The body was then taken away in Garvie's car and hidden in the tunnel. In a book she later wrote, *Marriage to Murder* (1980) Sheila would insist that she took no part in planning the murder, but merely agreed to take part in a cover-up to protect her lover.

The trial opened in the High Court in Aberdeen on Tuesday, November 19, 1968, and the eager public began to queue more than two hours before it began. The swinging 60s had not yet reached this part of Scotland, which had always been inclined to sexual Puritanism, and the interest was feverish. They were not disappointed, as Sheila Garvie revealed how her husband had begun to show an interest in

kinky sex five years after their marriage, and had spent a large sum of money opening a nudist camp amid a forest of newly planted trees.

It became clear that Garvie had connived at the affair with Tevendale because the idea of having sex with his wife immediately after another man had possessed her intensified his excitement; when Tevendale and Sheila had spent the night lovemaking, she had to get into bed with Max for more sex. They even had three-in-a-bed sex. (Sheila would claim that her husband admitted to being in love with Tevendale.)

Trudy Birse, it seemed, was happy to supply the kind of sex Garvie wanted – he told Sheila Trudy had given him more pleasure in two weeks than she had in 10 years.

However, things went badly wrong when Sheila and Tevendale fell in love with eachother and ran away. Suddenly Garvie realized that he did not want to lose his wife. But it was too late – he had already lost her. And now the only concern of her lover was how to get rid of his rival. They went on to commit an almost perfect murder

Happy Ever After?

It would seem that the love between Sheila Garvie and Tevendale did not survive their ten-year imprisonment, which ended in 1978. Sheila then went to Aberdeen to manage a guest house owned by her mother's sister, but in 1979, married a Rhodesian called David McLellan. This lasted only a short time. In 1992 she married again, this time to a drilling engineer named Charles Mitchell, and at the time of writing is living in Stonehaven near Aberdeen.

Brian Tevendale had resolved to seek a new life in Gambia when he died of a heart attack at the age of 58, in 1993.

In 1999 it was reported in newspapers that playwright and actress Fiona Ormiston had contacted Sheila Garvie to ask for her co-operation in a play about the murder, but since nothing more has been reported of this project, it has presumably fallen through. It hardly seems likely that Sheila Garvie would have wanted to see the sordid and tragic story represented on stage.

– spoiled only by her attack of conscience.

Brian Tevendale and Sheila Garvie were each sentenced to life (which in practice meant 10 years), while Alan Peters was acquitted on a Scottish verdict of Not-proven.

Trudy and Alfred Birse were chased down the street by a jeering mob and had to take refuge in a newspaper office.

A large crowd of onlookers gather outside the court. People were scandalized at the goings-on of the Garvie household.

1970s

THE CAPE TOWN SCISSOR KILLING

Marlene Lehnberg started work as a clerical assistant and receptionist at the Red Cross Children's Hospital in Rondebosch, Cape Town, in February 1972. An attractive girl of 16, she was told that one of her duties would be to assist the chief technician of the orthopaedic (artificial limb) workshop, Christiaan van der Linde. Marlene later admitted that her heart beat faster the moment she was introduced to the fatherly, 47-year-old van der Linde.

Marlene's own father was a cold and distant man, more inclined to discipline her for the slightest infraction than to show her any affection or kindness. Christiaan van der Linde, a good-natured father of three, proved an irresistible attraction for the teenager. He later claimed that he had not aimed to have an affair with Marlene, but "a determined, intelligent woman in love is difficult to contain". Nevertheless, Christiaan and Marlene managed to work together for over a year before, in April 1973, beginning a secret, but passionate sexual relationship.

The affair lasted just under a year before van der Linde began to get cold feet. People at work had guessed what was going on, he told Marlene, and an anonymous telephone call had alerted his wife to their affair. Marlene begged him to come and live with her, but he flatly refused to leave his wife. If his wife were to die, he said, he would marry Marlene like a shot, but he would not divorce the mother of his children.

He had promised his wife, Susanna, that he would end the affair with Marlene, but insisted that, the girl being so young, he would have to do so slowly and gently. He therefore continued to see the teenager, and to sleep with her. Eventually Marlene decided to bring matters to a head herself. She telephoned Susanna and arranged to meet her. To her surprise, Susanna told her that she could live with the present situation: she loved her husband too much to lose him, so was willing to "play

second fiddle" if that would keep him with her. Marlene saw that this would actually mean she was the "second fiddle" – the occasional lover who was blocked from setting up home with the man she loved – so she decided to kill Susanna.

Her chosen weapon was an unlikely candidate – a destitute, one-legged patient of the orthopaedic workshop, Marthinus Charles Choegoe. He was a black man, and this was apartheid South Africa, so his word would be unlikely to be taken against that of a white woman if he chose to go to the authorities.

Eventually, on November 4, 1974, Marlene drove Marthinus to the van der Linde house herself. Mrs van der Linde was terrified when she saw the pair walk in, and tried to telephone the police. Marlene, according to Choegoe, tripped the older woman, who hit her head on a door as she fell. Marlene then hit Susanna on the head with the butt of the pistol she had

brought along, and ordered Marthinus to strangle her. When this seemed ineffectual, she ordered him to stab their victim with a pair of sewing scissors she had just found. He stabbed Susanna seven times in the chest, killing her.

Marlene had promised Marthinus a car in payment for committing the crime, but now rewarded him with a threat. She had found an anti-mugger paint gun, belonging to Susanna, and squirted the telltale dye on to her accomplice. He could hardly go to the police and claim innocence with that marking. She then drove him home and told him to get rid of her pistol and the paint gun.

The police soon picked up both Choegoe and Marlene. It apparently hadn't occurred to her that she would be an obvious prime suspect for the murder. It didn't take long for both the 19-year-old girl and the terrified cripple to be pressured into confessing. Marthinus hadn't even disposed of the guns. The trial caused a storm of publicity in South Africa, and few were surprised that, when found guilty, both were sentenced to be hanged.

However, the death sentences were withdrawn the next year following psychological reports. Choegoe served 11 years of his 15-year sentence, becoming a preacher on his release. Marlene served 12 years of a 20-year sentence. Christiaan van der Linde, an emotionally broken man, moved house to be near enough to put flowers on his wife's grave every day. He died in 1983 of a stroke. After the trial he had told a reporter: "I sincerely wish to God that I had never set eyes on Marlene Lehnberg."

LADY IN THE LAKE

Retired teacher, Gordon Park, nursed a grim secret for two decades after killing his unfaithful wife and dumping her body in a lake. In July 1976, he bludgeoned her to death with an ice axe, carefully trussed up her body and pushed it from the side of a boat into the murky depths of Coniston Water in England's Lake District. He thought he had got away with murder, but his luck ran out 21 years later when amateur divers stumbled across the remains of the 30-year-old mother-of-three.

Coniston Water where Carol Park's body was discovered 21 years after she first went missing. For years Gordon Park, Carol's husband, convinced his family and the community that Carol had walked out on him and their children.

Outwardly, Gordon and Carol Park appeared to have the perfect marriage. Both were teachers who holidayed in France and Britain; he was a member of the local Round Table, and she belonged to the Ladies' Circle. But beneath this seemingly happy, respectable veneer, Carol Park was a restless spirit. Whereas she was bubbly and vivacious, her husband was more controlled and careful, and their conflicting personalities led to discord in the relationship. During their nine-year marriage, she had several affairs and twice left the family home in Leece, Barrow-in-Furness, to live with other men. In 1974, she moved in with a man named David Brearley, who she had met on an Open University course, but returned to Park in the summer of 1975 after failing to win custody of the children. Although Park would later claim that they had begun to "pick up the pieces again", the arguments continued unabated.

On the scorching hot day of 17 July, 1976, Carol Park vanished. Gordon Park subsequently testified that he had taken the children to Blackpool for the day at the start of the summer holidays

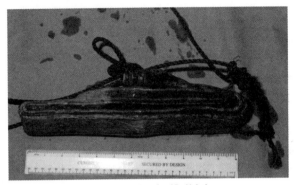

The lead weight and ropes used to weigh down Carol Park's body.

Carol Park, the "Lady in the Lake", who was brutally murdered by her husband.

and that his wife, who was feeling unwell, had stayed at home. When they arrived back at Bluestones, the bungalow that he had built himself, there was no sign of her. He told neighbours that she had left him, but he did not contact her former lover, David Brearley, to try and find her. There was no farewell note and, unlike on previous occasions when she had walked out, she left her wedding and engagement rings behind. She also left behind most of her clothes, all of her money and made no attempt to access the bank account. It was not until six weeks later that Park told her family that she had gone, and it was only then that he reported her disappearance to the police.

While Carol Park was listed as a missing person, Gordon Park got on with his life. He remarried twice and continued with his sailing hobby. The children grew up and left home, and he sold Bluestones in 1991.

Then, in August 1997, while he was on a cycling holiday in France, his ex-wife's trussed-up body, clad in a nightdress and weighed down with lead piping, was found by divers 25 metres down in Coniston Water, resting on the top of an underwater slope. Ironically, if he had dropped it over the side of his boat a few feet further out, it would have sunk much deeper and would probably never have been discovered. She was identified by dental records. The cold and damp had helped preserve much of the body, revealing injuries to her face caused by a weapon with a sharp edge. A finger on her left hand had been fractured as she tried to fight off her killer. On his return to Britain, Gordon Park was arrested on suspicion of murder but the case was dropped due to lack of evidence.

Just when he must have thought he was in the clear, Park was re-arrested in January 2004 and charged with murder. Now 60, he denied everything. During the ten-week "Lady in the Lake" trial at Manchester Crown Court, the jury heard how a search of Park's new home had uncovered an ice axe. All of the items hauled up from the lake were consistent with having been in use in the mid-1970s, and the ropes and knots used to tie up the body were identical to examples found at Park's house and on his boats. A wide range of climbing knots had been used and Park had been a keen climber in his youth. It was suggested that her rings had been removed to prevent identification. Even more damningly, stones examined from where the body had lain matched ones taken from the walls of Bluestones. Alerted by the publicity, a new witness came forward to say she had seen a man matching Park's description dumping a bulky item in Coniston Water from a dinghy back in July 1976. "He was wearing a wet suit," said the prosecution. "Gordon Park had at least one wet suit. He was of slim build, as was Gordon Park. He was wearing spectacles, as did Gordon Park."

After two days' deliberation, the jury found Park guilty of murdering his errant wife. Sentencing him to serve at least 15 years, the judge described the murder as "violent", but said he was not sure that there was a "significant degree of planning." Exactly why Gordon Park finally snapped all those years ago will probably never be known.

Gordon Park arrives at Manchester Crown Court for the start of his trial. Upon arrest, Park denied all charges against him.

JOYCE MCKINNEY AND THE MANACLED MORMON

The first indication of a bizarre scandal came on September 15, 1977, when Scotland Yard officers announced to the press that a visiting Mormon missionary – 21-year-old Kirk Anderson from the town of Provo in Utah, USA – had been abducted the previous day from outside his church in East Ewell, near Epsom to the south of London.

A young American calling himself Bob Bosler had telephoned Anderson a week before, asking to be schooled in, and hopefully accepted into, the Church of Jesus Christ of the Latter-Day Saints (the Mormons).

On Wednesday September 14, "Bosler" had pulled up at the front of the East Ewell Mormon Church in his car, got out and chatted pleasantly with both Anderson and another missionary. He had then asked Anderson to get into the car with him to point the way to the local Mormon headquarters on a road map he had there. Moments after both had got into the vehicle, the car suddenly sped away. The police were called in when it did not return.

Then, two days after the police announcement, on Saturday 17, Kirk Anderson reappeared. He was physically unhurt and had been returned to his lodgings in Epsom without a ransom being paid

or even demanded. Nevertheless, he insisted that he had been kidnapped.

The official police spokesman told the press that Kirk Anderson was helping them with their inquiries and that they were also seeking a woman called Joyce McKinney. She was described as American in her mid-20s, average height with shoulder-length blonde hair and a distinct Southern accent. She was believed to be in the company of another American – the sandy-haired, mustachioed young man who had called himself "Bob Bosler". Police now believed Bosler's real name to be Keith May.

Off-the-record journalistic niggling of the investigating officers also revealed that Kirk Anderson had claimed to have been manacled to a bed for at least part of his three-day abduction. This, combined with the fact that Joyce McKinney was said to be strikingly attractive, was more

than enough for news editors to work up some highly speculative but eye-catching front-page stories.

On Monday 19, Joyce McKinney and Keith May were

> 66 **HE HAD SEX WITH ME FOR FOUR DAYS. PLEASE GET THE TRUTH TO THE PUBLIC. HE MADE IT LOOK LIKE A KIDNAPPING.** 99

picked up in a police road-block on the A30 in Devon. Police soon found the cottage McKinney and May had rented – an isolated place on the edge of Dartmoor, near Oke-hampton. Inside there was evidence of recent habitation, including a pair of hand-cuffs, a set of foot manacles and a length of heavy chain attached to a double bed. Anderson's claim to have been held against his will seemed to have been confirmed.

Joyce was placed in a win-dowed police van, to be taken to the preliminary magis-trates' hearing on October 12. Turning to the van window closest to the eager press photographers outside the court she pressed an open bible to the glass. Written over the pages of the *Book of Job* were the words: "HE HAD SEX WITH ME FOR FOUR DAYS. PLEASE GET THE TRUTH TO THE PUBLIC. HE MADE IT LOOK LIKE A KIDNAPPING."

The first preliminary hearing was rather dull compared to the scene that had taken place outside the court. Joyce's profession was described as "model" and Keith May's as "trainee architect". Both pleaded "not guilty" on charges of kidnapping, but admitted to entering the country on false papers.

Joyce's counsel later made a statement to the press concerning her false pass-ports: she lived in fear of the Mormon church, he stated,

The Mormon beauty queen

Joyce McKinney turned out to be from a small village called Minneapolis in North Carolina (not to be confused with the city of Minneapolis in Minnesota). To the delight of the tabloids, she was found to be 27 years old, sported a "38-inch, C-cup bosom" and had been a successful beauty queen – Miss Wyoming 1974.

Joyce had apparently converted to the Mormon church after leaving Tennessee University and had moved to the town of Provo in Utah to immerse herself in her new faith. Joyce's mother told pressmen that her daughter had met Kirk Anderson in Provo in 1975, and soon after had announced that they were engaged to be married. However, Kirk had apparently broken off the engagement immediately thereafter and had subsequently gone away without telling Joyce where he was going. Joyce had been making frantic efforts to find him ever since.

Investigators found this all rather inconsistent. Joyce's choice of such a strait-laced religion and her mother's description of her as an "introvert" seemed rather at odds with her winning the Miss Wyoming beauty contest – not to mention her involvement in an alleged kinky kidnapping.

Joyce McKinney, out on bail, attends the gala opening of the movie *Saturday Night Fever*.

and carried false papers to hide herself from them. She believed, he went on, that the Mormons sought retribution on her as a convert who had later renounced the faith. Her continuing love and pursuit of Kirk Anderson only increased her fear that the Mormon hierarchy would seek to harm her in some way.

Joyce also made her own direct statement to the press when again being transported in a police van. She pressed a piece of card to the window, revealing the hand-printed message: "KIRK LEFT WITH ME WILLINGLY! HE FEARS EXCOMMUNICATION FOR LEAVING HIS MISSION AND MADE UP THIS KIDNAP-RAPE STORY."

The prosecution's chief witness was Kirk Anderson – the man whose charms had drawn a beauty queen across the Atlantic. In fact, Kirk Anderson cut a remarkably unstriking figure. His bespectacled, average-looking face topped a big body – at least 17 or 18 stone. Although he appeared to be more big-boned than actually fat, Kirk moved in a gawky, flat-footed shamble. He was arguably a fine example of a milk-fed young Mormon missionary, but he hardly looked the

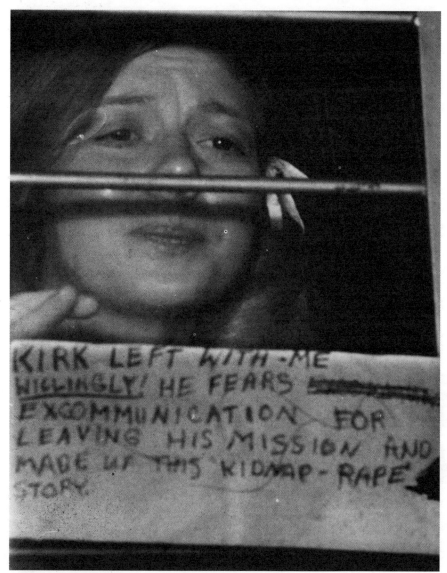

Joyce holds up a message to press photographers while being driven in a police van to her first court appearance.

to California to begin his missionary work early. But Joyce's continuing hounding of him had then driven him to relocate from California to Oregon, then eventually to Epsom in England. It was there that she abducted him.

Kirk went on to describe the actual kidnapping. He had met with Keith May and had agreed to point out the location of the Mormon Southern England headquarters on a map in "Bosler's" car. As they moved out of view of Kirk's missionary partner, May had pushed a gun into Kirk's ribs.

"He took me over to the car, that was parked 50 yards away, and I got into the rear seat. Joy was in the front seat wearing a dark wig and she had another gun.

"She said something like: did I think 8,000 miles of ocean was going to keep us apart?" May had then driven them to the Dartmoor cottage.

"I was taken to the bedroom and allowed to sit while Joy cooked dinner," Kirk continued. "She told me she still loved me and wanted to marry me."

That night, while Keith May had politely slept in another room, Joyce and Kirk had shared a bed, but nothing sexual happened that night. The next day May attached a leather strap to Kirk's ankle and ran a long chain from the strap to the heavy bed frame – "for Joyce's protection", Anderson was told.

catalyst of so much trouble in two countries.

Kirk described meeting Joyce at a Provo drive-in ice cream parlour. Joyce had liked Kirk so much that she had suggested marriage on only their third meeting. But Kirk had doubts, not only because he hardly knew Joyce, but because he was already signed up to do his tour of missionary work. He was also worried because he and Joyce had broken the rules of premarital chastity.

Kirk had confessed to his mother then to his bishop about his dalliance with Joyce, and was firmly told to break off his relationship and to ready himself spiritually for his missionary tour.

Joyce, Kirk told the court, "did not accept that position". She had made several embarrassing scenes in public and, to avoid further such problems, Kirk had been sent

1977

Joyce McKinney with her friend and co-defendant Keith May. Just what May's motivation was to help a woman kidnap another man so she could have sex with that man, has never become fully clear.

> **SHE WAS WEARING A NEGLIGEE. SHE CAME TO ME AS I LAY ON THE BED. I COULD TELL SHE WANTED TO HAVE INTERCOURSE. I SAID I DID NOT AND SHE TRIED TO CONVINCE ME. SHE THEN LEFT THE ROOM AND RETURNED A FEW MINUTES LATER WITH MAY. MAY WAS CARRYING CHAINS, ROPES AND PADLOCKS.**
>
> **Kirk Anderson**

"I had thought of escape," Kirk explained to the court, "but I didn't really know where I was."

Joyce emphatically told him that the price of his freedom – short of full matrimony – was to "give her a baby".

"That night [September 15] she spent the night with me in bed. I kissed her and held her in my arms. But there was nothing else."

The metaphorical gloves came off, he said, on the third night of his incarceration. "She was wearing a negligee. She came to me as I lay on the bed. I could tell she wanted to have intercourse. I said I did not and she tried to convince me. She then left the room and returned a few minutes later with May. May was carrying chains, ropes and padlocks."

The pair then tied and chained Kirk, spread-eagled on his back, to the four bedposts. Keith May left and Joyce ripped off Kirk's pyjamas and forced him to have full,

penetrative sex. The next morning, May and Joyce had driven Kirk back to Epsom and released him.

Prosecuting counsel Neil Denison asked Kirk: "You mentally didn't want it to happen, so how could it physically have occurred?" Anderson sheepishly replied that "she had oral sex" with him, to stimulate an erection.

Stuart Elgrod, counsel for the defence, cross-examined

Kirk. He asked Kirk how many times he and Joyce had made love on the night before he was released.

"Three times," Kirk replied. During the second two times he had been just as unwilling, he stressed, but allowed himself to be coaxed by Joyce because she had threatened to have Keith May chain him to the bedposts again.

"I am suggesting," Elgrod continued, "that at no stage were you ever tied up in that cottage except for the purpose of sex games." Kirk flatly denied this.

Elgrod's questioning later turned up the fact that Keith May had politely left Kirk and Joyce alone in the cottage for around 24 hours, but Kirk had made no attempt to escape, even though he must have guessed that Joyce would never shoot him (in fact, the guns turned out to be harmless replicas). "I was bolted in," Kirk replied, referring to his ankle chain.

Following his appearance in the witness box, Kirk Anderson did not return to the court, although his fellow Mormon representatives were always there in force.

The defence case emphasized that Joyce and Kirk had been lovers and, if Kirk had been less in thrall to his faith, would probably have been man and wife. However, under pressure from his religious superiors, Kirk had been forced to abandon Joyce and go abroad. Over the following year, Joyce had tirelessly sought out her lover and, when she discovered his location in England, had hurried to be reunited with him. He had gone *willingly* to Devon with Joyce and her friend Keith May. All three had regarded the trip as a rescue

from a heartless religion, not a kidnapping.

Unfortunately, after they had returned to London, Kirk's fear of excommunication from the Mormon church had overcome his happiness at being with Joyce. Instead of facing up to his religious superiors and insisting that he and Joyce were not going to be forced apart again, he had cravenly filed a claim of kidnapping and sexual assault against her. Elgrod ended on a Shakespearian note with a modified line from *Hamlet:* "Methinks the Mormon doth protest too much."

If Kirk Anderson had been a rather unimpressive figure in court, the same could not be

> **I WAS SUPPOSED TO PLAY-ACT THE PART OF A BEAUTIFUL WOMAN WHO HAD HIM IN HER LOVE PRISON. HE LAID DOWN ON THE BED FOR ME AND LET ME TIE HIM UP. I DID SO BY MYSELF – NOT WITH THE HELP OF KEITH MAY – AND PUT FAKE STAGE BLOOD ON HIM.**
> Joyce McKinney

said for Joyce McKinney. While wearing the sort of sober clothes that emphasized her claim to still be a deeply religious person – if not a Mormon any more – she still managed to show off the good looks and strong personality that had helped her win the title of Miss Wyoming three years earlier.

She had a rounded, pert face, a broad, winning smile and a slightly up-turned nose, all surmounted by surprisingly dark brown eyes for someone who claimed that her honey-blonde hair was to-

tally natural. She made the same claim for her apparently gravity-defying breasts. As she was being led back to the police van to be returned to Holloway prison, tabloid journalists shouted bawdy compliments. She paused, presented her full profile to the photographers and, indicating her upper body, shouted: "All mine!"

Neither Joyce nor Keith May gave evidence at the magistrates' trial, but following her defence lawyer's summing-up, Joyce announced that she would like to read a prepared statement to the court. She made her way to the witness stand with an ominously thick folder in her hand. Printed on the folder cover were the words: "THE GREATEST LOVE STORY EVER TOLD."

Joyce launched into what she plainly meant to be her big scene. For over an hour, she painted a picture of herself deeply in love: "I loved him so much that if anybody had tried to shoot him, I would have stepped in front of him and stopped the bullet."

But Joyce was scathing of Kirk's version of events. She and Keith May had carried guns, she admitted, but only to frighten off any Mormons who tried to rescue them from rescuing Kirk. He had guessed that the handguns were fake the moment he saw them. Climbing into the car of his own volition, Kirk had grinned at Joyce and said: "Hi, pintsize. Are you going to fight the whole Mormon army?"

Joyce positively scoffed at the idea that Kirk had been dragged away and held against his will. "I picked a romantic little honeymoon cottage because I wanted to get away from the smog of

Los Angeles. You should have seen the place when we walked in. There were presents everywhere for him and his slippers under the chair. I had a solid, 18-carat gold ring for him. It cost me over £1,000, but I wanted him to have the best. I just loved cooking for him, fixing his favourite meals and massaging his back.

"We made love several times at the cottage," she read on. "If he didn't like it, why didn't he just walk up to the people next door and say: 'Excuse me? There's a girl in the cottage next door and she's kidnapped me! She's there making my favourite meals and baking me chocolate cake, giving me better back rubs than my mother and making love with me!'

"Why didn't he do that?" she demanded. "Because nobody would believe him. They'd think he was a fool."

Concerning his claim of sexual assault, Joyce was positively scornful. "A woman raping a man? Him 18 stone and me eight stone? Come on! Who is kidding whom? His claim that he was unwilling makes me laugh!

"I was supposed to play-act the part of a beautiful wom-

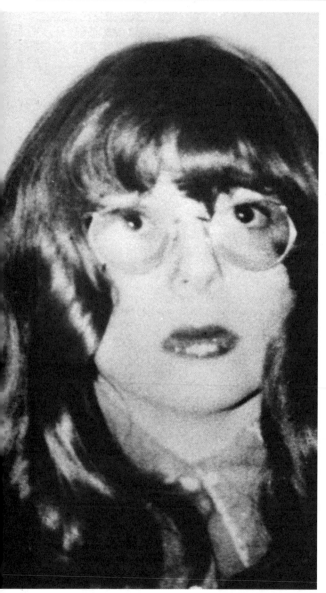

Tabloids in turmoil

Once Joyce was out on bail, the papers were frantically competing to buy her exclusive story. The editor of *The Sun* was said to be especially keen to pay Joyce to pose for the paper's "art" photo on page three. Specifically, he wanted her on a fake mountain, wearing nothing but skis and a carnation – although presumably he did not want her to push the flower up her nose. Joyce – in full religious maiden mode – indignantly refused the offer, insisting that she could never pose nude, whatever the payment. She *was* interested, however, in selling her story.

The *Sun*'s chief rival tabloid was *The Daily Mirror*, but they couldn't marshal the money to win Joyce's exclusive story. So, instead, they sent out a two-man team to California to dig for dirt in Joyce's past... and they found it. Joyce had funded her hunt for Kirk by posing for hardcore pornographic magazines and by acting as an "escort" to men with a taste for sadomasochistic pleasures. To her credit, however, the journalists could find no evidence that Joyce had actually had sex with anyone during this time – she had remained faithful to Kirk, in her own way.

Delighted by this scoop, and the damage it would do to Joyce's exclusive in *The Sun*, *The Daily Mirror* prepared to publish the revelations. But Joyce beat them to it. She and Keith May skipped bail and escaped back to America via Ireland before the case could come to trial. She was eventually found guilty *in absentia* and ordered to serve a year in prison but, of course, never returned to suffer the token sentence.

an who had him in her love prison. He laid down on the bed for me and let me tie him up. I did so by myself – not with the help of Keith May – and put fake stage blood on him. Yes, I tore off his pyjamas and it was : 'Oh! You sexy tiger!' But I acted the whole scene out for him. The whole works on *his* request. If he was so unwilling, then why was he lying there grinning like a monkey? Why was he moving his hips with me? I said, 'Honey, does that feel good? Do you like it like this?' And he goes 'Phew! Hot!'"

She continued with her reading: "At this point I think I should explain sexual bondage and Kirk's sexual hang-ups. Kirk was raised by a very dominant mother. He has a lot of guilt about sex because his mother over-protected him all his life. He believes truly sex is dirty. Kirk has to be tied up to have an orgasm. I co-operated because I loved him and wanted to help him. Sexual bondage turns him on because he doesn't have to feel guilty. The thought of being powerless before a woman seems to excite him.

Joyce in 1985 while being held for questioning after Kirk complained that she was following him around Salt Lake City.

"It was just amazing," she added, apparently off-the-cuff and in a tone of wonder, "he just kept going and going…"

Then she returned to her main theme: her defence against the charges. "He's had all kinds of temper tantrums after sex. I guess putting me in prison is an extension of those tantrums."

She ended on a plea to the court that would have done credit to Scarlett O'Hara: "This man has imprisoned my heart with false promises of love and marriage and family life. He has cast me into prison for a kidnap he knows he set things up for. I don't want anything more to do with Kirk. He does not know what eternal love is.

"All I ask is that you do not let him imprison me any longer. Let me pick up the pieces of my life. I ask you to let me out of prison so I can get a counsellor to help me get over the great emotional hurt I feel inside."

The bemused magistrates took very little time, however, to decide that it would take a full trial at the High Court to winnow the truth out of such a bizarre case. Nevertheless, Joyce's pleas had moved them enough to allow the release of both Joyce and Keith May on bail.

The crowd of reporters following the story were, if anything, more confused after Joyce's lengthy statement than they had been before. On the one hand there was Kirk Anderson, who claimed that an experience that most men his age would have leapt at was, to him, a terrible ordeal. On the other was the

attractive Miss McKinney, who claimed to have spent her life savings of $17,000 tracking, "rescuing" and pampering a man who returned the compliment by having her thrown in jail. Certainly most sympathy lay with Joyce, as Kirk had not been hurt in any non-spiritual fashion, but that didn't mean that her story was taken at face value. She was a little too much of a drama queen – a demure southern rose one minute, a roistering gal-o'-the-world the next – to be automatically believed.

" I WOULD HAVE SKIED DOWN MOUNT EVEREST IN THE NUDE WITH A CARNATION UP MY NOSE. "
Joyce McKinney

Then there was the ultra-mysterious Keith May who, up until this point, had

remained silent. An educated Californian in his mid-twenties, he did not, on first sight, seem the type to cross the globe to help two other people find true love. Throughout the preliminary hearing Joyce had sat next to May and held his hand. The pair's affectionate body language clearly indicated that there was some sort of a close bond between them but, the reporters wondered, just how far did it go?

However, such uncertainties certainly made for good news copy, and a comment that Joyce had made off-the-cuff during her statement to the court had the infamously lowbrow British tabloids in an excited fever. Describing the depth and passion of her love for Kirk, Joyce had said that, for him, she would "have skied down Mount Everest in the nude with a carnation up my nose".

Kirk Anderson had been sent back to Utah well before Joyce and Keith did their moonlight flit from Britain, but, regardless of his fears, he was not excommunicated from the Church of the Latter-Day Saints. Eight years later, now married and a father, Kirk complained to the Utah police that Joyce was shadowing his movements. She explained, when questioned, that she was preparing her autobiography, and was simply collecting information. The autobiography has yet to be published.

Before skipping bail, the usually taciturn Keith May complained about the bizarreness of the case: "[Britain] is a pretty strange country. If Joy had been busted in the US for doing what she did to Kirk, the only thing the cops would have done before they let her go was make sure they had her phone number."

1978

SID AND NANCY

The mid-1970s British punk rock movement was iconic by its very nature. In an anarchist rejection of both bourgeois conservative values and hippy pacifism, punks dressed like urban savages, embraced a cynical nihilist outlook and played songs that raged against the world. The most iconic of the punk bands was the Sex Pistols – shocking the staid public with lyrics like "God save the Queen! She ain't no human bein'." And Sid Vicious – the Sex Pistols' bass player who could barely play the instrument and deliberately spat on audiences – was the avatar of punk in the flesh. So the news, in October 1978, that Sid had apparently stabbed his girlfriend to death while out of his mind on a cocktail of drugs seemed to sum up perfectly what he and punk stood for.

In fact Sid Vicious was usually far from being a vicious person. Born John Simon Ritchie in London in 1957, he was a shy and good-natured child. His father left his mother before John was born and his mother, Anne, became a heroin addict under the stress of bringing up a child on her own. By the time he was 16, John was injecting with her.

In 1976 he became mixed up with the emerging punk movement and was soon a dedicated follower of the Sex Pistols. He took to hanging around the fashion shop of the Sex Pistols' manager, Malcolm McLaren, and was given the title "the ultimate Sex Pistols fan" by the Pistols themselves. When the group's bass player left, McLaren took Sid on as his replacement, despite the fact that Sid had virtually no skill on guitar. During concerts Sid's bass amplifier was often turned down, but Sid sang backing vocals competently and, as McLaren pointed out, he *looked* perfect.

Punk had freed something in Sid's soul, and he fully embraced the anarchism, the dress and, to a certain extent, the violence of punk. Certainly, despite being lightly built, he was willing to portray himself as threatening and barely civilized – the Sex Pistols' signing with A&M Records, for example, was promptly cancelled when Sid trashed the managing director's office and vomited on his desk. Yet, despite the punk façade, Sid

was generally introverted and good-natured. In fact, he got the name "Sid Vicious" as an ironic joke: he was nicknamed after a pet hamster owned by the Sex Pistols' lead singer, Johnny Rotten. The peaceable animal had been named "Sid the Vicious", because it occasionally bit people.

The Sex Pistols' career was meteoric, in all senses of the

word: the group shot to fame, but soon came crashing down again. In 1976, following the unexpected success of their first single, *Anarchy in the UK*, they were interviewed on the *Today* early-evening television show. The interview made British television history when lead guitarist Steve Jones repeatedly said "fuck" – the interview was live, so the expletives went out "un-bleeped".

The Sex Pistols' second single, *God Save the Queen*, was released in May 1977, shortly after Sid had joined the band (although the bass guitar part of the recording is reputed to have been played by a session musician, not Sid). The satiric song was promptly banned from being played on the BBC, but that

Left: The Chelsea Hotel on 23rd Street, New York. A famous refuge for artists, by 1978 it was becoming increasingly run-down.

Right: Paramedics remove the corpse of Nancy Spungen from the Chelsea Hotel.

didn't stop it making number two in the pop charts. (Some claim the charts were rigged to avoid the embarrassment of the song reaching number one in the same week as the Queen's Silver Jubilee celebration.) The Sex Pistols' first album, *Never Mind the Bollocks, Here's the Sex Pistols*, was also a hit and – because it presumably wasn't Sid who recorded the bass tracks – is still considered a classic rock album.

Then Nancy Spungen turned up. Nancy was an American, born in 1958 in the suburbs of Philadelphia. Her middle-class parents had found her almost too much to deal with; a hyperactive and violent child, she was given her first medical sedative at four years old and was receiving psychotherapy by the time she was 14. Nancy occasionally attempted suicide and took as many illegal drugs as she could get her hands on. She left home at 17, at her parents' despairing request, and worked as a stripper and occasional prostitute in New York. With spiked hair dyed platinum blonde, she flew over to London in 1977 with the express intention of "fucking

a Sex Pistol". Given the band's reputation, this might not have seemed such a difficult task, but Nancy's rasping personality got her passed off by Johnny Rotten and nicknamed "Nauseating Nancy". Then she met Sid, and he couldn't get enough of her.

Sid and Nancy's relationship was strongly based on their shared love of sex and drugs, but they also seemed to have earned the title, "the Romeo and Juliet of Punk Rock". Sid seemed to love the fact that Nancy was vitriolic and rude to everyone, including him. Nancy, on the other hand, found in Sid a lover who accepted her and didn't try to make her behave. Their relationship was sadomasochistic – both enjoyed being beaten by the other during sex – but that doesn't mean that, in their own way, they weren't genuinely devoted to each other.

Some have blamed Nancy for the break-up of the Sex Pistols, but that is largely unfair. The group's two-week tour of the US in January 1978 was a disaster on many fronts, and that seems to have been the main cause of the break-up. Johnny Rotten had a stinking head cold, Sid was

beaten up by the bodyguards hired to protect the band, the sound systems at the gigs were often faulty and some of the venues on their packed tour should never have been booked – country-and-western-loving audiences in the deep south actually attacked them while they were playing. Finally, at their gig in San Francisco, Johnny Rotten stopped a short way into the performance, shouted "Ever feel you've been cheated?" to the audience and walked off stage. He made a press announcement that he was quitting and the band fell apart.

None of the above can be blamed on Nancy Spungen, who was banned from the US tour, but her sharp tongue had amplified the tensions already within the group. Sid was totally dependent on her by now and, after the break-up of the band, Nancy announced that she was going to be his agent instead

of Malcolm McLaren. They moved into the Chelsea Hotel, a famous, but rundown, stopover for artists in New York. Nancy took Sid to meet her bemused parents (Sid apparently behaved very politely – only saying "fuck" twice) and organized a couple of solo gigs for her lover; but drugs were their main interest now, and they spent much of their time stoned or trying to buy more. An attempt to kick their various habits at the Spring Street methadone clinic went badly when the other addicts, jealous of Sid's fame and annoyed by Nancy's comments, beat Sid up. The pair went back on the drugs.

Physically and mentally they were both in a bad way; although barely out of their teens, they looked haggard and burned-out. The drugs had given Nancy a painful liver condition and both of them sported cuts and bruises from their sadomasochism.

Sid's usually good nature was also darkening – he talked of suicide, yet lived in fear of being attacked again. So Nancy brought him a folding hunting knife with a five-inch-long blade and a jaguar carved on the black handle…

At around 11 a.m. on the morning of October 12, 1978, an outside call came in to the front desk of the Chelsea Hotel. The anonymous male caller simply said, "There's trouble in Room 100" before hanging up. Then, before a bellboy could get to Room 100 to tactfully investigate, Sid Vicious rang down, shouting "Someone's sick. Need help." The bellboy arrived as the evidently stoned Sid was still on the phone to the front desk. In the bathroom was Nancy – dead. She was lying on her back in a pool of blood, wearing only a black bra and panties. The cause of death was a single puncture wound to her lower abdo-

men, and the killing weapon appeared to be the knife that she had bought for Sid only the day before.

Sid was still stoned when the police arrested him, but was heard to mutter something about Nancy falling on the knife. At the station he confessed to killing Nancy, saying, "I did it because I'm a dirty dog", but he could give no details of what happened. Malcolm McLaren raised the $50,000 bail and Sid was released into the care of his mother. She tried to help him kick the heroin habit while he was awaiting trial, but Sid, still only 21 years old, was on a downward spiral. On the night of February 1, 1979, Sid took three doses of heroin in a row and died before morning. In Britain, grieving punks wore tattered T-shirts with the words "SID LIVES" scrawled across them.

Shortly before he killed himself, Sid wrote of Nancy:

Vicious yes – but a killer too?

No trial ever decided whether Sid Vicious was guilty of killing Nancy, but the New York police apparently made no effort to investigate anyone else as a suspect. This is a pity, because it seems possible that Sid was innocent. He is known to have been out wandering the hotel corridors for most of the night while Nancy was phoning around trying to buy drugs. The anonymous outside call, warning of trouble in Room 100, and the fact that the hundreds of dollars Nancy was seen to have earlier that night were not found at the murder scene both suggest she was actually killed by a thief or drug dealer. Sid may have just found her and, in his drug-addled state, blamed himself.

> **❝ YOU WERE MY LITTLE BABY GIRL, I KNEW ALL YOUR FEARS. SUCH JOY TO HOLD YOU IN MY ARMS AND KISS AWAY YOUR TEARS. BUT NOW YOU'RE GONE, THERE'S ONLY PAIN AND NOTHING I CAN DO. AND I DON'T WANT TO LIVE THIS LIFE, IF I CAN'T LIVE FOR YOU. ❞**
> Sid of Nancy

Sid's arrest photos. He was still thoroughly stoned on a cocktail of drugs when arrested. When asked why he had killed Nancy, he replied: "I did it because I'm a dirty dog".

JAMES AND FREDA WILSON

In Auckland, New Zealand, in January 1979, a woman named Freda Wilson began to complain of stomach pains; a few months later she died in agony. The post-mortem showed, as her doctor suspected, that she had died of arsenic poisoning – arsenic administered in fairly small doses over a long period.

The only suspect was her husband James Wilson. What is more, he was also suspected of killing his first wife Norah, with strychnine. Norah Wilson had been found dead in front of the television set, with a bottle of lemonade in front of her. Her husband had a perfect alibi – he had been in Wellington on business that day. But he admitted that her death was probably his fault as he kept strychnine for killing pests on his farm in a lemonade bottle in the kitchen. Somehow, his wife had mistaken the strychnine for lemonade.

It had been impossible to disprove Wilson's assertion, and the police were unable to charge him with her murder.

Soon after the death of his first wife – from whom he inherited the farm – James Wilson married Freda. He had been having an affair with her since 1962, two years before Norah's death – another reason for the police to believe that he murdered Norah.

Now his second wife had died of arsenic poisoning. The Auckland police soon uncovered a motive – Wilson had been having an affair with a beautiful young girl who lived nearby.

Wilson denied that he had poisoned Freda. He insisted that he did not even possess any arsenic. But under the pressure of police interrogation, he finally admitted that he had murdered his first wife Norah – and what's more, with Freda's knowledge.

Norah and James were childless, and she refused to have sex with him. He met Freda at a trade fair and within hours the couple were in bed. They seemed made for one another. One day, James Wilson told her he had decided to kill his wife. She owned the farm – he was penniless when he met her, and he married her largely because she owned a sheep farm. So he evolved a simple and foolproof plan. Every afternoon, Norah watched television and drank a bottle of lemonade – she kept a row of them on the larder shelf. All he had to do was to introduce strychnine into one of the bottles, and make an appointment for the day she would drink it – she always drank the bottles in sequence. This is how he had come to be in Wellington while Norah died in agony.

Yet even though he had confessed to killing Norah, James Wilson continued to deny poisoning Freda with arsenic. Why should he? he asked. In fact, this question also bothered the police. If Wilson did not want to marry his beautiful young mistress, then why poison his wife?

This was a point made by the defence at his trial. The prosecution countered that Freda knew he had murdered Norah, and may have used this as a threat to make him give up his mistress.

The jury agreed, and (not least because he had confessed to murdering his first wife) found him guilty of the second murder. In April 1980, he was sentenced to life imprisonment. He immediately had a heart attack, and the following month had another, which killed him.

Terrible revenge

After James Wilson's death, Freda's best – and only – friend came forward with the true story. Jessica Lacey told how Freda had learned of her husband's affair. She had been driving along the road when she saw her husband's car parked near some bushes. On the other side of the bushes, her husband was sitting beside a stream, and the naked younger woman was bathing in it. James Wilson was begging her not to keep him waiting. Minutes later, she came out of the stream and they made love on the grass…

Freda Wilson had chosen an interesting method of getting her revenge. She had poisoned herself with small doses of arsenic, knowing that her husband would be charged with her murder. For the pleasure of destroying her husband's love affair, she had endured months of pain, dying in torment. The only person she confided in was Jessica, the only woman in the area who did not ostracize her after Norah's death. Jessica kept silent until her friend's revenge was complete.

1980s

1980

JEAN HARRIS

Towards 11 o'clock on March 10, 1980, the police in Westchester County, New York, received a phone call telling them that there had been a shooting at the house of Dr Herman Tarnower in the exclusive suburb of Purchase. Tarnower was among its most famous residents, having become a millionaire as a result of his book *The Scarsdale Medical Diet*. He was also Purchase's most successful Don Juan, with a taste for blonde mistresses. Never having been married, he was able to play the field.

The police met a car driving away from the Scarsdale Medical Center, which did a U-turn and led them back. The middle-aged woman who got out of it had blood on her white blouse. Tarnower's housekeeper, Suzanne van der Vrekens, pointed at her and said: "She did it".

Tarnower himself was lying between the two single beds in the bedroom, dying from three bullets wounds.

Jean Harris, the 57-year-old headmistress of an expensive girls' school in Virginia, had been Tarnower's mistress for 14 years. She told the police: "He slept with every woman he could, and I'd *had it*."

When Jean Harris met Dr Tarnower in 1966, she was 42, the doctor 56. The son of poor Jewish immigrants who had settled in Brooklyn, the intensely ambitious doctor had "played life to win". So he got rid of his Brooklyn accent and developed the smooth manners of one who is accustomed to wealth. Indeed, he was so good at card games that he once supported himself by gambling. Yet he was a curiously superficial man, for whom introspection was frightening or boring. He never read novels or took much interest in psychology.

Always sexually successful, he ruthlessly terminated relationships when he was tired of them. He ran the Scarsdale Medical Center with the aid of his latest mistress and secretary Lynne Tryforos, who at 37 was 22 years his junior.

She had been introduced to Tarnower at a dinner party, and the two highly intelligent people had found eachother fascinating. Soon, Tarnower was proposing marriage. In fact, he had never been married, and had just broken his promise to another woman.

Jean Harris and "Hy" Tarnower travelled widely and often spent weekends together in the Hotel Pierre in New York. The idea of marriage was tactfully shelved, for she realized that he valued his freedom. In 1971 she improved her professional position by moving to Connecticut as headmistress of a private school, then in 1977 she moved again to the Madeira School in Virginia.

Even as early as 1972 she was aware that there were other women in Tarnower's life – in particular the 29-year-old divorcée Lynne Tryforos, whose letters often followed them around the world. Mrs Harris regarded Lynne Tryforos as "a vicious adulteress and

psychotic". But the adulteress had the advantage of being at Tarnower's side most of the time. In January 1980, Tarnower took Jean Harris to Miami for the New Year, but on New Year's Day her holiday was spoiled when she saw a message in the personal column on the front of the *New York Times*; it read: "Hy T. Love always. Lynne." Jean suggested acidly that next time she might think of advertising on the Goodyear blimp. She was so obviously depressed for the rest of that holiday that Tarnower feared she was thinking of suicide, and increased the anti-tension drug he had prescribed.

When they returned from a subsequent trip, she found the clothes she had left in

Tarnower's guest closet cut and ripped; the housekeeper said that only Lynne Tryforos had been in the house.

It was after this it became increasingly clear to Jean Harris that her lover "wanted out". When she went to stay the night, she often found Lynne Tryforos's nightgown and curlers in his bedroom.

The week of March 7, 1980, had been a time of emotional stress for Jean; she had decided to expel four seniors when drugs were found in the dormitory. After that, she wrote Tarnower a 10-page letter, which she sent by

Dr Herman "Hy" Tarnower: famous dietary expert, best-selling author and septagenarian philanderer. He once commented: "I don't love anyone and I don't need anyone."

recorded delivery - because he claimed that some of her previous letters had failed to reach him.

One writer on the case has spoken of its "insults hurled at Lynne Tryforos, its paranoid obsession with financial minutiae and its pitiable, distasteful grovelling". It was the letter of a woman who hated herself for her weakness, and hated - as well as adored - her lover. After sending it - on March 10 - she finalized her will, then rang Tarnower to tell him she was driving from Virginia to his home in Westchester. "Suit yourself," he said resignedly. He did not realize she had bought a .32 revolver.

That evening, Tarnower gave a dinner party at which Lynne Tryforos was one of the guests. There was a conversation about wives murdering their husbands, and Tarnower remarked: "That is one of the advantages of being a bachelor - that could never happen to me." The party was over by 9 p.m.; the guests - including Lynne - departed and Tarnower went to bed early, as was his wont.

Jean Harris arrived at 10.30 and went in through the garage. She almost certainly expected to find her rival in Tarnower's bed, and was prepared to kill them both - and then, probably, herself. In fact, Tarnower was alone, and that should have defused her murderous intentions.

Unfortunately, Tarnower made two mistakes that cost him his life - first, he had forgotten to conceal his other mistress's nightclothes and hair curlers. As the light came on, Tarnower woke up and said: "Jesus Christ, Jean, it's the middle of the night." He watched resignedly as

Jean Harris stormed around the bedroom and threw the nightgown and curlers out of the window.

When she went into hysterics he applied the recognized remedy and slapped her face; she stopped screaming. But the sight of the nightclothes had revived her jealous fury; she opened her handbag and took out the gun. As Tarnower grabbed it, it went off and shattered his hand. Still holding the gun, Tarnower picked up the telephone and pressed the button that would connect him with his house-keepers, the van der Vrekenses. That was his second mistake - he should have thrown the gun out of the window first. Jean Harris lunged for it and, as they struggled, she pulled the trigger three times. Tarnower slumped between the twin beds, dying.

When a police patrol-man arrived minutes later, summoned by the van der Vrekenses, he saw a car with Virginia licence plates making a U-turn to lead him back. As he jumped out, Jean Harris told him "Someone's been shot." She went back into the house and followed the patrolman, up to the bedroom. As he tried to revive the dying man, Jean Harris sat on one of the twin beds and asked "Hy, why didn't you kill me?"

Her story was that she had driven up to Westchester intending to kill herself - in fact, she had placed the gun to her head before Tarnower wrested it from her. When she had asked him to kill her, he had said: "Get out of here, you're crazy!" The gun had gone off accidentally as they struggled, then jammed. But even after Tarnower had collapsed, she had tried to kill herself - she went into the

Jean Harris, Tarnower's lover of 14 years, who shot him four times "by accident".

bathroom and banged it on the bath to try to unjam it.

Jean Harris was arrested and fingerprinted, then taken to court in White Plains. There she was granted bail. Instead of returning to Virginia, she then admitted herself to a local hospital "for rest and recuperation".

Tarnower's death gave his book a new lease of life; to the delight of his publishers, *The Scarsdale Medical Diet* rocketed once more up the best-seller charts.

Jean Harris's defence at her trial, which began on November 21 before Judge Russell B. Leggett, was that her only intention in going to see Tarnower was to commit suicide. But the fact that Tarnower had been shot four times undermined her story that the gun had gone off accidentally in the course of the struggle. And if she had intended to give herself up, as she alleged, why had she tried to escape, and only made a U-turn when she saw the

police car with its flashing red light? It seemed clear that she was hoping to escape unrecognized, and that she only changed her mind and decided to "come clean" when she saw there was no hope of keeping her presence a secret. It seemed equally obvious that she had then decided on the suicide defence.

Jurors were impressed by her calm, quiet demeanour. But all that changed as they listened to the letter she had sent to her lover by recorded delivery, with its hysterical accusations. This made it very plain that she had driven to see Tarnower with murder clearly in her mind. Jean Harris, as it appeared, was obviously a calculating woman who would tell whatever lies might influence the jury.

In fact, it took the jury eight days to finally reach their verdict. But on March 29, 1981, she was sentenced to 15 years to life imprisonment.

The evidence presented in court made it clear that Tarnower was a lifelong seducer who took pleasure in having mistresses shuttling in and out of his bed – he is quoted as saying: "I don't love anyone and I don't need anyone" – and that he had undoubtedly treated Jean Harris very badly indeed. But the guilty verdict demonstrated that her plea of being under intolerable emotional pressure failed to convince a jury who recognized her as a highly controlled woman who killed out of hysteria and a desire for revenge.

She was eventually pardoned by Mayor Mario Cuomo on December 29, 1992.

Jean Harris' story has been filmed twice: as *The People vs Jean Harris* in 1981 and as *Mrs Harris* in 2005.

1980

DEATH OF A PLAYBOY CENTREFOLD

Dorothy Stratten's life was the American dream, crossed with the Hollywood nightmare – a Cinderella story with a monstrous ending.

She was born Dorothy Hoogstraten in 1960, in the British Columbian town of Coquitlam, near Vancouver. White settlers had named Coquitlam after the local Native American name for the area, apparently unaware that the word meant "stinks of rotting fish". The ironically named town was considered a rough neighbourhood by British Columbian standards but, nevertheless, Dorothy grew up a wholesome, sweet-natured girl. She was not noticeably pretty until she was about 16, when she suddenly bloomed into the sort of beauty that makes gawking men walk into lampposts.

In 1977 she got a job at the local Dairy Queen ice cream parlour, and was soon spotted by her future Prince Charming – at least, that's how small-time promoter Paul Snider saw himself. Nine years Dorothy's senior, Snider had little trouble sweeping the teenage girl off her feet. They started dating and Snider persuaded Dorothy that he could open up a glittering new world for her as a fashion model. In fact, he just sent her photo to *Playboy* magazine: a soft-core pornographic publication with a very

large readership. *Playboy* was then running a 25th anniversary new talent competition. Snider was disappointed that Dorothy wasn't chosen to be the "Playmate of the Year 1979", but was mollified with the offer for Dorothy to be the centrefold for the August edition.

Dorothy was mortified; she had been brought up to have a small-town girl's modesty, but the chance fof fame and the dreams of Hollywood imagined by Snider convinced her to agree. She posed for the naked photo shoot and suddenly she had Hollywood – or at least *Playboy* owner Hugh Hefner's fabled mansion – at her feet. She married Snider soon after and they set up home in Los Angeles.

The success continued for Dorothy, who now sported the professional surname Stratten. She was named the 1980 Playmate of the Year after another nude photo shoot, though she never felt happy as even a famous porn star. But by then the movie offers had started to come in. In 1979 she had played roles in *Skatetown, Autumn Born,* and *Americathon.* Admittedly none was a great movie

Dorothy Stratten and her husband Paul Snider celebrate Dorothy's 20th birthday in their West Hollywood home. Within seven months, Sneider would brutally kill Dorothy in that same home.

and her parts were not starring, but at least she got to keep her clothes on and better things beckoned. At 20, Dorothy Stratten was hot property in Hollywood.

All this was not entirely to

Dorothy poses for the cameras at the celebration of her winning the *Playboy* magazine title, "Playmate of the Year 1980".

the delight of her husband. Paul Snider now showed

170

his possessive, control freak streak. He forbade her to drink coffee in case it stained her teeth, fussily interfered with her acting on movie sets and, it is rumoured, poisoned her dog because he was jealous of the love she showed to it. Little surprise then that when director David Bogdanovich offered her the title role in the science fiction movie *Galaxina*, Dorothy not only took the part, but also moved in with Bogdanovich.

Snider was furious, but could do nothing but hire a detective to follow Dorothy; all this proved was that she was sleeping with her director, which Snider knew already. As a promoter Snider was totally out of his league in Hollywood, so he decided to experiment with his other talents. He built a prototype "bondage bench" – a love seat for sadomasochists, complete with numerous leather restraining straps. Not even LA sex shops wanted the bench, however, so the prototype gathered dust in his now lonely bedroom.

Late in the morning of August 14, 1980, Dorothy visited Snider at his home. She had withdrawn $1,000 earlier that day, and it is thought that she intended the money for her husband, possibly to buy his agreement not to oppose their impending divorce.

Snider was sub-letting the upper floor of his house to a doctor called Steven Cushner, but only Paul was at home when Dorothy called. At 12.30 p.m., Snider's private detective telephoned him, and was told

One of Dorothy's publicity photos. By 1980 her career as a nude model was over as she aimed to make a splash in the movie world.

"everything's going fine". Dr Cushner didn't come home until 7 p.m. and, seeing both Dorothy and Paul's cars in the driveway, took the outside stairs to his apartment to give them some privacy. He was telephoned at 11 p.m. by Snider's private detective. The man was worried because he had been trying to call Paul all afternoon, but nobody was answering.

Dr Cushner let himself into Snider's half of the house and, finding nobody about, cautiously peeped into the bedroom. They were in there and they were both dead. Dorothy was lying on

the waterbed, her head covered in blood. Paul was lying on the floor, on top of the Mossberg shotgun that had

killed them both. The bodies were crawling with black ants that had come in from the garden.

How she died

Police scene-of-crime officers reconstructed the murder. Blonde hairs from Dorothy's head were found in Snider's left hand, suggesting that he had forced her to sit on the edge of the bed, gripping her hair with one hand and pressing the shotgun against her left cheek with the other. Dorothy raised her hand to the gun and Snider fired, destroying the tip of her left index finger and killing her instantly. Bloody handprints on Dorothy's buttocks and the state of Snider's "bondage bench" suggested that he then had rear-entry sex with her corpse. Then, having returned her body to the waterbed, Snider killed himself.

The West Hollywood house where Paul Snider murdered Dorothy, sexually violated her corpse, then killed himself.

1981

SUSAN BARBER'S POISONED PIE

Michael and Susan Barber married in 1970, when he was 24 and she was 17. Susan already had a six-month-old baby that Michael thought was his, but it was actually that of Susan's previous lover. They had two more children and a lot of arguments over the next 10 years. Over that time Michael got into trouble with the police several times – for car-theft and indecently molesting his six-year-old niece – and Susan left her husband twice, but both times came back.

The Barbers were hardly an ideal couple but, by 1980, Michael at least had settled down; he brought in a regular wage from his job, packing cigarettes in a nearby factory, and was the well-liked captain of his local pub darts team. On that team was Richard Collins, married though only 15 years old, and also living on Osborne Road.

Every weekday morning, Michael would go off to work at 5 a.m. Richard Collins would leave home at the same time, even though his job started an hour later than Barber's. As soon as Barber was safely out of sight, Richard would let himself into Michael's house and into Susan's bed. This arrangement worked well, and Michael Barber might have carried on having no idea what was happening, if the lovers hadn't become over-ambitious…

On Saturday, March 31, 1981, Michael set off at 4 a.m. to go on a fishing trip. Why not treat the day like a weekday, the lovers thought, but with an extra few hours in bed together? Richard made an excuse to his wife and crept down the street

as soon as Barber had gone. But it was too windy for fishing that morning and Michael, returning much sooner than expected, walked into his bedroom to find his wife naked in bed and her teenage lover desperately dragging on his clothes. Barber punched Collins in the mouth and boxed Susan across the ear hard enough to leave a bruise: the latter blow was to cost him his life.

Despite the teetering state of their marriage, Michael and Susan decided to try to stay together – with Susan still secretly writing love letters to Richard Collins. On Thursday, June 4, Michael reported to his works clinic with a severe headache. The next day it was just as bad, accompanied by nausea. On Saturday he was sick enough to call out his GP. The doctor gave him a bottle of liquid antibiotic.

The next day Michael was having breathing difficulties and was rushed to intensive care. There his condition continued to worsen and a severe liver complaint was detected. His doctors thought that he might have a rare condition known as Goodpastures

Syndrome, but one registrar suggested that Barber might instead be suffering from poisoning – specifically, weed killer poisoning, which the doctor had read caused similar symptoms.

Blood and urine specimens were ordered to be sent to the specialist poisons' unit at New Cross Hospital. Whoever was supposed to do this, however, never got around to sending the samples. Then, when asked by the doctor if the results had returned, they covered their mistake with a lie: they said that yes the test results had come back, and they were negative. Thus, denied proper treatment, Michael Barber died on June 27.

While Susan was enjoying the good life, however, the wheels of justice were slowly turning. Four months after Barber's death, a pathologist finally examined the organ samples from the autopsy, and spotted possible evidence of poisoning. The records were checked and the lie about a negative test result from the poisons' unit discovered. Unfortunately the preserved organ slices were not enough to run a proper analysis, so it looked as

if the case would stop there. Then, eight months after his death, someone found Michael Barber's guts sitting in an anteroom of the mortuary; they had been dropped into a labelled bucket of preserving fluid during the autopsy. Testing these showed that he had, in fact, died of a lethal dose of weed killer.

Susan Barber and Richard Collins were arrested on April 5, 1982. Collins immediately admitted that Susan had told him that she wanted to kill her husband. Susan then admitted putting the weed killer in her husband's dinner of steak-and-kidney pie, but she insisted in court that she hadn't meant to kill him; just punish him for catching her in bed with Collins. "[I] just wanted him to suffer as I'd suffered," she said. But the fact that she had re-dosed Michael with weed killer in his antibiotic medicine showed that she had clearly meant him to die. Collins received a lenient two years for conspiracy to murder, thanks to the fact that he hadn't actually had a hand in the killing. Susan Barber served 10 years of a life sentence for murder.

COLIN THATCHER

On December 17, 1982, Colin Thatcher, the Canadian minister for energy and mines, was forced to resign from the cabinet of the then Conservative government. The causes of Thatcher's political downfall were his disreputable private life, his insufferable arrogance and his brushes with the law in his continuing battles with his ex-wife. Usually the aftermath of such a misfortune for a politician is a period in the political wilderness. But, in this case, within a week of his resignation Colin Thatcher would be arrested as a murder suspect.

Thatcher, born in 1938, came from a political family – his father Ross had clawed his way up the political greasy pole from small-town politics to become the premier of Saskatchewan – but Colin got little encouragement in his own political career from his dismissive and unaffectionate father. The older man often belittled his son's efforts and would coldly insist that one politician in the family was all that was required. It was only after the older man's death, in 1971, that Colin Thatcher seemed to come out of his shell and make real headway in politics.

Mr "right"

It was perhaps the unhappy relationship with his father that made Thatcher into what a psychologist would call a "right man". Right men can be utterly charming, provided nobody dares cross them, but if anyone that they consider inferior to themselves contradicts them, they can fly into an irrational rage: they are "right" men, because they cannot bear to be proved wrong. Adolf Hitler was a right man and a perfect example of why such people should be kept out of politics.

Another likely catalyst for Thatcher's increasingly arrogant and bullying demeanour was his new success in politics. Certainly his relationship with his wife had been generally a happy one before he got himself elected as member for the riding of Thunder Creek in 1975, but thereafter he treated her with a mounting coldness that verged on contempt.

Colin and his wife JoAnn had met while both were attending courses at Iowa State University. JoAnn was a brilliant student and, even in the patriarchal early 1960s, could have had a brilliant career in any one of a number of areas. But, on marrying Thatcher shortly after they left university, she had happily moved to his hometown of Moose Jaw in Canada, and took a low-prestige job teaching home economics to high-school students. Unlike Colin's father, JoAnn did everything she could to help his career in politics. She became the quintessential politician's wife, organizing public events and making social connections to boost his standing in the local community. Thatcher's election in 1975 owed much to her efforts, not least because she was now the main breadwinner of the family, having abandoned teaching to run a successful interior design company.

After his victory, Thatcher started staying out later and later and JoAnn guessed, correctly, that he was seeing other women behind her back. When she confronted him with her suspicions he would bellow abuse and threats at her and, on at least two occasions, blacked her eye. But it was a political betrayal that marked the beginning of the end for their relationship.

Thatcher, like his father, had run on the Liberal Party ticket but, in 1977, he defected to the Conservative Party – an act of self-interested career boosting, rather than of principle. Not only did all JoAnn's hard work making connections with Liberal supporters go down the drain but, at a stroke, Thatcher had wiped out many of the family's friendships. He hadn't spoken to his wife before his defection, so JoAnn naturally felt betrayed.

The marriage staggered on for another two years, with Thatcher becoming so blatant in his extra-marital affairs that not only his wife, but also his work colleagues and the media began to comment. Eventually, JoAnn could take no more.

In August 1979, Thatcher went on a five-day golfing holiday in California with his latest lover, and a friend called Ron Graham. Halfway through the trip, Graham made excuses and flew back to Canada, leaving Thatcher with his girlfriend.

It is a typical trait of right men personality types that

they have many extra-marital affairs themselves, but refuse to believe it possible that their spouse might do likewise. Thatcher was flabbergasted, when he got back to Moose Jaw, to find that JoAnn had run off with Ron Graham. His next reaction was also typical of a right man – he flew into a towering, hypocritical rage that his wife could dare to betray him in this way.

In fact, JoAnn had tried to be as fair as she could, under the circumstances. She could have taken all three of their children with her when she left, and would have been reasonably certain that the courts would have awarded her full custody. But she decided to leave their eldest son with her husband, since she saw what a close relationship the pair had. Colin Thatcher reacted by kidnapping the other two children from JoAnn and telling her, over the telephone, that she would "never find them".

The courts disagreed and awarded JoAnn weekend visiting rights while the matter of custody was settled. Despite this minor victory, JoAnn soon realized that Thatcher was poisoning their children's minds against her: the younger son and daughter were cold during her visits and the eldest boy flatly refused to see her. Thatcher himself was just as unpleasant and overtly threatening.

In 1980 the court ruled that JoAnn should have custody of the two younger children and awarded her $820,000 in the divorce settlement – this was the highest figure yet reached in a Canadian divorce case, but reflected the fact that it was actually JoAnn, through her interior design company, who had made much of the

money in the Thatcher bank account. Thatcher blocked payment and appealed. He then persuaded their second son to run away from JoAnn and took him out of Canadian jurisdiction to live with Colin's mother in the USA. Despite being charged with child-snatching and contempt of court for refusing to reveal the boy's whereabouts, Thatcher continued to be pugnaciously defiant.

On the evening of May 17, 1981, four months after marrying businessman Tony Wilson, JoAnn was standing in the kitchen of their house when she was suddenly knocked to the floor. She initially thought that the dishwasher door had burst open, then realized that someone out in the darkened street had shot her in the shoulder. She survived and the bullet proved to have come from a .303 hunting rifle, of the sort Thatcher had recently bought for their eldest son. Although Thatcher was an obvious suspect, the police made no effort to charge him. Some suspected that his political position was protecting him.

Thoroughly cowed, JoAnn agreed a divorce settlement of just $500,000 and also that Thatcher should have custody of the two boys. But Thatcher, according to friends and his new girlfriend, Lynne Dally, continued to be obsessed with his hatred for JoAnn. He even bragged to Lynne that it was he who had shot JoAnn. Unfortunately, according to her, she was so frightened she didn't dare go to the police.

Thatcher's appointment as minister of energy and mines, in May 1982, even further enhanced his arrogance and self-righteousness. Over the months that followed, his ques-

tionable political decisions, his unconcealed sex affairs and the persistent rumour that it was he who had shot JoAnn badly undermined his standing. But this did not stop him openly attacking the policies of his boss, Conservative premier Grant Devine, and few were surprised when Thatcher was forced to resign on January 17, 1983. But this was the sort of insult that no right man could easily take in his stride. Someone would have to pay…

Four days later, on January 21, JoAnn Wilson was attacked as she got out of her car in the garage of her house. Her assailant grabbed her by the hair and struck her repeatedly over the head with a heavy, bladed weapon, cutting ruts in her skull and, as she tried to protect herself, breaking the bones in her forearm and partly severing her left little finger. JoAnn fell screaming to the floor and her attacker shot her in the head with a pistol. A passer-by, Craig Dotson, was alerted by what he thought were the cries of a child. He saw a man of Thatcher's build, wearing shabby clothes and an odd-looking beard, running from the garage. Investigating further, Dotson discovered JoAnn's dead body.

Police naturally suspected Colin Thatcher, but had little to go on. Several neighbours had seen a furtive man with a beard lurking in a parked car before the murder took place, but none had got a good look at him. (Thatcher was beardless, but it seemed likely the murderer had worn a disguise.) Investigators also found a discarded credit card slip near the crime scene. The printing was partly illegible, but the readable letters "C. THATCH" suggested Thatcher

had been in the area recently. He was arrested but, with so little evidence, the police had to release him again.

The case gathered dust for six months before investigators got the break they had hoped for. An ex-criminal called Gary Anderson approached them and freely admitted that he had known Thatcher had planned to kill his wife. In fact, Thatcher had tried to hire Anderson to commit the murder for him, but Anderson had refused. Anderson now contacted Thatcher, claiming to be worried that the police might accuse him of the murder. During their conversation, which the police taped through a wiretap, Thatcher came close to admitting that he was the murderer.

Even so, the case against him was largely circumstantial. Such an experienced politician might easily convince a jury to give him the benefit of the doubt. Investigators delayed arresting him until May 1984, in the hope that more evidence might come to light but, as it turned out, Colin Thatcher was the best friend the prosecution had in the court.

On the stand, Thatcher was predictably charming and elder-statesman-like. However, when the prosecution lawyer, Serge Kujawa, suggested to him that defence witnesses, including Thatcher's sons, might have been persuaded to give false evidence, Thatcher flew into an immense fury. Bunching his fists he roared at Kujawa: "It's easy to say that my sons have lied. Why don't you step out of the courthouse and say that where you don't have immunity?" The jury were visibly shocked by this werewolf transformation.

Colin Thatcher was eventually found guilty and was sentenced to life with a minimum of 25 years to serve. He remains, at the time of writing, in a minimum-security prison, but is unlikely to be fully paroled becauseas he continues to refuses to admit his guilt.

Colin Thatcher achieved a cabinet level post in the Canadian government, but was unlikely to have gone any further. While his rampant egotism was quite exceptable in a political career, his brutal temper made him too many enemies.

THE PROFESSOR AND THE PROSTITUTE

One evening in March 1982, after working late, Professor William Douglas of the Tufts Medical School, New York, decided to unwind by picking up a prostitute. This was easy, since a red light district nicknamed the Combat Zone was next door to the medical school. In a bar called Good Time Charlie's, he was approached by a slim, beautiful 20-year-old named Robin Benedict. Douglas accompanied her back to her "trick pad" and paid her $50 for half an hour of sex. He found her so delightful that he visited her three times more in the next two weeks.

Forty-year-old Douglas was one of the brightest stars of the medical school, and was relatively famous in his own field of tissue research. He and his wife Nancy had three children, but had not had sex in years.

Robin soon had Douglas hopelessly enthralled. In spite of his professional pre-eminence, he lacked self-esteem – to begin with he was hugely overweight – and Robin made him feel good. He longed to spend time with her, as lov-

Professor William Douglas was a highly respected expert in the field of human tissue research. His obsession with a prostitute emptied his and his wife's bank account and eventually drove him to murder.

A middle-class prostitute

Robin Benedict's background was middle-class. Her father, a Hispanic from Trinidad, was a commercial photographer, while her mother managed a jewellery shop. A naturally gifted artist, Robin had attended a technical high school, and had fallen in love with a football player she had met after his team had played the school faculty team. She had no difficulty seducing him, and soon they were living together. But he was engaged to a black girl in Mississippi, and after a while his conscience had led him to abandon Robin and return home. Robin plunged into depression, and somehow became re-acquainted with a pimp she had met at a party with her former lover. So when Bill Douglas met her, she was making a thousand dollars a day.

ers do. At a hundred dollars an hour, she had no objection. So they took walks on the common and fed the ducks, went to films, and ate meals in her room – all at her professional rate. Soon he had emptied the joint bank account he shared with his wife of their total savings – $16,000.

He now thought of a way of saving himself some of the expense; he got a grant for Robin to work on his staff as an artist making sketches of specimens, for which she received $200 a week.

By now his obsessive love had turned to something more ambivalent. One night, he and Robin were picked up by a patrolman in a cruiser, and – as instructed by her – he denied giving her money and insisted she was his assistant; finally, they were allowed to go. Yet it was Douglas himself who had tipped off the police. Was this a way of making her grateful to him for his loyalty? Or maybe to make her give up prostitution?

In due course his wife Nancy found out. He admitted

Professor Bill Douglas being led into court in handcuffs. He claimed to have killed Robin with a sledgehammer "in self-defence".

everything and asked if she wanted a divorce. She said no, and he promised to give up Robin. But he did nothing of the sort.

His colleagues at Tufts soon learned what was happening, and assumed it was a middle-aged crisis. Then a check of financial records revealed that Douglas had been raiding the money intended for grants for the whole team. He was informed that he was under investigation.

There may have been another reason for the embezzlement: drugs. Robin was addicted to cocaine, and soon had Douglas trying it, too.

Now his resentment found another form; he broke into her apartment and stole $300 and an answering machine he had given her. And a message on this made him aware that she had a pimp. This was the real turning-point in their relationship. The $5,000 she said he owed her for past services may have helped.

With $25,000 Douglas had given her, Robin took out a mortgage on a house, and decided it was finally time to break off with him. She rang Douglas and told him they were finished.

On the last weekend in January, 1983, Douglas rang her and promised to give her

all he owed her if she came out to his home. When she arrived, he invited her upstairs. What happened next is moot, but the end result was Robin being battered to death with a sledgehammer. Douglas then placed her body in her Toyota, and took it to a garbage dump in Brookline, where he left it. It was never found – almost certainly destroyed by a garbage compacter. He drove her car to New York, removed the number plates, and left it in a garage.

Alerted by her pimp, the police went to Douglas's home and found Robin's jacket and personal belongings. They arrested him.

In court, in May 1984, Professor Douglas's defence was that he had killed her in self-defence when she had attacked him with the sledgehammer that she had brought to his house. Despite this unlikely scenario – Robin had little motive to attack Douglas, let alone with such an unwieldy and unfeminine weapon – the jury believed the professor and he was sentenced to 18 to 20 years for manslaughter. In fact, he was out in less than half that.

Robin Benedict was no common streetwalker. College educated with a good family background, she slipped into prostitution while in a state of depression following the failure of a relationship.

THE FATAL ATTRACTION OF CAROLYN WARMUS

It became known as the "Fatal Attraction" murder case because of its resemblance to the film in which the mentally unstable mistress of a married man tries to kill his wife.

Carolyn Warmus, the innocent-faced young teacher, at her first trial for the murder of Jean Solomon.

On the evening of January 15, 1989, a teacher named Paul Solomon ate dinner with his mistress, a sexy blonde named Carolyn Warmus, in the Holiday Inn in Greenburgh, near Yonkers, NY. At 41, he was 16 years her senior, and they had been sleeping together, on and off, for more than a year. His wife Betty Jeanne thought he was out bowling.

At 10.30 p.m., the meal over, they went out to his car – or rather, his wife's car, which he had borrowed – and after some petting in the car park, Carolyn fellated him. Finally he drove home at about 11.40 p.m. He found Betty lying on the floor, and closer examination showed she was dead, having been shot many times and clubbed on the back of the head. When police moved the body, they found a black glove underneath it, but, since an on-the-spot test for blood was negative, it was somehow forgotten and mislaid.

Money lying round the apartment indicated that the motive had not been robbery, and although semen was found inside the victim, this proved to be the result of

some last-minute lovemaking between the couple before Paul Solomon went out.

A check with telephone records revealed that an emergency services operator had taken a call from the Solomons' flat at 7.15 p.m., and that a woman had been screaming that someone was trying to kill her. But police had sent a patrol car to the wrong address. At that time, Betty Jeanne's husband had been leaving a bowling alley, where he had been watching the game, to go and meet his mistress. Although he had arrived five minutes before they were due to meet at 7.30 p.m., Carolyn had kept him waiting for 20 minutes. But she had seemed perfectly normal and cheerful, not in the least like someone who has just killed a love rival.

The case stalled. There was no evidence that Paul Solomon had formed a closer relationship with Carolyn Warmus – on the contrary, he took up with a fellow schoolteacher named Barbara Ballor. However, this caused Carolyn to behave in a way that directed the suspicions of the law in her direction. A

spoilt girl, daughter of a rich businessman, she was also intensely possessive, and her reaction to learning about Paul Solomon's new affair was to fly to Puerto Rico, where he was spending a weekend with his new girlfriend, and try to find out which room they were in – she had already found out which hotel. But Solomon had by this time begun to suspect that Carolyn was the one who had murdered Betty Jeanne. His reaction to the discovery that she was now trying to find

him was panic; he fled on the next flight out, even persuading the Puerto Rican police to give him an armed escort to the airport.

Carolyn now made her major mistake. She telephoned Barbara's mother and warned her that her daughter was mixed up with a man suspected of shooting his wife *nine* times. But the police had never released the information as to the number of shots fired at Betty Jeanne. They began to investigate her more closely, and learned that she had persuaded a private detective to obtain for her a silencer for a Beretta .25, the same type of gun that had killed Betty Jeanne. (Carolyn had hired the detective to watch another errant husband with whom she was committing adultery.) And her telephone records revealed that she had phoned the detective the day after the murder, apparently to ask him to hide the Beretta. It was also discovered that she had bought .25 cartridges on the day of the murder, using a stolen driving licence as identification.

After the second trial, the jury went out on May 21, 1992, and deliberated for six days, with many requests to look back at evidence and ask for legal advice. But in the end, they returned with a guilty verdict. The "poor little rich girl" was sentenced to 25 years to life – although, oddly enough, for second-degree murder. First-degree murder in New York state, because of a historic and legal anomaly, is reserved for the killing of policemen, court officials and other specific circumstances.

Below: Carolyn Warmus at her second trial in 1992.

Right: Paul Solomon, the husband of the murdered woman and the former-lover of the suspected murderer.

Return of the glove

The "Fatal Attraction" case generated tremendous publicity. But when the trial opened on January 14, 1991 a brilliant lawyer, David Lewis, succeeded in raising so many questions about police incompetence and muddle that it ended with a hung jury. Lewis also suggested that the glove found beneath the corpse –which, although mislaid, was visible in a police photograph – was a man's.

When the second trial opened a year later, the glove had not only been recovered, but proved to be a woman's. And testing with more sensitive equipment revealed the victim's blood – evidence that Betty Jeanne Solomon had grabbed it at the wrist with bloody fingers. Moreover, its fabric matched scrapings from below the dead woman's fingernails.

BK 40 13970 06-17-94

1990s

1991

THE PAM SMART CASE

In March 1991, a pretty 23-year-old widow was accused of persuading her 16-year-old schoolboy lover to murder her husband so that she could claim his insurance money.

It had all started on May 1 of the previous year, when neighbours of Greg and Pam Smart in Derry, New Hampshire, were electrified by a series of piercing screams. "Help! My husband, my husband..." When two men went to investigate, they saw her husband Greg lying face down on the floor, with blood running from his nose. The police who were summoned quickly established that he was dead. The post-mortem revealed that he had been shot in the top of the head.

Apparently the murder had been committed by a burglar, or burglars. The house was in wild disarray. Greg's wallet was empty, and various items – such as a TV and video – had been placed near the doors as if for quick removal.

When marijuana was found in Greg Smart's pickup truck, neighbours developed a new theory – that he had been killed by drug traffickers to whom he owed money. More than a month passed with no leads. Then, in the second week of June, the case broke open, creating a scandal that stunned New Hampshire.

Pam had many admirers at the school where she worked in Hampton. One good-looking 15-year-old called Billy Flynn turned to a friend after she had been introduced to his class and murmured: "I'm in love." And another student, 15-year-old Cecelia Pierce,

Pam and Gregory Smart on their wedding day in 1989. Within six-months, both were cheating on each other and within two-years, Pam had killed Greg.

also developed a crush on the young publicity director.

Both teenagers had a chance to get to know Pam better

when they collaborated with her in a competition to make

Bound to clash

Even as a high school student in Miami, Florida, Pam (or Pame, as she preferred to spell it) Wojas had acquired a reputation as a nymphomaniac. Her father, an airline pilot, alarmed by Miami's rising crime rate, had moved the family to New Hampshire.

On New Year's Eve 1985, Pam attended a party at the home of a young man called Greg Smart, who had a reputation as the local stud – at one party, he was said to have "scored" with three girls in the course of the evening, none of them knowing about the others. These two intensely egotistical young people saw one another as a natural challenge, but Pam seemed the more smitten of the two. Then, when she returned to the University of Florida, in Tallahassee, Greg startled his friends by announcing that he was moving to Florida to be near her. In January 1988, when Pam was 20 and Greg 22, they decided to get married.

The problem was that two such dominant personalities were bound to clash. Pam was determined to "be on top"; Greg had no intention of letting her.

Back in New Hampshire, the Smarts moved into Summerhill Condominiums, in the small community of Derry, and Greg quickly became a promising insurance salesman, while Pam took a step towards realizing her TV ambitions by becoming the director of the media centre at School Administrative Unit 21 in Hampton. Her job was to "generate positive publicity". Their condominium cost $750 a month, and they ran two cars. In their first year of married life, Greg earned $42,000, and Pam more than $29,000.

of a friend. He finally admitted that he had spent the night with another woman. Pam was outraged.

Pam's obvious revenge was infidelity. But with whom? Billy Flynn was the nearest choice. One day she asked him: "Do you ever think of me when I'm not around?" "Sure," said Billy. "I think of you all the time." Soon after this conversation, they drove to Billy's house when no one else was home. They went up to his bedroom to play records, and Billy locked the door. Tentatively, they exchanged their first kiss. Pam seems to have felt instinctively that she should move slowly.

In mid-February 1989, when Greg was on a skiing holiday, Pam invited Billy and Cecelia to her condominium. After they had listened to records for a while, Pam and Billy went upstairs; he stripped naked, and she went into the bathroom and put on a filmy nightdress. Then the two had sex. It was to be the first of many occasions.

Billy Flynn, Pam's teenage lover and one of the eventual killers of Pam's husband Greg.

a video commercial to advertise the nutritive qualities of orange juice. Pam enjoyed being group leader, and she accepted Cecelia's adoration as casually as she accepted Billy's obvious devotion. Billy was not happy at home – his father, an alcoholic, showed him little affection, but when he was killed in a crash caused by drunkenness, Billy was shattered.

Just before Christmas 1989 – when the Smarts had been married a little over six months – Greg came home at 6 a.m. claiming that he had spent the night at the home

A photo of Pam Smart, found in Billy Flynn's possession. The prosecution claimed it was evidence of the school teacher's sexual manipulation of her teenage lover.

Ralph had heard rumours of the killing from another youth. It seemed that the deal to murder Greg Smart had been discussed around the area for at least a month before it happened. Billy's affair with Pam was also common knowledge. So when Ralph Welch confronted JR and Pete with questions about the murder, they at first denied it, then told him the whole story. Ralph Welch was horrified, and told them that he could not keep silent. There were angry words. The following day, further arguments ended with Ralph being knocked to the ground. Ralph went to JR's parents and told them that their son had been involved in the murder of Greg Smart, and that Billy Flynn had killed Greg with a gun belonging to JR's father Vance.

Around midday on Sunday, June 10, Vance and Diane Lattime, determied to get to the truth, called at the police station and told them the whole story. Meanwhile, JR and Pete called on Billy Flynn, who had spent the night with Pam, and told him that all hell was about to break loose.

Later that day, the three boys fled in the car belonging to Pete's mother. But when they called on Pete Randall's grandparents in Connecticut, his grandfather called Pete's father, and Pete was ordered to return home.

What followed was inevitable. The boys were arrested. Cecelia finally gave in to police pressure when she realized she could also end up in jail, and agreed to ring Pam and try to get her to incriminate herself. Suspecting she was being taped, Pam would not even admit she and Billy were lovers.

Soon Pam was telling her lover that, if they were to be together for ever, they would have to kill Greg. At first he thought it was a joke, but her persistence made it clear that she was serious. Her plan was that Billy should go to their home and kill Greg while she was at a school meeting, to establish an alibi.

Oddly enough, Cecelia was also told about the plan. She pooh-poohed the idea. Billy, she said, was too gentle by nature. She later explained that she did not take the plot seriously. But Pam was deadly serious - as Cecelia realized on May 2, 1990, when Greg Smart was killed.

For a month the case marked time. But on the evening of Saturday, June 9, a youth named Ralph Welch listened with incredulity as two of his close friends, Pete Randall and JR Lattime, described how, together with Billy Flynn, they had murdered Greg Smart.

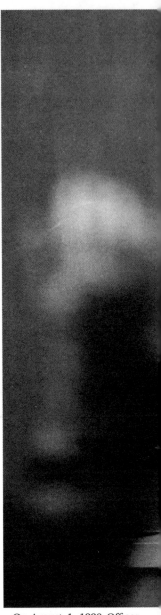

On August 1, 1990 Officer Dan Palletier called on Pam at work. "Well, Pam, I have some good news and some bad news. The good news is that we've solved the murder of your husband. The bad news is that you're under arrest."

Vance "JR" Lattime, the get-away driver, gave evidence for the prosecution against Pam Smart and won himself a lenient sentence.

Pam Smart takes the stand at her trial, clearly hoping that her conservative outfit might, to some degree, counteract the effect of her salacious reputation.

sentence. JR and Billy Flynn decided to follow suit.

On March 5, the prosecution began to tell the story of the murder. Later in the day, Pete Randall took the stand, and described in a flat voice how, on May 1, 1990, he had gone to pick up the car belonging to JR's grandmother, "in order to go to Derry to kill Greg Smart".

Three days later, Billy Flynn described how he and the other two boys had driven up to the empty house, and gained entry by an unlocked door in the basement. They lay in wait until Greg Smart finally came home, then Billy Flynn grabbed him and began to hit him; Pete Randall threatened Greg with a knife and made him get down on his knees. It was then that Greg pleaded for his life. This actually moved the boys – so much so that Pete Randall, who was supposed to slit Greg Smart's throat, could no longer bring himself to do it.

Pete then signalled to Billy Flynn, who took his revolver out, held it a few inches above the kneeling man's skull and squeezed the trigger. As he described the terrible scene, Billy Flynn cried uncontrollably.

When Pam Smart took the stand, she flatly denied her guilt. Her line was that her jealous schoolboy lover had carried out the murder without any of her knowledge.

On March 22, 1991, the jury was out for 13 hours. When they filed in, none of them looked at Pam Smart – a sign that they had voted for a guilty verdict. In fact, they had found her guilty on three counts: conspiracy to commit murder, accomplice to murder, and tampering with a witness. (She had asked a boy to give false evidence implying that Cecelia was a liar.) The verdicts were unanimous. Judge Grey sentenced her to life imprisonment without possibility of parole. Pam commented about her lover: "I can't believe Billy. First he took Greg's life. Now he's taking mine."

But for their plea bargaining, the three youths would also have received the same sentence. In fact, the two active participants in the murder – Billy Flynn and Pete Randall – each received 40 years, with 12 years deferred for good behaviour, a minimum of 28 years each. JR Lattime received 30 years with 12 deferred.

Pam Smart proved to have many friends, who defended her vociferously. But on January 22, 1991, these supporters were dealt a heavy blow when Pete Randall agreed to a deal with the prosecution in which he would testify against Pam in exchange for a more lenient

1992

AMY FISHER, THE LONG ISLAND LOLITA

On the morning of May 19, 1992, a teenage girl got out of a car outside a house on Adam Road West, Long Island, walked up to the porch and rang the bell. A housewife, Mary Jo Buttafuoco, answered the door and looked at the girl without recognition. The girl asked if she was the wife of Joey Buttafuoco and, when Mary Jo said that she was, the teenager told her that Joey was having an affair with her "16-year-old sister".

Shocked and angered, Mary Jo demanded to know just who the girl was, and what evidence she had to back the outrageous claim. The girl said that her name was "Ann Marie" and, as evidence, pulled out a T-shirt marked "Complete Auto Body and Fender, Inc" – the name of Joey's business. As proof of an affair the shirt was ridiculous – Buttafuoco regularly handed the T-shirts out to customers – so Mary Jo turned on her heel to go and telephone her husband.

At that moment "Ann Marie" pulled out a Titan .25 semi-automatic pistol and hit Mary Jo on the back of the head with it. Mary Jo fell to her knees, "Ann Marie" aimed the pistol at her victim's right temple and fired a single shot. She then dropped both the pistol and the T-shirt and ran to the waiting car. The man behind the wheel refused to leave until "Ann Marie" went back for the gun and shirt, then they sped away, just as neighbours were coming out to investigate the noise.

Mary Jo Buttafuoco did not die, although she came very close to doing so. Surgeons at the Nassau Community Medical Center operated on her for hours, stabilizing her condition, but were unable to remove the bullet from her head without the risk of killing her. She was taken to intensive care, where she remained unconscious.

In the meantime, police were interviewing Joey Buttafuoco. Nobody around Adam Road West had seen the shooting, but plenty of witnesses could testify that Joey was working in his auto body shop at the time. The police asked Joey if he could think why somebody would shoot his wife, and Buttafuoco gave them two names: Amy Fisher and Paul Makely. Amy was Paul's girlfriend, Joey said. Paul had asked Amy for money and Amy had turned to Joey for advice. Joey, who claimed to be just a friend to Amy, had advised her not to give Paul the money, but she had done so anyway. Maybe, Joey told police, Paul had heard about his advice not to lend the money, and had come gunning for revenge…

Investigators found this explanation unbelievable, so did not follow it up until, the following day, Mary Jo regained consciousness. She managed to tell the police what had happened and described the girl who had shot her: the description matched that given by Joey of his "friend" Amy Fisher.

With Joey's help, the police located and arrested Amy. She turned out to be a 17-year-old from a normal, middle-class Long Island family. But the story she told the police was far from normal. Amy had met the 35-year-old Joey Buttafuoco in May 1991. She had accidentally sheared the side mirror from the car her father had bought for her, and was frightened that he would be furious with her when he found out. So she secretly went to Joey's auto repair shop for advice. Joey calmed her, charmed her

Mary Jo Buttafuoco, with her husband Joey and daughter Jessica, shortly after Mary Jo left hospital. Against the odds she achieved a high degree of recovery, but suffered permanent paralysis down the right side of her face.

and helped smooth the matter over with her father. After that, Amy had started to hang around Joey's auto shop after high school…

By July 1991 the pair had become lovers, Amy told investigators. They would meet in local motels and, after lovemaking, Joey would complain about his relationship with his wife. He also, according to Amy, hinted several times that he wished to "get rid" of his spouse. Two weeks after they had started their affair, Amy discovered that Joey had given her herpes, but her feelings for him remained undimmed. By September Amy was worrying about money. She had lost her summer job as a shop assistant and owed a lot for a new car she had bought on credit. Amy claimed that Joey talked her into becoming a prostitute with a local "escort agency". She was soon making lots of money, but her education and her more conventional friendships suffered.

In November 1991, Amy claimed, she had given Joey an ultimatum: "your wife or me". Joey chose his wife. Amy reacted by trying to cut her wrists, but lost her nerve before she did any serious damage. Her family, unaware of her secret life, did everything they could to support her emotionally, but Amy could not let go of her obsession with Joey, or her jealousy of Mary Jo. At one point she even posed as a girl scout selling candy door-to-door, just to get a look at her hated rival.

Amy was continuing her part-time prostitution all this time, and had also started a relationship with the owner of a local gym, Paul Makely. In January 1992, according to Amy, she and Joey patched up their relationship, but she continued her prostitution and to see Paul Makely. Joey was apparently unconcerned by the whoring, but became very jealous of Paul. Was this, investigators wondered, why

> ## 66 WHEN [MARY JO] ANSWERS [THE DOOR], DON'T EVEN WAIT FOR HER TO OPEN THE SCREEN DOOR. JUST SHOOT AND KEEP SHOOTING. 99
> **Joey Buttafuoco**

Joey had clumsily tried to implicate Makely in the shooting?

It was an appointment at a beauty salon, on May 14, 1992, that proved the catalyst to attempted murder. Amy was having her hair done when the stylist, a schoolfriend of Amy's, complained that her boyfriend was seeing another woman. At one point, Amy's friend said something along the lines of: "if she doesn't leave him alone, I'll get a gun and blow her head off". It was the sort of thing people say all the time in anger, without actually meaning it, but it set Amy thinking… She asked her friend where she would get a gun, if she wanted to do something like that, and the name of a man called Peter Guagenti was mentioned.

Known to his friends as "Peter G", Guagenti was a 21-year-old college dropout from Brooklyn. He was contacted and agreed not only to provide a weapon, but also to drive the getaway car. That night, Amy told the police, she met with Joey and told him

---

Amy Fisher is taken into custody on a charge of attempted murder. The apparently normal, middle-class college student turned out to be a part-time prostitute.

Record-breaking bail

The story caused an international stir. The press headlined it as a "Fatal Attraction" case – after the hit 1987 movie about a murderous jilted lover. Amy herself was dubbed the "Long Island Lolita", after the Vladimir Nabokov novel about an under-age affair. The prosecution at the grand jury trial successfully painted Amy as a threat to the community: a self-confessed prostitute who even cheated the escort agency she worked for (Amy would see some customers privately, thus avoiding having to pay the agency a fee). The judge set her bail at a record-breaking two million dollars.

her plan. He, according to her, agreed wholeheartedly and even advised her on the best assassination technique: "When [Mary Jo] answers [the door], don't even wait for her to open the screen door. Just shoot and keep shooting."

The next day, according to phone company records, Joey contacted Amy on her pager, asking her to ring him. During that call, Amy said, Joey asked her again if she could get her hands on a gun. He did not try to dissuade her from shooting Mary Jo, she said.

Peter Guagenti picked Amy up on the morning of May 19, and gave her the gun. Amy claimed to have been surprised, because she had hoped Peter was going to do the actual shooting.

Amy gives evidence at her trial. Her good looks all but guaranteed a press feeding-frenzy.

Nevertheless, she steeled herself and walked up to the Buttafuoco house…

Joey Buttafuoco escaped without charge of complicity in the murder attempt on his wife, but was later convicted of the statutory rape and sodomy of Amy Fisher — at the time, a legal minor.

permanently paralysed, stood by her husband.

By the time Amy came to trial in December 1992, her name had been thoroughly blackened in the media. A former client released a pornographic tape he had made of her, and Paul Makely, on a prison visit, secretly recorded Amy saying that she deserved a Ferrari for all the pain and misery she was going through. Perhaps this was why Amy's plea that the gun had gone off accidentally cut no ice with the judge and jury. She was sentenced to 15 years in jail for attempted murder. Peter Guagenti was given six months for driving the getaway car and illegally obtaining a gun.

But if Joey Buttafuoco thought he was getting away scot-free, he was in for a nasty surprise. The following year he was charged and convicted, on Amy's testimony and the evidence of numerous motel registers, of statutory rape (sex with a legal minor) and sodomy. He served a four-month sentence.

Joey denied everything. He knew Amy, but had never been her lover. She certainly hadn't told him that she was planning to kill Mary Jo, and he had no idea why Amy had done it. Police were sceptical, but had no material evidence to link Joey to the killing.

Joey, still denying everything, was not charged at all. Mary Jo, now out of hospital but with the muscles down the right side of her face

Fame and fortune

While in prison, Amy filed a $220 million suit against the prison authorities, claiming to have been raped by prison guards. She was released, seven years into her sentence, shortly after deciding to drop the suit. After writing a book about her story, she went on to write a regular column in the *Long Island Ear* newspaper, finished her education, married in 2002 and started a family. Joey and Mary Jo Buttafuoco divorced in 2003.

JOHN AND LORENA BOBBITT

Despite, or perhaps because of, the amount of violence in the modern world, it's fairly rare for a criminal trial to shock the global media, let alone cause millions of men to automatically wince and cross their legs. The case of John and Lorena Bobbitt managed to do just that.

On the night of June 26, 1993, the emergency services in Manassas in northern Virginia received a hysterical 911 call from a payphone. At the address the woman caller had given, horrified paramedics found John Wayne Bobbitt lying on the floor of his bedroom, drenched in blood and clutching the stump of his severed penis. The end of his penis was nowhere to be found.

He was rushed to hospital where, while waiting for emergency surgery, Bobbitt was told by a doctor that he would never be able to have sex again and that he would have to get used to urinating while sitting down. At that moment Bobbitt decided that, as soon as he got out of the hospital, he would buy a gun and kill himself.

But both he and the doctor had judged the matter too soon. Police officers, doubtless moved to greater efforts by empathy, conducted a foot-by-foot search of the sides of the roads leading away from Bobbitt's house. After several hours, they found the decapitated member lying in a field. They packed it in ice and rushed it to the hospital. After a nine-hour operation the penis was successfully reattached, and doctors were confident that Bobbitt might fully recover its use.

The woman who had cut off Bobbitt's penis was his wife, Lorena. She was from Ecuador, and had married John in 1989, when she

was 19 and he was 22. The Manassas police picked her up soon after she made the 911 call and asked her why she had emasculated her husband. Her heavily accented reply was: "He always have orgasm and he doesn't wait for me to have orgasm. He's selfish." They charged her with malicious wounding.

Later Lorena claimed that she had attacked her husband in a state of temporary insanity, brought on by years of abuse and marital rape. She then charged John Bobbitt with marital sexual abuse. This was be a mistake, as he was acquitted, in late 1993, for lack of evidence. This meant that entering her trial for malicious wounding, beginning in January 1994, Lorena was potentially stripped of her main defence against the charge.

On the stand, Lorena insisted that John had habitually tortured her, both physically and mentally. An ex-Marine (he said the only reason he hadn't bled to death was due to his military training in pressurizing arterial wounds) John Bobbitt would, she claimed, often knock her to the ground and practise

Lorena Bobbitt: "He always has an orgasm and he doesn't wait for me."

Left: the prosecutor holds up a photo of the severed penis.

Below left: the knife Lorena used on John.

painful hand-to-hand capture techniques on her, some nearly strangling her. At other times he would show her photos of women that he claimed to be sleeping with. If she refused to sleep with him herself, he sometimes raped her, and when she became pregnant by him, she said, he had forced her to have an abortion.

On the night of the attack, Lorena continued, John had come in drunk, raped her and passed out on the bed. Lorena had gone to get a glass of water from the kitchen and, in a shattered state, had seen the beckoning gleam of a carving knife… She had come to her senses as she drove away, and discovered she was still holding John's severed penis. In horror she had automatically thrown it out the window, then driven to the nearest payphone.

Now friends of Lorena gave evidence that they had often seen her sporting bruises, and even several of John's friends admitted that he liked to brag about forcing his wife to have sex. John again denied ever abusing his wife, but was unimpressive on the stand and allowed Lorena's defence lawyer to catch him out in several contradictions. The fact was that nobody could believe that she would cut his penis off just because he always stopped making love before she achieved orgasm. The jury acquitted Lorena on the grounds of temporary insanity, brought on by marital abuse. After a 45-day evaluation period in a mental hospital, she was released scot-free.

Upright citizens

From the beginning the media had given the case enormous coverage. In a US poll, 60 per cent of people admitted to closely following it. Suddenly Lorena Bobbitt was a feminist icon – a woman who had struck at the mainspring, so to speak, of a phallocentric, male-dominated society. And afterwards? Following a lengthy period of recovery, John Bobbitt's penis was healthy enough for him to star in three hardcore pornography movies: *Frankenpenis, John Wayne Bobbitt: Uncut* and *Buttman at Nudes a Poppin' 2*. Lorena rather disappointed her feminist adulators when, in 1998, she was reported to have been arrested for punching her mother.

1994

THE TRIALS OF OJ SIMPSON

Just after midnight on Monday, June 13, 1994, a howling, blood-spattered Akita dog attracted investigation by neighbours of 35-year-old Nichole Brown Simpson. They found her lying dead in the garden of her luxurious Santa Monica condo in a partially enclosed area near the entry gate. Lying nearby was the corpse of 25-year-old Ronald Goldman, also murdered. Both had been dead for just over two hours.

Los Angeles Police scene-of-crime officers quickly reconstructed the events of the murders from the evidence. The angle of the wound on Nichole's neck indicated that she had been standing near and was probably conversing with the killer when he struck her with a long-bladed weapon, nearly severing her head from her body and killing her almost instantly. The 25-year-old Goldman then struggled with the murderer and was stabbed and slashed over 30 times. The murderer then escaped.

Even from this sparse evidence the police could some preliminary guesses: the killer was probably known to Nichole Brown Simpson, as he had been standing close to her when he attacked – people, especially women, tend to keep over an arm's length away when talking to total strangers. The killer was also almost certainly a man and, to judge by the strength needed to make such brutal and damaging attacks on two unrestrained adults, a very strong man at that.

(Right) OJ and Nichole Simpson appear here to be a happy couple at the opening of the Harley Davidson Café. Despite appearances, however, Nichole was soon to file for a divorce from OJ.

(Below) Nichole's blood soaked corpse. She had been killed by a single, powerful blow with a bladed weapon to her throat that almost severed her head from her body.

Ronald Lyle Goldman was an innocent victim. He was killed while he was trying to return a pair of sunglasses that Nichole had left in the restaurant where he worked as a waiter.

Life imitating art

Before he fell under suspicion as a double murderer, OJ Simpson's life had been a classic American success story. Starting his public career in American football in the 1970s, he was soon one of the most famous players in the game's history. Also, the fact that he was black and from a relatively poor background made him a living icon of the American Dream: that pure talent could take anyone, from any background, right to the top.

OJ retired from professional football in 1979, but maintained his public career and high popularity. His pleasant, affable demeanour made him a popular TV personality and he eventually branched out from the usual profession of retired sports heroes – sport commentary – to start a new career as an actor. His success in the role of an inept, accident-prone policeman in the hit comedy movie *The Naked Gun*, in 1988, made OJ a hot property in Hollywood. He followed this with another acting success, playing a black man framed by a racist cop in *The Klansman*. OJ also landed a lucrative advertising contract as the endorsing celebrity for Hertz car rental – in one TV advert for the company, OJ was shown desperately running through an airport, trying to catch a departing plane. The irony of these TV and movie images was later to be much commented upon.

Finally, although much more speculatively, there was the possibility was this was a crime of passion: a savage attack on an attractive woman and a young man, who might have appeared to a jealous killer to be her lover. (In fact Ronald Goldman was a waiter from a nearby restaurant who was – as far as we know – simply returning a pair of dark glasses that Nichole had left there earlier that day.) All the initial evidence seemed to point to Nichole's ex-husband: football hero and movie star Orenthal James "OJ" Simpson.

OJ Simpson married Nichole Brown in 1985. He had originally met her waiting tables in 1977, when she was 17 and still in high school. The simple fact that Nichole was white only served to highlight OJ as an example of the modern American Dream: in this case, showing that prejudice against mixed-race marriages was a thing of the past (in the well-off part of Los Angeles, at least). However, all was not as perfect in the relationship as was shown in the glossy magazines.

Nichole told friends and family members that OJ was violently jealous of her. She also showed them bruises that she claimed had come from beatings OJ had given her for playfully flirting with other men. OJ later denied ever hitting Nichole, insisting that the bruises had resulted from friendly games of "wrassling", but the very fact that Nichole was making such claims indicated deep problems in their marriage.

Few friends of the pair were surprised, therefore, when Nichole filed for divorce from OJ in 1992. She won a $433,000 cash settlement, plus $10,000 a month in child support for their two children. Some might consider the saving of $120,000 a year to be a further motive for OJ to have murdered Nichole.

OJ Simpson was in Santa Monica at the time of the murders – his house was only a few blocks from Nichole's – but he was not there when police called to inform him of the death of his ex-wife. He had caught a flight to Chicago at 11.45 p.m. – less than two hours after the killings.

A limousine booked to take him to the airport had arrived at 10.25 p.m., but the driver, Allan Park, failed to get any response when he rang the doorbell. Used to the often-eccentric behaviour of LA's upper crust, Park went back to the limousine and waited.

At 10.56 p.m. Park saw a big man in dark clothes walk up the drive and enter

The infamous "slow-motion" car chase: dozens of police cars follow as AC Cowlings drives Simpson around the LA freeway system. OJ spent much of it ducked out of sight, as in this picture.

concern", and phrased in such a way as to hint that OJ had killed himself, but without actually saying so directly.

OJ was soon spotted being driven by a friend, AC Cowlings, on the nearby freeway in a white Ford Bronco. There followed a farcical "slow-motion" chase in which dozens of police cars and a swarm of news helicopters followed the Bronco as it drove around the Los Angeles freeway system. Police negotiators talked to both men via mobile phone and OJ eventually had himself driven to his home, where he was finally taken into custody. The car was found to contain a gun, $8,750, OJ's passport and a false beard.

A 133-day "trial of the century" followed, starting on July 24, 1995. Television cameras were allowed in the court by Judge Lance Ito, and from the beginning the often tedious courtroom developments got as much news coverage as a war or a natural disaster. Asked how he pleaded, OJ Simpson replied emphatically: "Absolutely 100 per cent not guilty."

> ## " ABSOLUTELY 100 PER CENT NOT GUILTY. "
> OJ Simpson

The prosecution sought to show that Simpson was a jealous and abusive husband who had preferred to murder his estranged wife rather than see her with another man. He had, they said, con-

Simpson's home. He assumed that this was OJ, though it was too dark to make a positive identification. A few minutes later OJ opened the front door and told Park that he had been inside all the time, but had dozed off and had not heard the doorbell. They then drove to the airport and OJ caught his flight to Chicago without incident.

The police tracked Simpson to the O'Hare Plaza Hotel the following morning. The officer assigned the task of telephoning to inform OJ that his ex-wife had been murdered noted that OJ did not ask how, when or where Nichole had died – the usual questions immediately asked by a relative of a murder victim. He didn't even ask if the murderer had been caught.

Homicide officers questioned OJ for about half an hour later that day. He denied any knowledge or involvement in the killings but was, at the same time, vague about his movements on the previous evening. The investigators failed to press him on these points. Many people later thought this interview was too easy-going on Simpson. Follow-up questions were not asked and several obvious lines of enquiry were not pursued at all. The interviewing police did notice, however, that OJ had a bandage on his left hand. He told them that he had a deep cut to the palm, but claimed not to remember where he got the wound. OJ later claimed to have cut his hand reaching into his Ford Bronco car on the night of the murders. He had reopened the wound, he said, when, stricken by grief at the news of Nichole's

death, he had crushed a hotel water glass. The prosecution at his later trial claimed that this injury had actually been sustained while he was committing the murders.

The police allowed OJ to remain free, an almost unheard-of leniency for a person suspected of violent homicide. In fact, even after amassing enough evidence to issue a warrant for Simpson's arrest, the LAPD allowed him to remain at large until after Nichole's funeral. They simply asked the man they had charged with a savage double killing to hand himself in at his local police station at 10 a.m. the following morning.

Simpson failed to turn up. The police and Simpson's lawyer drove up to OJ's house, but found it empty. However, a note was discovered, prefaced: "To whom it may

Nichole Brown had been a 17-year-old high school girl when she first met OJ Simpson. Eight years later they married, and nine years after she was brutally murdered.

OJ Simpson's arrest mug shot. Despite the fact that he was strongly suspected of two extremely violent homicides, LA police allowed OJ to remain free until after Nichole's funeral; an unheard of lenience that led to accusations of "kid glove treatment".

belonged to Nichole Simpson. Furthermore, blood found at the murder scene had been DNA tested and, the prosecution claimed, had been positively proved to be OJ's.

Firstly, the prosecution presented witnesses to OJ's willingness to kill Nichole and of his predilection to marital violence. Nichole's sister, Denise Brown, described seeing OJ pick up Nichole and throw her against a wall. Denise also described seeing OJ at his daughter's school dance recital only a few hours before the double murder. She told the court that he looked "scary", like a "madman". Ron Shipp, a friend of Simpson, described OJ telling him: "I've had dreams of killing Nichole."

Next, and visibly disturbing to the jury, the prosecution played a tape of an emergency services 911 call made by Nichole before her divorce from Simpson. The eerie sound of the dead woman's voice filled the court, begging for assistance because, she said, that her husband had just

fronted Nichole and Goldman after letting himself into her garden. OJ had clearly planned to commit murder because he had brought a long-bladed weapon with him. After the brutal killings he had then made his way back to his own

estate, hurriedly disposed of some, but not all, of the evidence, then had caught a flight to Chicago.

The chief evidence for their theory, aside from numerous witnesses who had seen or heard OJ threatening Nichole

at one time or another, was the cut on Simpson's hand, dating from the night of the murder, and a pair of socks and a leather glove found in Simpson's home. These latter were stained with blood that DNA testing showed

beaten her and was threatening to do it again. OJ himself could be heard shouting furiously in the background of the recording.

Finally, the prosecution offered evidence that OJ Simpson had actually committed the murder. The limousine driver, Allan Park, testified to the apparent absence of OJ from his home at 10.25 p.m. – approximately half-an-hour after the murders – and the arrival of the unidentified man at 10.56 p.m. He added that when OJ had finally emerged from the house to go to the airport, he had been carrying a small black bag. At the airport, Park offered to carry this bag along with the other luggage, but Simpson refused

the offer. An airport staff member testified that he had seen OJ approaching a litterbin shortly after he had arrived, and OJ was not carrying the bag when he checked on to his flight a few minutes later. The implication was that this was how Simpson had got rid of the murder weapon.

OJ Simpson's house had not been empty on the night of the killing; there was a house guest called Kato Kaelin staying there. He testified that he and OJ had gone on a "run for Big Macs and French fries" at around 9.30 p.m. He had not seen OJ again after they got back. Then, just before 11 p.m., Kaelin had heard several loud thumps on his wall. Again, the prosecution

wished the jury to infer that after the food run, Simpson had slipped out, committed the murders and had been crashing about when he got back, trying to deal with the bloody evidence.

The physical evidence was the final, possibly clinching, proof that the prosecution presented to the court. First there was the wound on OJ's left palm. His vague explanations to the police could not hide the fact that the cut looked very much like a knife wound, perhaps sustained accidentally during a frenzied attack on someone.

Many technical experts were called to testify that hair, clothing fibres and footprints found at the murder scene

indicated Simpson's presence during the murders. There was also the blood of a third person found at the crime scene – DNA testing showed that only 0.5% of the population could have deposited this blood; OJ Simpson was one of this very select group.

The police had found a pair of bloodstained socks at the foot of OJ's bed and, even more damning, an extra large Aris Light leather glove, of a type Simpson was known to wear, was found at the murder scene. Another such glove – apparently the partner of the murder scene glove – was found soaked in blood, in a hallway of OJ's house. The inference was that OJ had attacked his victims wearing

An unfair cop

OJ Simpson's defence team – dubbed the "Dream Team" by the press, because they comprised some of the best lawyers in the country – sought to sow a seed of doubt in the jury's mind. In this task they were given invaluable help by one of the prosecution's star witnesses: Officer Mark Fuhrman of the LAPD (pictured right).

During the prosecution's questioning of Fuhrman (the officer who had found the glove in Simpson's house) he had been presented as a model policeman. The defence cross-examination, however, soon exploded this image. They asked him if he had ever used the "N-word" (nigger) to which he immediately replied that the word had never passed his lips. The defence then played an audio tape, which was made while he was acting as an adviser for a TV show about the LAPD, in which Fuhrman not only used the "N-word" with racist abandon, but also admitted to being willing to plant evidence to help secure convictions.

The Dream Team built much of their defence argument on Fuhrman's racism and admitted evidence-planting. The glove in Simpson's house, they insisted, had originally been at the crime scene with the other, but Fuhrman had dipped it in Nichole's blood and had transplanted it to OJ's hall. Presumably he also took a pair of OJ's socks back to the murder scene, dipped them in gore and then transported them back to be found by another officer under OJ's bed. Predictably (and arguably with good reason) the prosecution objected repeatedly to this purely theoretic line of defence, but, despite the lack of supporting evidence, Judge Ito allowed it to go into the record.

only his right-hand glove (there was no cut to the palm of the left glove), had sustained the wound to his left hand and had dropped the left glove at the crime scene. He then accidentally dropped the blood-soaked right glove in his hall during his efforts to clean himself up to catch his flight to Chicago.

DNA testing pointed to a 6.8-billion-to-one likelihood that the blood on the gloves and the socks belonged to Nichole Simpson Brown – she was probably the only person on the Earth with blood to match the samples. The prosecution case could not have had stronger supporting evidence … at least, that is what the numerous press commentators following the case believed before the counsel

for the defence began their attack on the state's case.

The prosecution attempted to win back the lost ground by getting OJ to put on the gloves in front of the jury. This was a crashing mistake because the gloves were self-evidently too small for him. Visibly shocked and demoralized at the complete reversal of their attempted coup, the prosecution team later pointed out that a leather glove soaked in blood would have shrunk, but the damage could not be undone.

Even what might have been a case-winning stroke in other circumstances could not save the prosecution. The defence called a doctor to state that, despite his bulk and regular golfing activity, OJ was a martyr to arthritis – he

OJ Simpson tries on the "murder gloves" at the request of the prosecution team. They seemed too small for him, but they may have shrunk after being soaked in blood.

was described as having a physique less like that of Tarzan than of "Tarzan's grand-father". The prosecution then played a recent commercial exercise video in which OJ was to be seen doing very vigorous exercises. At one point he even performed a number of punching movements while joking to the camera that this was one to try "with the wife".

The defence team argued, with little or no supporting evidence, that there was a racist conspiracy to convict the innocent OJ Simpson. They also presented character witnesses who swore to OJ's gentle nature and called their own forensic expert, Dr Henry

Lee, who rubbished the DNA evidence of the prosecution's blood samples. Today his evidence can be seen to be far from incontrovertible, but in 1994 accurate DNA profiling was still partly unproven and the science was mistrusted by members of the general public, so Dr Lee's gentle refutation of the prosecution evidence, despite having little or no conclusive evidence on which to do so, seems to have carried a lot of weight with the jury.

In the final summings-up, the difference between the prosecution and defence teams was thrown into sharp relief. Prosecution leader Marcia Clark spent much of her time attacking one of her own witnesses: Mark Fuhrman. He was the "worst type" of cop – one you wouldn't want "on this planet" – but Fuhrman's personal faults did *not* add up to proof of a criminal conspiracy to convict an innocent man or, indeed, prove that OJ Simpson was guiltless. The entire speech sounded defensive, even though her logic could not be faulted.

On the other hand, Johnny Cochran, for the defence Dream Team, was anything but defensive. He too attacked Officer Fuhrman, comparing him to Hitler. From there Cochran proceeded to attack Hitler's racism and "anti-religionism". What this had to do with the murders of Nichole Brown Simpson and Ronald Goldman is hard to see, but Cochran certainly managed to underline the dangers of white racism to a jury of which nine members were black. (Fellow Dream Team member Robert Shapiro later accused Cochran of "not only playing the race card, but playing it from the bottom of the deck".)

Cochran concluded by stressing that the jury should not convict if there was a shadow of a doubt in their minds. Harking back to the moment OJ put on the gloves and showed they were too small (or shrunken) for his hands, Cochran repeated several times: "If it does not fit, you must acquit."

The jury took just three hours to acquit OJ Simpson on all charges.

In his post-trial statement, OJ Simpson insisted that he would dedicate the rest of his life to tracking down the actual killer of his ex-wife. He got little time to do this,

however, as the bereaved families immediately filed a civil suit, demanding damages from OJ for killing their loved ones (civil cases can only award financial penalties).

Whereas Judge Ito in the criminal trial was very often criticized for letting lawyers on both sides wander off on wild and unproved theories, Judge Hiroshi Fujisake, who sat on the civil proceedings, kept a tight ship. All attempts by OJ's defence team to suggest that their client was the victim of a huge, if unprovable, racist conspiracy were instantly quashed by the bench. Only actual, solid evidence was accepted on to the court record this time.

Some new evidence at the civil trial showed that OJ Simpson had lied to police in one important matter – the footprints found around the murder victims. The prints of the murderer proved to have been made by a pair of

size 12 Bruno Magli shoes. Simpson had denied ever owning such a pair of shoes, but pictures taken before the murders were found by the newspapers, clearly showing Simpson wearing Bruno Magli shoes of the type that had made the prints. Simpson's feet were size 12.

OJ Simpson had not been called to give evidence in the criminal trial, but was forced to in the civil case. He made a bad impression on the stand, mumbling replies to questions and looking furtive.

After 17 hours, the civil jury concluded that Simpson was guilty of the "wrongfully caused deaths of Ronald Goldman and Nichole Brown Simpson". He was ordered to pay compensatory damages of $8.5 million to the bereaved families and $25 million in punitive damages. This did not reduce him to a pauper because, under California law, he was able to set up a $25,000-a-month pension

fund that could not be touched by any legal judgment against him.

In America, as under most legal systems, OJ Simpson cannot be put before a criminal court twice for the same crime without dramatic new evidence coming to light that calls for a verdict of "mistrial" on the first case. He is, therefore, likely to remain in legal limbo – found both guilty and not guilty of savage murder.

It is perhaps indicative that, despite his promise to "hunt down" his ex-wife's killer, OJ Simpson has apparently done nothing visible towards that end. It is also interesting that Johnny Cochran – the man most responsible for getting OJ acquitted in the criminal trial – is said to have told a friend: "OJ is in massive denial. He obviously did it."

OJ Simpson on hearing his acquittal at his criminal murder trial. He was less happy at the verdict of his subsequent civil trial for "wrongfully causing death".

1994

SUSAN SMITH

At around 9 p.m. on October 25, 1994, Shirley McCloud was sitting reading the newspaper in her South Carolina home, close to John D Long Lake and the town of Union. Suddenly there was a pounding on her front door. She opened it to find a hysterical young white woman who wailed: "Please help me! He's got my kids. He's got my car."

While her husband called the police, Shirley calmed the woman down enough to find out what had happened. The woman, called Susan Smith, said that she had been driving through nearby Monarch Mills and had pulled up at a red light. Out of the night a strange man had pulled open the front passenger door, climbed in and menaced her with a gun. After forcing her to drive four miles to the turn-off sign to John D Long Lake, he had told her to stop and had forced her out of the car. She had pointed to her two sons – Michael, aged three, and Daniel, aged just 14 months – strapped into the back seat, and begged him to let her take them with her. He replied: "I don't have time. Don't worry. I won't hurt your kids." Then he had driven away.

It was a heart-rending story, but it was a lie. Michael and Daniel were already dead, and their mother was perfectly aware that they were.

The local sheriff, Howard Wells, arrived and took Susan's statement. In fact he knew her – her brother Scott was an old friend of his – so he was initially inclined to believe every word. He was more worried that she claimed that the kidnapper was black. South Carolina had come a long way from the racist heyday of the Ku Klux Klan and the official repression of black civil rights, but something as shocking as an African-American kidnapping two helpless white children was bound to escalate race tensions in the community. On the positive side, black men very rarely drove around with white children, so Wells was reasonably confident that the kidnapper would soon be spotted and the children returned to their mother.

That confidence flagged over the coming days, as did his belief that Susan Smith was telling the whole truth. The sketch artist who made up the picture of the kidnapper told investigators that Susan had been vague in giving his description, despite the fact that the faces of strangers who menace people with guns tend to be burned into their victims' memories.

And the police were soon fairly certain that Susan knew more than she was saying about where the boys were. Over the next week she was given over half a dozen lie-detector tests, all of which proved indecisive except over one question: she was clearly lying when she said that she didn't know the boys' location. An initial hope that she had hidden the boys in some safe but secret place, because of a presumed custody battle with her estranged husband, soon collapsed. David and Susan Smith had a fairly equable relationship and David had no intention of trying to take the boys from their mother's home. Police divers, fearing the worst however, searched

John D Long Lake twice, but found nothing.

Another cause of suspicion was Susan's insistence that there had been no other cars about when she pulled up at the red light at Monarch Mills: Sheriff Wells knew for a fact that that traffic light was set be permanently green, unless a car coming crosswise triggered the other lights – this couldn't have happened if there were no other cars (or witnesses) about. Confronted with this fact, Susan changed her story, now saying that the carjacking had actually been at the Carlisle intersection. But Wells also knew for a fact

Everyone agreed that Susan Smith (left), 23, was a model mother. She was hard-working, dedicated to her two children and even maintained a good relation with her estranged husband, David, so that the boys wouldn't feel the lack of a father.

that, on October 25, there had been an undercover police anti-drugs operation going on at the Carlisle intersection, and that officers there would almost certainly have spotted a carjacking.

Finally, there was the question as to why Susan Smith had been out with her boys in the first place. She said that she had gone shopping in a Wal-Mart store and then had been driving to visit a friend when the carjacker struck. The friend in question denied any knowledge that Susan was coming round, and all the employees of the Wal-Mart insisted that they hadn't seen a woman with a little boy and a baby. Susan then admitted that she had actually been driving around at random for over an hour.

The reason why came out when her boss, Tom Findley,

told police that he and Susan had openly dated, on-and-off, for the past few months. Susan had recently separated from the boys' father, David, and clearly hoped to start a long-term relationship with Findley. But, Tom said, he had broken off the relation-ship just before the night of the supposed carjacking. The reason: Findley hadn't wanted to be deeply involved with the mother of another man's children. The two boys had been the main bar to Susan marrying a handsome, rich and important man…

Susan Smith finally cracked on the ninth day of the investigation, admitting that she had killed her own children.

She had been depressed by Findley's rejection, she

told investigators. That night she had strapped the boys into the car and had driven randomly, wondering what she could do with what she saw as her empty life. She considered suicide, but couldn't bear the thought of Michael and Daniel growing up without a mother: so she decided to take them with her "into God's hands".

She had pulled up at the top of the 75-foot boat ramp running down into John D Long Lake and let the car trundle forward with the automatic gears disengaged. But she couldn't do it and handbraked to a stop after travelling just a few feet. She got out of the car and looked at the boys still sleeping peacefully on the back seat.

(Below) Susan's two sons: Michael, aged three, and Daniel, aged 14 months. Had their mother callously drowned the children on a mere whim?

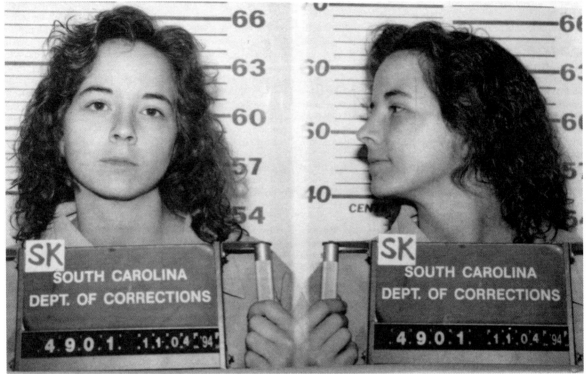

Then she reached through the open driver's door and released the handbrake. The car rolled on to the water and floated out into the lake. The nose quickly sank, under the weight of the engine, but the back, containing the terrified boys, took some minutes to sink out of sight.

If Susan had intended to kill herself immediately after killing her boys, she now abandoned that plan. She ran to the nearest house, half a mile away, concocting the carjacking story as she went.

The confession and arrest over, Sheriff Wells now had the terrible task of informing the other family members. David Smith, despite being estranged from his wife, had steadfastly stood by Susan when, in recent days, the press had speculated that she

might be involved in the boys' disappearance. Now he had to be told that the woman he had so firmly defended had in actual fact sent their sons to a horrible death.

Police divers descended into John D Long Lake a third time and this time found the car, with the dead boys still strapped into the back seat. The divers had earlier searched too close to the bank, thinking that the car might have been driven in at speed: such momentum, ironically, creates an impact buffer in the water that sinks a vehicle quickly, but near to the shore. Susan Smith's Mazda had rolled comparatively slowly into the water, allowing it to float some distance out into the lake before it sank. In fact, she must have watched until her

Susan Smith's arrest mug shots. Nine days of police interrogation and intense press interest broke her down and she confessed to killing her children.

car disappeared beneath the water, because she was later able to point out the exact spot where the divers could find it.

During the pre-trial preparation, the police reconstructed the crime scene – rolling an identical-model Mazda down the boat ramp and into the lake. A camera strapped to the back seat of the reconstruction vehicle showed the water rising inexorably up inside the vehicle – the last view the boys would have had as the nose-diving car sank into the lake. The reconstruction Mazda took six minutes to fill with water. The boys would then have died of drowning about two minutes after the car filled and sank.

The case had already made the national news, largely because of the race element – Susan's claim that an African-American had stolen her kids. With her confession the case made headlines around the world. It all seemed impossible to understand: Susan Smith, all who knew her agreed, had been a model mother up to that terrible night. Added to this shock was the indignation of the African-American community: Smith had claimed a black man took the boys and she had, presumably, meant to stick to this story when the car was eventually found. Smith was apparently a baby-murdering racist – about as low as anyone could get in modern society

– and the world watched her trial with a mixture of horror and bilious fascination.

Smith pleaded not guilty. Against the prosecution's case that she was a totally selfish woman who would rather kill her children than miss a chance to marry a rich man, the defence claimed that she was suicidally depressed when she killed her sons, and not in full control of her actions. The jury found for the prosecution, and it was only the fact that Susan's stepfather came forward to admit that he had sexually abused her since she was 14 that helped her avoid a death sentence. She was given life.

The police reconstruction of the death of the two boys. The car would have taken over five minutes to fill with water, with the boys conscious the entire time.

Accidental murder?

The police forensic report on Susan's Mazda showed it to have had a faulty handbrake at the time it entered the lake. Experts concluded that it was highly unlikely that she could have released the handbrake and then closed the car door before the vehicle rolled down the slope (the driver side door was firmly closed when the car hit the water). At least one researcher is now suggesting that the car suddenly rolled down the slope of its own accord, while Susan was standing outside contemplating suicide. She was a non-swimmer, so couldn't have saved her boys once the car floated away from the edge (trained emergency rescuers often find it impossible to save people in similar circumstances). She had contrived and was then trapped by the kidnapping story and, after nine days of intense interrogation, she confessed to what her own depression-twisted conscience insisted – that she was a murderer in all but fact.

Whether or not this version of events is true remains a moot point – Susan Smith has made no effort to appeal her life sentence, and is unlikely, for her own protection, ever to be paroled.

CURRY WARS AND RED HERRINGS

A badly incinerated corpse was found in a burned-out Mitsubishi Pajero on March 18, 1999, in Hillfield Lane near Bushey, Hertfordshire. The victim turned out to be an Indian restaurant owner called Tahir Butt, and investigators were initially flummoxed as to why the 49-year-old entrepreneur should have met such a grisly end. The autopsy showed that he had been tied up, beaten, then strangled to death before being incinerated in the Pajero.

The newspapers speculated, on no supporting evidence, that he might have been a victim of the gangland violence that occasionally flared up in nearby North London. It was suggested that the apparently legitimate businessmen might be involved in drug dealing, or even restaurant rivalries: the so-called "curry wars". Police looking into his life found that Butt had been involved in a dizzying array of business activities – ranging from his restaurant, The Karahi Queen in Wembley, to his management of traditional Asian "mujra" dancers. Any one of these activities, or none of them, might have held the clue to the motive of his killer(s), so all had to be carefully investigated.

Then the letters started to arrive. One was sent to Butt's grieving widow, Rafia, another to a friend of the dead man and a third to the chief superintendent at Harrow police station. All were in the same handwriting and claimed to be from a member of the Chinese "Tong" mafia. Tahir Butt, the letters claimed, had been involved in drug dealing, and had owed the Tongs over a million pounds.

But the police found the letters themselves to be suspicious. The Tongs are famously tight-lipped; members don't send helpful letters to the police. And if Butt had been involved enough with such gangs to owe them a million pounds, then why was there no evidence of such activity in his – admittedly complex – financial arrangements? It's one thing to live a double life, but quite another to have arranged such good double book-keeping that a large police investigation could find no sign of illegal activities.

So if the letters were deliberate "red herrings" – designed to throw investigators off the correct scent – then what was the letter-writer trying to hide? One thing that the late Mr Butt had not managed to cover up was that he had been having an affair for over 10 years. This was an obvious line of enquiry, but the lover, Mrs Aruna Joshi, had recently moved to Gujarat in India. The police nevertheless looked into Mrs Joshi's past and found some interesting facts.

Not long after Butt's murder, Aruna Joshi sold her house in Wembley and spent £40,000 of the proceeds on buying a house in India. She and Manoj Minstry, another lover, had moved out there to live permanently, but four years after the murder, the couple returned to England on a visit and were promptly arrested.

Investigators took DNA samples from Minstry and compared them with DNA traces found on the "red herring" letters. They were not surprised when they did not match – Manoj could barely speak any English, let alone write it – but the genetic test showed that the letters had been handled by someone who was probably closely related to him. Handwriting and DNA comparisons pointed

The victim, Tahir Butt (top), was found partly incinerated in the burned-out wreck of his car. The autopsy showed, however, that he had been beaten and strangled to death before being burned.

to Manoj's younger brother, Kiran, as the letter-writer.

At the subsequent trial, Aruna's own son was a chief witness for the prosecution. He told the court that on the night of the murder, March 17, 1999, he had seen Tahir Butt arrive, then heard a loud argument between Minstry's brother Milan and Butt. The row had ended suddenly with an ominous "thud".

The jury found Aruna Joshi guilty of luring Tahir to her house, then of helping Manoj and Milan to kill him. Both Manoj and Milan were also found guilty of attempting to pervert the course of justice by sending the "red herring" letters. Their brother Kiran, the actual letter-writer, was also found guilty of perverting the course of justice, but not guilty of involvement with the actual murder.

Butt out

Born in 1959 in India, Aruna Joshi had gone through an arranged marriage in 1975 and had moved, with her husband, to London the following year. The couple were apparently happy until, in 1985, Aruna's husband started to suffer from a degenerative mental disorder. She then found herself looking after not only their two sons, but also her increasingly child-like spouse.

She found comfort with Tahir Butt in 1988, and the pair maintained their illicit affair for 10 years. But then, in 1998, Aruna met a mechanic called Manoj Minstry and started a second extra-marital affair. Minstry was six years Aruna's junior, while Butt was six years her senior, but she was happy to try to maintain both relationships. The men were less accommodating, however, with Minstry demanding she remain faithful only to him and Butt refusing to back out gracefully.

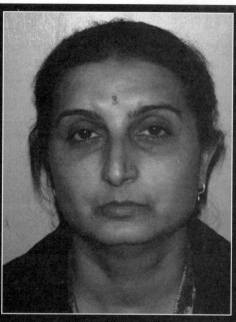

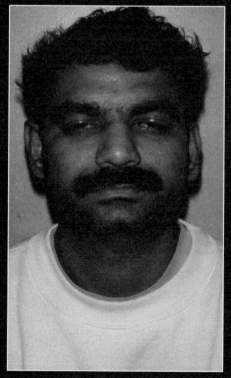

Aruna Joshi (above) lived an unhappy life, with a mentally ill husband and two children to bring up on her own. She found solace with lovers, but when her lovers became jealous of each other, murder was the result.

Manoj Mistry, Aruna's younger lover (left). He couldn't bare to share her with the older but richer Butt, so the couple turned to murder. But they were clearly the most likely suspects in the crime. How could they put the police off the scent?

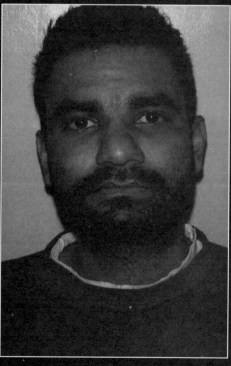

Milan Mistry (right), Manoj's brother, helped to try to conceal the true motive of the murder by writing false letters to the police, claiming that Tahir Butt had been killed by drug dealers.

2000s

JANE ANDREWS, DRESSER TO THE DUCHESS

As we've often seen in this volume, fairytale lives can sometimes end in nightmares, and this was grimly true in the case of Jane Andrews – plucked out of obscurity and placed among the top of British society, only to be coldly ejected and to end up in a prison cell.

Andrews was born in Cleethorpes in 1967 into a poor Lincolnshire family. Her father was a carpenter, but was frequently out of work. Her mother, an infant school teacher, was the main breadwinner, but couldn't bring in enough for the family to live in a house with either a bathroom or an indoor toilet. It was a grim upbringing. Jane later claimed to have been sexually abused as a child, and certainly tried to commit suicide at least once during her teens.

By the time she was 21, Jane was working as an assistant in the local Marks & Spencer and living in no doubt that she would be a poor nobody all of her life. Then she noticed an anonymous advert in the magazine *The Lady* for a "dresser". Well, Jane knew the fashions – she daydreamed over fashion magazines all the time – so she put in for the job.

She heard nothing more for six months then, out of the blue, a letter arrived: Her Royal Highness, the Duchess of York, had requested an interview with Miss Jane Andrews. Unable to believe it was really happening, Jane caught a train to London and arrived with just £10.00 in her pocket. At any other time and, arguably, with any other member of the royal family, Jane wouldn't have even got her nose through the door, but the Duchess (nicknamed "Fergie" by the media, after her maiden name, Ferguson) was remarkably fun-loving and easy-going. She and Jane got on immediately, and the schoolteacher's daughter from Cleethorpes became the Duchesses dresser.

Eventually the Duchess's marriage to Prince Andrew began to founder. As it became increasingly obvious that the marriage was coming to an end, the tabloid press

The social climb

Jane Andrews soon became more than a servant and fashion adviser; as the years went on she became one of the Duchess's closest confidantes. She also hobnobbed with royalty, statesmen, diplomats, celebrities and multi-millionaires, so it wasn't too surprising that Jane dropped her Lincolnshire accent and became increasingly "posh". In 1989 she married a wealthy IBM executive, 21 years her senior, but the marriage broke up amicably after several years. Another break-up with a rich boyfriend, a couple of years later, was less pleasant. The man rang the police to report that Jane had "trashed" his flat in her fury.

gave "Fergie" an increasingly hard time. And she apparently came to rely more and more on her friendship with Jane. But the Duchess was also up to her neck in debt so, in 1997, she was forced to sack most of her personal staff, Jane included.

Andrews was shattered by the rejection. The Duchess didn't even break the news in person, but sent a palace flunky to fire her friend. Jane, suffering from depression, had difficulty finding another position, but eventually got a job selling silverware in a

Knightsbridge jewellers – she must, however, have felt that she was slipping away from the glamorous world that she had happily inhabited for nine years.

In 1999 she was introduced to Thomas Cressman, a rich, well-connected playboy, five years Jane's senior. The resulting relationship has been described in two very different ways. Andrews claimed that Cressman was a sexual predator who tried to force her into anal sex, bondage games and bizarre role-playing, all of which she found abhorrent. When she rebuffed him, she later claimed, he threatened her and was capable of violence.

If this version of their relationship was true, others – even close friends – saw no signs of Cressman's cruel behaviour towards Jane. On the contrary, it seemed to be Jane who was highly possessive of Tom, jealously fending

Jane Andrews and Thomas Cressman. She later claimed that he was a bullying pervert. Others claimed that it was Jane who was unstable and over-possessive.

off any women who looked too interested in him.

In the summer of 2000 the couple went on holiday to the south of France, and Jane appeared to be convinced that Thomas was about to propose marriage to her. When he didn't, a friend later reported: "Jane asked Tom a blunt question about marriage, and Tom gave her a blunt answer. He didn't want a family with Jane because he thought that she was unstable."

On the evening of September 17, 2000, Jane and Tom had a showdown. She later claimed that he attacked her, raped her and then accidentally fell on the knife that she was defending herself with. The prosecution claimed that, infuriated by a further refusal by Tom to marry her (and

The stair landing in Cressman's flat where police found his dead body. Jane claimed that he had attacked and raped her, then fell on a knife.

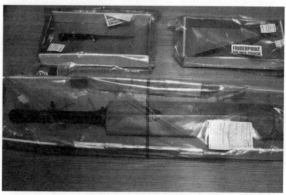

Forensic examination showed that the cricket bat had been used to strike Cressman on the head and that one of the two knives was then used to stab him to death. Jane's fingerprints were on both weapons.

thus keep her in the manner to which she had become accustomed), Jane cracked Tom over the head with a cricket bat, went to the kitchen to get a carving knife, then stabbed the unconscious man in the chest.

The jury agreed with the prosecution and Jane Andrews was given a life prison sentence for murder.

2003

THE PETERSON CASE

In some cases a "crime of passion" actually shows the criminal to be strikingly cold-hearted, at least as far as their victims go. The murder of Laci Peterson, a heavily pregnant Californian housewife, by her supposedly loving husband is a case in point ... if he actually did it, that is.

In late 2002, Scott Peterson and his wife Laci were living a comfortable life in the town of Modesto, California. Scott, aged 30, and Laci, 27, had been college sweethearts. They had been married for five years and lived well on Scott's income as a fertilizer salesman and Laci's wage as a substitute teacher. Best of all, their first child was due to be born in early February 2003. Then suddenly, on Christmas Eve, Laci disappeared.

Scott told police that he had gone out fishing for the day, sailing his boat from the marina at Berkley. When he returned that evening, his wife was missing, leaving behind her car, her mobile phone and her purse. Laci's only known plan for that day had been to go to buy some groceries and to walk the dog in the nearby park.

Neighbours had found the Petersons' dog wandering in the street at 10 a.m., just half an hour after Scott had left for his fishing trip. Laci didn't answer the door when they called to return the animal and, unusually for a California home even in December, all the curtains were closed. So they had left the dog tethered in the Petersons' backyard.

The police immediately suspected that Mrs Peterson had met with foul play. Heavily pregnant women do not wander far from home

Scott and Laci Peterson, photographed just days before Laci disappeared. The couple appeared completely happy to all who knew them.

without money or transport. Neither did it seem likely that she had run away; family friends and Laci's own mother all insisted that the couple were very happy and had a "honeymoon" relationship.

Laci's disappearance moved everyone in Modesto: leaflets were handed out and thousands interrupted their holiday plans to help the police comb first the city, then the local

countryside. Within days a $500,000 reward for finding Laci was posted, much of it donated by concerned citizens.

Through all this Scott refused to give press interviews, insisting he was too upset, but he was very active in the search for his wife and unborn baby. Yet the police

almost immediately decided that he was the prime suspect in Laci's disappearance. Away from the public eye, investigators found Scott too relaxed and even prone to laughter – hardly the image of an anxious husband. He had also taken out a $250,000 life insurance policy on his wife, so stood to gain substantially if the police were forced to proclaim her "missing and presumed dead".

Nobody but Scott admitted to having seen Laci on the day she disappeared. Police bloodhound handlers insisted that she had not left on foot, but in a vehicle. Since the Peterson dog had been found wandering just half an hour after Scott had driven from the house, it seemed most likely that Laci – alive or dead – had left with him. A neighbour told police that she had seen Scott leave the house on the morning Mrs Peterson vanished; Laci had not been with him but, ominously, Scott had loaded something bulky and apparently heavy into the truck before driving away.

Yet relatives, including Laci's mother, continued to insist that Scott could never have harmed his pregnant wife. They insisted that the Petersons had an idyllic marriage, and Scott was keen to be a father – lovingly decorating a nursery for the son that they had decided to call Conner. How could such a man be a wife- and baby-murderer?

Then a woman came forward to reveal that Scott Peterson was not the model husband that everyone had believed. Amber Frey, a 28-year-old massage therapist, had met Scott the previous November, introduced to him by a friend who had, in turn,

met him at a business conference and believed that he was an eligible bachelor. Amber was a lonely single mother with a two-year-old daughter, so the kindly, educated, well-off, supposedly single Scott appeared a perfect catch. In short, they began a love affair that Scott failed to tell Amber was adulterous.

In fact, the friend who had introduced them, Shawn Sibley, discovered in early December that Scott was married and threatened to tell Amber. Peterson convinced Sibley that he had "lost his wife", and had found the subject too painful to talk about. To placate Sibley, Peterson told Amber the same lie, stressing that all he wanted now was a loving relationship with her. Chillingly, Scott had added that, come January, he would have a lot more time

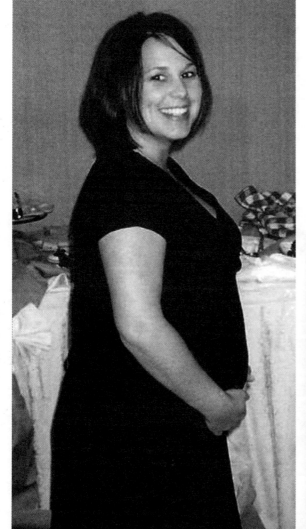

Laci Peterson was eight-months pregnant when she disappeared. Police immediately suspected foul play: heavily pregnant women don't just wander off without any transport or money.

Amber Frey (below) was Scott's lover – quite unaware that he was not only married, but was about to become a father. It was only when she saw Scott on TV that she realised the horrible truth and alerted the police.

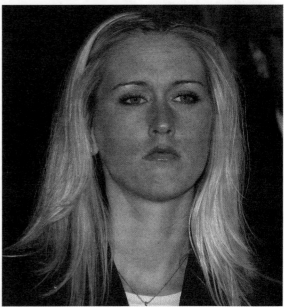

to spend with Amber and her daughter – the exact opposite of the likely situation *if* he expected to soon be helping care for his newborn son. As soon as Amber saw Scott on television, described as Laci Peterson's anxious husband, she had put two and two together and rang the police.

Police forensic teams checked the Peterson house and Scott's truck and boat for signs of foul play. Scott reacted by secretly selling his wife's Land Rover to buy a replacement for the truck impounded by the police. The car dealer who bought the car was so horrified to discover Peterson's actual identity that he immediately sold the vehicle to Laci's family for the nominal sum of one dollar. Scott Peterson was also reported to be making enquiries with local estate agents about selling the house. It appeared that he didn't think that his wife was coming home.

In the face of these negative revelations, Scott broke his media silence, allowing himself to be interviewed on ABC News by anchorwoman Diane Sawyer. There he insisted that there was nothing suspicious about the life insurance on his missing wife – they had bought equal policies on each other over two years previously. The house curtains had been left closed on the day Laci disappeared because she had felt cold that morning, he said, and the "heavy object" his neighbour had seen him loading into his truck that day was a bundle of umbrellas he gave out as free gifts to customers of his fertilizer business.

As to his love affair with Amber Frey, he admitted that it was indeed true, but that

Scott Peterson at the time of his arrest. He had grown a beard, dyed his hair and just happened to be carrying $10,000 on his person.

he had told Laci all about it in early December and she "had come to terms with the situation." Just why she had not mentioned this earth-shaking revelation to her mother, or anyone else, he did not say.

Laci's due date, February 10, 2003, came and went with still no sign of her. It took a further two months before there was a further development in the case, but when it came, on April 13, it was horrible. The decayed corpse of an eight-month male foetus washed ashore just south of Berkley marina, where Scott had gone fishing the day his wife vanished. The next day the headless, limbless body of a woman was found near

where the baby had been washed ashore.

DNA tests proved that the corpses were those of Laci and Conner Peterson. The cause of death could not be ascertained, but they had been dead since Christmas. Gas from the decay process had forced the foetus from the mother's body while still at sea, and the torso had originally been weighted down, but had escaped its anchor.

The police arrested Scott Peterson shortly after the bodies were found. Despite already having heard the news of the gruesome discoveries,

he was calmly playing golf when officers came for him. He had grown a beard and dyed both it and his naturally brown hair blond – to avoid harassment by members of the press and the increasingly hostile public, he explained. He was also found to be carrying $10,000 – the legal maximum that can be taken over the border into Mexico without having to declare it.

The circumstantial case against Scott Peterson seemed damning, but one important thing stood in his favour: the police had failed to find any physical evidence to show that he had been involved in the killings. Usually, the dismemberment of a body tends to leave a wealth of evidence for forensic officers to pick up on, but all that the Modesto police could find was a single strand of Laci's hair, stuck to the tip of a pair of pliers in Scott's boat. This merely showed, however, that Laci had probably been in the boat at some time, and not that she had been dead in the boat.

The prosecution's case was that Scott had wanted to start a new life with Amber Frey; Laci and the unborn baby had stood in his way and so he had killed them. But this was only a theory. They had no witnesses and no physical proof beyond the single hair. In an attempt to strengthen their case, the prosecutors brought in an expert witness, hydrologist Ralph Cheng, an expert on the tidal patterns in and around San Francisco Bay. Cheng testified that the location of Scott's boat on his "fishing trip" and the probable dumping point for Laci's corpse were likely to be one and the same. However, under cross-examination, Cheng was forced to admit that the tidal patterns in the area were too chaotic to allow anything but a "probable, not precise" estimate of the body's movements.

But if the prosecution's case was flimsy and almost purely circumstantial, the story the defence offered the jury was little less than fantastic. Scott's lawyer told the court that roving, murderous Satanists could have kidnapped Laci as she walked her dog in the park: who else *could* so brutally murder a heavily pregnant woman?

Unfortunately for Scott, this defence was about 10 years too old. California in the early 1990s had indeed been rife with fear that gangs of Satanic ritual abusers were stalking in the night, murdering babies and hypnotizing witnesses into forgetting what they had seen. But that particular belief had since fallen out of fashion due, in no small part, to a total lack of supporting evidence.

The jury eventually found Peterson guilty of first-degree murder for killing Laci and second-degree murder for killing Conner. The judge took their recommendation and sentenced Scott to death by lethal injection.

Peterson, following his conviction, is escorted to Death Row in the San Quentin Prison. Few doubt that he was guilty of double murder, but the police never found any firm evidence to link him to the crime.

Shadow of a doubt

Justice seems to have been served but, then again, it should be remembered that there was absolutely no physical or conclusive witness evidence to indicate that Peterson killed his wife and unborn son. Many people believed that, although not necessarily innocent, Peterson should have been released under the "shadow of a doubt" rule. Following his conviction, several websites sprang up to support Peterson, one of which pointed out that "it seems now there is a legal precedent that if your wife turns up dead and you happen to be a sleaze, then it's sufficient grounds for a death sentence".

There still remains the disturbing possibility that Scott Peterson — as unpleasant a personality as he certainly appeared to be — had nothing to do with the double murder.

THE SIDE EFFECT

Fiona Paramour met Adrian Hodge in 1988, when she was 17 and he was 26. She was immediately swept off her feet by the older man who was a successful computer software entrepreneur, drove a Ferrari, earned over £100,000 a year and showered her with gifts. But when the pair moved in together, Fiona was unaware that Adrian had been jailed for beating up a previous girlfriend.

Hodge's true nature soon came out, however, and Fiona found herself in the vicious circle that traps so many abuse victims: the violence leads to depression and a feeling of helplessness in the victim, which are reinforced by threats and belittlement by the abuser.

"He was hardly ever at home," she later told a reporter, "and when he was, all he was interested in was knocking me about. I've still got the scars. He always punched me on the same eye. I've been told to wear glasses to help me, but I can't bear to put them on because it reminds me of him."

Hodge was not above dragging the police in as unwilling accomplices in his abuse of Fiona. When she gave birth to a premature baby, who died soon afterwards, Hodge first failed to attend the funeral, then reported the death as murder by the baby's mother. Although the medical records clearly showed that the death had been natural, with no suspicious circumstances, police procedures forced them to conduct an investigation, further increasing Fiona's grief and misery.

Neither was Hodge any easier on their children. He punched his third son, Moses,

in the face when the boy was just 10 months old. He then tried to make the toddler walk from one end of the room to the other. When Moses didn't make it Hodge declared that he couldn't be his son, but the bastard of another man, and whipped the boy's legs with a telephone flex until they bled. Hodge then forced his two older boys to watch as he showered the blood off the howling child, telling them: "That's what happens when you don't listen to daddy."

Fiona Paramour tried to run away several times during the eight years she was with Hodge, taking shelter with friends and family but, according to Fiona, "every time he found me and ordered me back home. He said he'd kill me and the kids if I didn't."

Fiona finally broke away from Hodge in 1996, taking the children with her. She attempted to go to the authorities over his abuse of the children, but dropped the charges when threatened by a friend of Hodge's. She did report him to the Child Support Agency to get him to pay family maintenance. "He had two houses and a flash car and spent hundreds of pounds on prostitutes and champagne. I even sent them a picture of him with his Ferrari 456. But all they told him to pay was £11 a week."

So Fiona had to get a job, and there met Alvin Timothy. Within a year they were married, but that didn't solve Fiona's problems. Adrian Hodge was infuriated to hear that his ex-lover had married another man, and began a three-year campaign of harassment against the couple. He made abusive telephone calls, broke into their house and falsely accused Timothy of sexually abusing the children. On one occasion Hodge bashed on the their front door, armed with an axe and two carving knives. But he hid the weapons before the police arrived and no charges could be pressed. On another occasion Fiona claims she saw a man with a rifle standing on a nearby garage, peering into her house. This harassment eventually drove Fiona to take an overdose of sleeping pills but, fortunately, paramedics managed to save her life.

One evening in November 2002, a stranger knocked on the front door of the Timothys' Basingstoke home. When Fiona answered, he asked to see her husband. As Alvin stepped up to the front door, a second man jumped out and shot him in the face. Fortunately the gun, a lethal air pistol, misfired. Although Alvin's face was a mass of blood, he survived with only shrapnel wounds.

Police arrested the would-be assassins: Derek Danso, William Phillips and Mushbir Hussain. Charged with attempted murder, they admitted that Adrian Hodge offered them £7,000 to kill *either* Alvin or Fiona. Hussain, the driver and organizer, was given 18 years; Danso, the gunman, got 13 years; and Phillips, the lookout, got nine years.

Sentencing Adrian Hodge to 16 years, Judge Michael Astill pointed out: "Never have you expressed the slightest regret. In fact your only expression is one of disgust that Alvin Timothy has not died."

Tragic postscript

There is a dreadful postscript to this case. Over the years of abuse and harassment, Moses Paramour – the boy Adrian Hodge had called a bastard and whipped until he bled – had been showing signs of increasing mental disorder. He was eventually taken into the care of Hampshire social services after he set fire to Fiona and Alvin's house in 2001. In October 2004 his foster parents found him dead in his bedroom: he had hanged himself with the belt of his dressing gown. He was only 12 years old.

Fiona Paramour (left) suffered years of cruel abuse at the hands of her violent lover, Adrian Hodge.

Moses Paramour (right) had deep mental scars after witnessing and suffering Adrian Hodge's abuse. Scars that eventually led Moses to kill himself.

2005

MURDER AT TREWINNICK COTTAGE

At 11.25 a.m. on the morning of April 26, 2005, North Cornwall Emergency Services received a 999 call from a payphone. The male caller told the switchboard: "There's been a murder. She's been beaten around the head. The baby's had a plastic bag put over its head." He then gave the address of the crime scene as Trewinnick Cottage in the tiny village of St Ervan. When the police operator asked what exactly had happened, the man simply said: "I don't know. I haven't got a clue. I found her in the back bedroom. She's lying on the bed. There's blood everywhere. She's my girlfriend and fiancée." Then he rang off.

The first emergency vehicle to arrive was an ambulance, driven by paramedic Mike Ford. It was only as he pulled up outside Trewinnick Cottage that he realized with horror that it was the home of the parents of his daughter's fiancée. Ford's partner held him back from entering the cottage as arriving police officers hurried in.

In a rear bedroom they found the walls and ceiling spattered with blood. Mike Ford's 19-year-old daughter, Claire, was lying in bed clearly having suffered severe head injuries. Nearby was Claire's 18-month-old daughter, Charlotte, with similar cranial injuries. A plastic bag had also been placed over the baby's head and taped closed around her neck. Both victims had been dead for some hours.

Charlotte's father, 26-year-old Christopher Adams, was

The quiet Cornish lane leading to Trewinnick Cottage, St Ervan, where Claire and Charlotte were brutally murdered.

Claire Ford, 19, and her eighteen-month-old daughter Charlotte. Both lived happily with Chris, Charlotte's father.

nowhere to be found. He worked as a pub manager, and most of the time the little family lived in a flat above the pub, the Market Inn, in the village of St Cleer. On Christopher's days off, however, they stayed in the spare room of Trewinnick Cottage, to escape the noise of the pub.

Christopher's father, Martin Adams, had been at home that night, and told the police he had heard odd noises coming from the spare room just after 6 a.m. that morning. He had met his son in the kitchen at around 7 a.m. and had asked if everything was all right. Christopher told his father that Claire had had a nightmare and had been moaning loudly in her sleep. Christopher left the cottage at 9 a.m. and did not return. Forensic examination of the bodies showed that Claire had been killed by three "substantial blows" to the head, around 6 a.m. that morning. She also showed evidence of blows to the shoulders, arms and hands – what are known to forensic scientists as "defensive wounds" – resulting from her attempts to protect herself from her attacker.

Baby Charlotte had also suffered "massive head injuries", which probably would have killed her, but it was the plastic bag, placed over her wounded head and secured tightly with tape around her neck that had been the cause of Charlotte's death.

Christopher Adams was a devoted father and fiancé who worked long hours to support his family. Nobody could understand how such a man might harm those he loved most dearly.

Christopher Adams did not claim diminished responsibility over the killing of Claire and Charlie, insisting on pleading guilty to murder. Yet he could give no reason as to why he had killed his family.

Charlotte, nicknamed Charlie, had been born. He himself had no previous record of violent or anti-social behaviour, had no drink or drug problems, and apparently loved his fiancée and baby dearly. But he was also the main suspect in their murders.

A nationwide hunt was now launched to find Adams. After making the telephone call to the emergency services – some five and a half hours after the time of the murders – he had driven off in his mother's Peugeot car. Given the savage violence of the killings, the police were extremely concerned that he might harm others or himself. Over the next week he was seen twice, near Exeter in Devon and later near Bristol, both times at motorway service stations, suggesting that he was sleeping in the car and keeping on the move. He was eventually caught in Hampshire, and made no effort to resist arrest. As police handcuffed him, Adams said: "I don't know what happened, mate. I just lost it."

Despite initially – in his call to the emergency services – claiming to have "found" the murder victims and not to have a clue as to what had happened, under interrogation Adams freely admitted to the murders. He had had little sleep the night before the killings, he told investigators, because baby Charlie had kept waking up and crying. At around 6.15 a.m. he had again got up to bottle-feed Charlotte, then woke Claire.

He went on: "I suppose we had a falling-out. We've had falling-outs before. Nothing major. Nothing violent. Usually about the hours I work and things like that. "Claire got up. I pushed her down. The bat

The wounds had all been inflicted with a heavy, blunt object; a cricket bat, found in the blood-spattered bedroom, was shown to have been the murder weapon. Fingerprints on the bat proved to be those of Christopher Adams.

At first, neither the Ford nor Adams families could believe that Christopher had murdered his fiancée and baby. Claire and Christopher had met when she was 16 and he was 24. They had formed a close and loving relationship and, six months later when Claire realized that she was pregnant, had been happy at the thought of starting a family together. Adams worked hard to support his partner and had been "over the moon" when baby

was there. I just swung round to hit her with it. I don't know why I did it. I hit her again. I brought it back round and hit Charlie. I didn't mean to do it."

Despite Adams' candour, his confession clearly lacked an adequate explanation as to his motive. Why had he lost his temper so violently? The autopsy showed evidence of not just two impacts to Claire Ford, as he had described, but a positive rain of blows directed at her head and upper body. And if he had accidentally hit baby Charlie with the bat in the course of the attack on her mother, then why had he not rushed to get help? Instead of calling for medical aid, he had instead deliberately suffocated the infant.

During the subsequent trial, Christopher Adams refused to enter a plea of diminished responsibility due to temporary insanity, despite the fact that, given his previous clean record, such an explanation might well have reduced his charge to manslaughter (a term equivalent to second-degree murder in the US). He doggedly insisted, however, that he was guilty of murder, although he still could give no substantial reason for killing his family.

Adams' defence counsel, Geoffrey Mercer, QC, underlined this ambiguity in his statement to the court. "If one looks for an explanation as to why these offences happened, it is very difficult to find one." Mercer stressed that: "[Adams] does not seek to exaggerate the tensions that led to this terrible loss of control, or to place the blame elsewhere… Temporarily, at least, his mind must have been very disturbed at the time [of the killings]…

This was a single occasion of unpremeditated violence, entirely out of character, resulting in the deaths of the two people he loved most."

Sentencing Adams to life imprisonment, with a minimum tariff of 20 years to be served, Judge Graham Cottle said: "Apart from the fact that you murdered two people, the description of the offence in connection to the murder of [baby] Charlotte in particular reveals aggravating features." In other words, the fact that Adams had deliberately suffocated his daughter, and had then delayed over five hours before calling for help, indicated that he had been fully intent on murder, even if he apparently had no motive.

"The devastation," Judge Cottle went on, "that you have brought upon the lives of those who loved and cherished Claire and Charlotte, and on your own family, is quite incalculable." The judge added that he might have insisted that Adams serve a minimum of 30 years, but he had taken into account the young man's evident shame and horror. Adams' guilty plea to murder, rather than trying to wriggle out of his responsibility for the deaths or trying for a manslaughter verdict, saved him a possible extra 10 years in prison.

So why did Adams murder the two creatures he clearly loved more than any others in the world? His own and Claire's family had absolutely no idea. They described Christopher as "a thoroughly decent, hard-working young man, cheerful, mild-mannered and placid". He worked long hours as a pub manager to support his family, and played an active and cheery role in caring for the baby. Not a

Blood simple

Perhaps Christopher Adams' state of mind – during the murders and immediately afterwards – might have been what the 1930s author Dashiell Hammett called "blood simple" in his novel, *Red Harvest*. Hammett described such a mindset as an irrationally cold or savage rage that leads a person to commit murder, followed by an addled, frightened and yet dreamlike foolishness, which often gets them caught immediately.

Perhaps such murderous irrationality is the most disturbing aspect of "crimes of passion". It's not that relationships sometimes get so poisoned that one partner eventually decides that the other has to die. It's not that some people are selfish and unwise enough to hope they can get away with the murder of someone that they are clearly connected with – although they are thus the first to be held under suspicion by investigators. It is the grim fact about human nature that even the most loving spouse, romantic lover or devoted parent can, in a fit of ungoverned rage, destroy the creatures they love most in the world … and often for little or no reason.

Before April 26, 2005 nobody – especially Christopher Adams, his fiancée and daughter – could have believed him capable of deliberately murdering his family. It reminds us that similar seeds of "blood simple" madness potentially lurk in anyone's heart, even our own.

hint had come out during the police investigation to suggest that either he or Claire were unfaithful to each other, or were unhappy with their relationship.

The police, despite their interviews with Adams and his openness in confession, remained similarly in the dark. Detective Inspector Karl Fellows, a senior officer on the case, told reporters: "For every member of [police] staff involved it was particularly difficult and challenging. We've all got families and this is probably the most devastating sort of crime for anybody to come across. We still don't have a full explanation as to why Christopher Adams did what he did. I can only hope that, in the fullness of time, he can explain that to help both families concerned."

INDEX

A

Adams, Charlotte 218–20, 221
Adams, Christopher 218–19, *219*, 220–1, *220*
Agostini, Antonio 71–2
Agostini, Linda 72
aircrash 108–11
Algarron, Jacques 122–3, *123*
An American Tragedy (Dreiser) 20, 21
Anderson, Kirk 153, 154–9
Andrews, Jane 210–11, *210*
arsenic 7–8, 10, 163

B

Bahmer, Pearl 38
Bailly, Felix 118, 119
Barber, Michael 174
Barber, Susan 174
Bartlett, Adelaide 8–10, *8*
Bartlett, Edwin 8, 9
battery 6, 58, 74, 77, 84, 95, 98–9, 100, 101, 102, 124, 125, 176, 179, 194, *194*, 196, 197, 198, 199, 219, 220
Beadle, James 60, 61
Benedict, Harriet 20
Benedict, Robin 178, *179*
Birkett, Norman 79, 84, *85*
Birse, Trudy 146, 147
Blakely, David 6, 127–9, 130, 131
Bobbitt, John Wayne 192–3, *193*
Bobbitt, Lorena 192–3, *192*
Boldizs, John 140
Boldonado, Gus 139
Bosevsky, Alexis 31, 32
Brearley, David 151, 152
Brook, Maggie 103, 105
Broughton, Diana Delves 89–90, *89*
Broughton, Henry 'Jock' Delves 88, 89, *89*
Brown, Denise 198
Brown, Grace (Billie) 20, 21
Bruce, Lillian 104
Butt, Rafia 206
Butt, Tahir 206, 207
Buttafuoco, Joey 188, 189, 190, 191
Buttafuoco, Mary Jo 188, 189, 190
Bywaters, Frederick 46, *46*, 47–8, 49, *49*

C

Caillaux, Henriette 34, *34*, 35
Caillaux, Joseph 34, *34*, 35
Calmette, Gaston 34–5
Camb, James 106, 107
Cameron, Elsie 54, *54*, 55, *55*
Carberry, June 89, *89*
Casserley, Georgina 'Ena' May 80–1, 82, *82*, 83, 84, 85
Casserley, Percy 80, 81, 82–5
Chaplin, Edward Royal 80–2, 83, 84–5
Cheogoe, Marthinus Charles 150
Chevallier, Pierre 116
Chevallier, Yvonne 116–17, *116*, *117*
chloroform 9, 10
Clark, Lorraine 6, 126
Clark, Melvin 126
Crane, Cheryl 132, *133*, 134, 135, *135*
Cressman, Thomas 211
Crippen, Harvey Hawley 26, *26*, 27, 28, 29, 48, 76
Cross, Dr Philip 10
Cross, Laura 10
Cussen, Desmond 129, 130, 131
cyanide 21

D

Davis, Fred 14, 17
Deluzy, Henriette 10–11
Dimmock, Phyllis 22, *22*, 23
Dobkin, Harry 92–3, *93*
Dobkin, Rachel 90–3, *90*, *91*, *92*
Douglas, Professor William 178–9, *178*, *179*
Dreher, Dr Tom 60–1, *61*
drowning 202–5, *205*
Dubuisson, Pauline 118, *118*, 119
Duc de Choiseul-Praslin, Charles-Louis Theobald 10–11
Duncan, Elizabeth 138–9, *138*, *139*
Duncan, Frank 138–9
Dyson, George 9

E

Edmands, Violet 21
Ellis, George 128
Ellis, Ruth 6, 127–31, *127*, *128*
Elmore, Belle 26, 27, *27*, 28, 29
Emmett-Dunne, Sergeant Frederick 120, 121
Erroll, Lord 88–9, *89*
explosives 108–11

F

Fahmy, Marguerite 50–1, *50*
Findley, Tom 203
Fisher, Amy 188–9, *188*, 190, 191
Flynn, Billy 184, 185, 186
Ford, Claire 218, 219, *219*, 220–1
Ford, Mike 218
Frey, Amber 213–14, *213*, 215
Fuhrman, Mark 199, *199*

G

Gardiner, William 14, 16
Gardner, Eric 94, 95
Garvie, Maxwell 146–7
Garvie, Sheila 146
Geist, Louise 39, 40
Gibson, Gay 106, *107*
Gibson, Jane ('Pig Woman') 39, 40, *40*, 41
Gillette, Chester 20–1, *20*
Glaister, John 76, 77, 79
Goldman, Ronald 194, *194*, 196, 198, 201
Graham, Ron 175–6
Gray, Henry Judd 56, 57, 58, *58*, 59
Graydon, Avis 47, 48, 49
Griffiths, Tom 71
Guagenti, Peter 189–91
Guay, Joseph Albert 108, 109, *109*, *110*, 111, *111*
Guay, Rita 109, 111
Gump, Fred 19
Gunnell, Clive 127, 129, 131
guns 11, 18, 33, 38, 43–4, 51, 58, 60, 63, 71, 80, 81, 82–3, 85, 116–17, 118, 126, 127, 131, 139, 140, 142, 146, 150, 166,

168–9, 184, 187, 189, 190, 191
air pistol 217
Beretta .25 180–1
Browning revolver 34
Colt .32 revolver 89
rifle 147, 176
shotgun 98, 173
Titan .25 semi-automatic pistol 188
Webley and Scott .25 automatic 83, 84

H

Hall, Edward Wheeler 38
Hall, Frances 38, 39, *39*, 40, 41
Halliwell, Kenneth 144–5
hammer 68, 69
Harris, Carlyle 21
Harris, Jean 166, 168–9, *168*, *169*
Harsent, Rose 14, *15*, 16, *16*, 17
Harsent, William 14, *15*, 16
Hix, Theora 6, 62, 63
Hodge, Adrian 216, 217
Hulme, Juliet 124–5
hyoscine 28, 29, 48

I

ice axe 151, 152

J

Jones, Alfred 53
Jones, Mabel Theresa 52–3, *53*
Jones, Patricia 140
Jones, Walter 140
Joshi, Aruna 206, 207

K

Kamarovsky, Count Paul 30, *31*, 32–3
Kamel, Prince Ali 50–1, *50*
karate chop 121
Kaye, Violette 66–70, *66*
kidnapping 153, 154, 155, 156, 157, 158, 159, 202–3
Kinne, James 140

Kinne, Sharon 140, *141*, 142, *143*
knives 6, 11, 14, 38, 46, 47, 63, *96*, 97, 134, 150, 192, *192*, 193, 194, 198, 199, 162, 211, *211*
Kupczyk, Olga 138, 139

L

L'Angelier, Pierre 6–7, 8
Labbé, Catherine 122–3
Labbé, Denise 122–3
Lattime, JR 186, 187
Le Boeuf, Ada 60, 61
Le Boeuf, Jim 60, 61
Le Neve, Ethel 26–8, *27*, 28, 29
Lehnberg, Marlene 150
Ley, Thomas 102–3, 104–5
Linnell, Avis 21
Lombard, Monique 118

M

Mackay, Bill 71–2
Makely, Paul 188, 189, 191
Mancini, Tony 66–8, *68*, 69
Manton, Bertie 100–01
Manton, Rene 99, 101
Manton, Sheila 100
Maslow, Abraham 6
May, Keith 153, 155–6, 157, 158, 159
McCloud, Shirley 202
McKinney, Joyce 153–9, *154*, *155*, *156*, *159*
mercury poisoning 9, 57
Miller, Bill 62, 63
Mills, Eleanor 38, *38*, 40, *40*, 41
Mills, James 41
Minnoch, William 7
Ministry, Kiran 206, 208
Ministry, Manoj 206
Ministry, Milan 206
morphine 21
Mougeot, Bernard 118, 119
Moya, Luis 139
Mudie, John McMain 102, 103, 104, 105

N

Naumov, Dr Nicolas 30, 32–3

O

O'Rourk, Count 30, 31
Ordonoz, Francisco Parades 142

Orton, Elsie 144
Orton, Joe 144–5, *144*
Osterreich, Fred 42, 43, 44–5
Osterreich, Walburga 42–3, 45, *45*

P

Paramour, Fiona 216–17, *216*
Paramour, Moses 216, 217, *217*
Park, Carol 151–2, *152*
Park, Gordon 151–2, *152*
Parker, Honora 124, 125
Parker, Pauline 124, 125
Perreau, Jeanette 116, 117
Peters, Alan 146, 147
Peterson, Laci 212–13, *212*, *213*, 214, 215
Peterson, Scott 212–15, *212*, *214*, *215*
Pierce, Cecelia 184, 185, 186, 187
Pitre, Marie 108, 109, 111
poisoning 7–8, 9, 21, 28, 29, 47, 48–9, 53, 163, 174
Potts, Helen 21
powdered glass 47, 48
Prilukov, Donat 30, 32, 33
Puglise, Sam 140–1

R

Randall, Pete 186, 187
Rattenbury, Alma 73–5, *73*, *74*
Rattenbury, Francis 73, *73*, 74
Richeson, Rev. Clarence 21
Riehl, Arthur 39
Riggs, Irene 73, *73*, 74
Robitaille, Marie-Ange 108–9
Rogerson, Mary 78, 79
Ruest, Genereux 109
Ruxton, Buck 77–9, *78*
Ruxton, Isabella 77–8, 79, *79*

S

Sangret, August 95, 96, *96*, 97
Sanhuber, Otto 42, 43–4, *44*, 45
Schneider, Albert 56–7
Schneider, Raymond 38
Scott, Lydia 80, *80*, 82
Shaw, Bert 22
shootings 33, 34, 38, 51, 60, 63, 71, 80, 81, 82–3, 84, 85, 89, 98, 116–17, 118, 126, 127, 140, 142, 146, 147, 150, 166, 168–9, 173, 176, 180–1, 184, 188, 190, 191, 217

Simpson, Dr Keith 90–1, 92, 93, 94, 95, 97, 98
Simpson, Nichole Brown 194, *195*, 196, 198, *198*, 199, 201
Simpson, OJ *182*, 194, *195*, 196–201, *198*, *200*, *201*
Skinner, Effie 10
sledgehammer 179
Smart, Greg 184–5, *184*, 186–7
Smart, Pam 184–7, *184*, *186–7*
Smith, Daniel 202, 203, *203*, 204
Smith, David 204
Smith, John 102, 103, 104, 105
Smith, Madeline 6–8, 7
Smith, Michael 202, 203, *203*, 204
Smith, Susan 202–5, *204*
Snider, Paul 170, 172–3
Snook, Professor James 6, 62–3, *62*, *63*
Snyder, Ruth *36*, 56–8, *56–7*, *58*, *59*, *59*
Solomon, Betty Jeanne 180–1
Solomon, Paul 180, 181, *181*
Spilsbury, Sir Bernard 55, 69, 70, 76, 81, 84
Spungen, Nancy 161–2
stabbing and knife wounds 6, 11, 14, 38, 46, 47, 63, 77, *96*, 97, 97, 126, 134, *134*, 135, 150, 151, 152, 162, 192, *192*, 193, 194, 198, 199, 211, *211*
Stahl, Dmitri 31–2
Steinhagen, Ruth *86*, 112, 113, *113*
Stevens, Willie 39–41
Stompanato, Johnny 132–5, *134*
Stoner, George 73, 74, 75, *75*
strangulation 77, 92, 101, 102, 106, 139, 150, 206
Stratten, Dorothy *164*, 170, *170*, *171*, 172–3, *172*
strychnine 10, 53, 163
suffocation 219–20

T

Tarnovska, Countess Marie 6, 30, *30*, 31–3, *33*
Tarnovsky, Count Vassili 30, 31
Tarnower, Dr Herman 166, *167*, 168–9
Tevendale, Brian 146, 147
Thatcher, Colin 175–7, *177*
Thatcher, JoAnn 175
Thaw, Evelyn *12*, 18, *18*, 19
Thaw, Harry 18–19
Theobald, Fanny 10–11

Thompson, Edith 46, *47*, 47–8, 49
Thompson, Percy 46, *47*, 47–8
Thompson, Richard 46
Thorne, Norman 54, *54*, 55, *55*
Timothy, Alvin 217
Tryforos, Lynne 166, 168
Turner, Cora *see* Elmore, Belle
Turner, Lana 132–4, *132*

V

van der Linde Christlaan 150
van der Linde, Susanna 150
Vaquier, Jean Pierre 52, *52*, 53
Vicious, Sid 160–2, *160–1*, *162*

W

Waitkus, Eddie 112–13, *112*
Warmus, Carolyn 180–1
Watters, Mia 120, 121
Watters, Sergeant Reginald 120, 121
weapons *see under individual name*
weed killer 174
White, Stanford 18, 19
Wilson, Freda 163
Wilson, James 163
Wilson, Norah 163
Wolfe, Joan Pearl 94–5, *94*, 96, 97
Wood, Robert 22, 23, *23*

Y

Young, Ruby 22, 23

PICTURE CREDITS

The Publishers would like to thank the following sources for their kind permission to reproduce the pictures in this book. The page numbers for each of the photographs are listed below, giving the page on which they appear in the book.

Location indicator:
(t-top, b-bottom, r-right, l-left).

AKG London: /Ullstein: 35; Ullstein Bild: 133 l; **Alamy Images:** /Den Reader: 150; **CP Images:** 177; **Corbis Images:** /Bettmann: 12, 18, 19, 36, 40t, 41, 42, 45, 54 tl, 55t, 56–57, 58, 63, 73 t, 73 b, 86, 107, 109, 110, 112, 113 l, 113 r, 114, 117 tl, 117 bl, 118, 135 b, 135 t, 136, 141, 142 tr, 142 tl, 142 b, 143, 170, 172, 178–179, 179, 181 l, 181 r; /J A Giordano: 188–9; /Hulton Deutsch: 160; /Pacha: 182, 198 l; /Reuters: 180–1; /Justin Sullivan/Pool/Reuters: 208, 215; /Maiman Rick: 189, 191; /Sygma: 190, 200; /Outlook/Sygma: 196–197; /Spartansburg Herald Journal/Sygma; 202; /Underwood & Underwood: 40 b; /Peterson Family/Zuma: 212; Rocha Family/Zuma: 213 l; **Empics:** /AP: 44, 69, 76, 77, 123, 132, 184, 186, 194 bl, 204; /G Paul Burnett/AP: 161; /Jim Cole/AP: 187; /Jon Pierre Lasseigne/AP: 186–187; /LAPD/AP: 194; /PA: 29, 49, 128, 131, 151, 154, 156, 158, 206, 207, 211 tr, 210–211, 217; /Barry Batchelor/PA: 218–9; /Devon & Cornwall Police/PA: 219 b; /Phil Noble/PA: 152 b; /Tim Ockenden/PA: 126; **Getty Images:** 159; /AFP: 198 tr; /Pool/AFP: 192 tr; /Express Newspapers: 124; /Edward Gooch: 26; /Yvonne Hemsey: 169; /Hulton Archive: 8, 18 b, 24, 27 t, 27 b, 30, 31, 32, 33, 46–47, 50 b, 51, 100–101; /Frank Barratt/Hulton Archive: 155; /Frank Edwards/Fotos International/Hulton Archive: 164, 171; /Fox Photos/Hulton Archive: 80, 82, 83, 85; /Becker/Fox Photos/Hulton Archive: 81; /General Photographic Agency/Hulton Archive: 64, 67; /Keystone/Hulton Archive: 99, 102, 103, 105 br, 148, 160–161; /Topical Press Agency/Hulton Archive: 53, 66, 68; /Firmin/Topical Press Agency/Hulton Archive: 52; /H Thompson: 144; /Stanislaus County Sheriffs Office: 214; /Time Life Pictures: 116, 117 r; /Robin Platzer/Twin Images/Time Life Pictures: 195; /Ted Thai/Time Life Pictures: 167; /Topical Press Agency: 34, 50 t, 78; /Kirby/Topical Press Agency: 55 b; **www.johnbarber.com:** 22, 23 t, 23 b; **Mary Evans Picture Library:** 7; /Barnabys Glass Negative: 35 tr; **Rex Features:** 219 t, 220; /Stewart Cook: 173; /MB Pictures: 162; /Steve Maisey: 211 t; /Charles Ommanney: 193; /Sipa Press: 185, 192 b, 199, 201, 203, 205; /Roger Viollet: 119 t; **Topham Picturepoint:** 15, 16–17, 20, 28, 46, 48, 54 br, 59, 61, 70, 74, 75 tl, 75 tr, 75 b, 79, 88 t, 88 bl, 88 br, 89 tr, 89 bl, 90, 91, 92–93, 94, 96 t, 96 b, 97, 98, 104 b, 105 tl, 108, 111, 120–121, 122, 125, 127, 130, 133 r, 134 tl, 134 tr, 138, 139 t, 139 b, 146, 147 t, 147 b, 152 tl, 168; /Photonews: 152 tr; /Roger Viollet: 119 b; **Wikipedia:** 38, 39, 62, 104, 108–9.

Every effort has been made to acknowledge correctly and contact the source and/or copyright holder of each picture. Carlton Books Limited apologises for any unintentional errors or omissions which will be corrected in further editions of this book.

Special thanks are due to Katie Johnson at Corbis Images, whose efforts greatly rendered the burdens of picture research.